Promoting Nonprofit Organizations: A Reputation Management Approach

Promoting Nonprofit Organizations is a practical guide to developing and implementing a strategic public relations program to enhance a nonprofit's reputation. The ways in which businesses—both for-profit and not-for-profit—communicate with customers has changed dramatically in recent years. Coupled with economic uncertainty, nonprofits have had to adopt a leaner operational mode, further underlining the need for organizations to take advantage of all the promotion strategies available to them.

This book:

- Discusses why public relations and reputation management go hand-in-hand with marketing efforts
- Offers a step-by-step guide to develop a public relations strategy
- Considers the importance of nonprofit sustainable citizenship
- Provides tips for reputation enhancement using a range of tools, such as social media and board ambassadorship
- Guides the reader in developing a reputation approach to crisis communication management

Highly practical in its approach, this book is a great guide for students in public relations and nonprofit management courses, as well as for professionals seeking to enhance the success of their nonprofit organization.

Ruth Ellen Kinzey, MA, is a reputation strategist with more than 35 years of communication experience in the corporate and consulting arenas. She is also founder and president of The Kinzey Company, a firm that develops comprehensive communication strategies. She has taught communication at the University of North Carolina, Charlotte, and authored the book *Using Public Relations Strategies to Promote Your Nonprofit Organization*.

Promoting Nonprofit Organizations

A Reputation Management Approach

Ruth Ellen Kinzey, MA

Routledge
Taylor & Francis Group

NEW YORK AND LONDON

First published 2013
by Routledge
711 Third Avenue, New York, NY 10017

Simultaneously published in the UK
by Routledge
2 Park Square, Milton Park, Abingdon, Oxon OX14 4RN

Routledge is an imprint of the Taylor & Francis Group, an informa business

Library of Congress Cataloging in Publication Data
Kinzey, Ruth Ellen.
    Promoting nonprofit organizations : a reputation management approach / Ruth Ellen Kinzey.
    p. cm.
    Includes bibliographical references and index.
    1. Nonprofit organizations. 2. Nonprofit organizations—Management. I. Title.
    HD62.6.K5358 2013
    659.2'88—dc23
    2012037334

ISBN: 978-0-415-89926-0 (hbk)
ISBN: 978-0-415-89927-7 (pbk)
ISBN: 978-0-203-14089-5 (ebk)

Typeset in Garamond
by EvS Communication Networx, Inc.

SUSTAINABLE
FORESTRY
INITIATIVE

Certified Sourcing
www.sfiprogram.org
SFI-00555
The SFI label applies to the text stock.

Printed and bound in the United States of America by Walsworth Publishing Company, Marceline, MO.

Contents

About the Author

Ruth Ellen Kinzey, MA

Ruth Ellen Kinzey, president of The Kinzey Company, is known for developing strategic and comprehensive communication strategies. She emphasizes the importance of linking communication, branding, marketing, and corporate responsibility in a manner that protects and enhances reputation. She has used this approach successfully with organizations to help them through crises as well as to make proactive reputational improvements.

Ms. Kinzey has worked in corporate settings within the retail grocery, trucking, natural gas, and healthcare computer software industries. During her prolific career, she has served as corporate spokesperson; prepared change management communication; launched brands; developed government relations strategies; collaborated with special interest groups; managed crises; established sustainable community partnerships; supervised corporate foundations; educated consumers; engaged employees; created corporate citizenship platforms; supported investor relations activities; and designed and executed strategic public relations and marketing campaigns. Early in her career, she was a radio news broadcaster.

Having worked for global companies both as an employee and as a consultant, Ms. Kinzey is familiar with diverse cultural environments. She has consulted in the travel and tourism, risk management, natural gas, grocery retail, manufacturing, business association, banking, and deconstruction sectors as well as assisted nonprofits. Her executive speech coaching sessions have helped business leaders improve their presentation skills and prepare for important meetings and media interviews.

Ms. Kinzey taught public relations, public speaking, and journalism at University of North Carolina - Charlotte. During her tenure, she established and chaired the Journalism Curriculum Committee and oversaw Communication Department internships.

Ms. Kinzey has conducted seminars for businesses and nonprofits on topics such as crisis communication, community relations, media relations, public speaking, internal communications, customer service, and personal branding. In addition, she has facilitated strategic planning sessions for board of director members.

A regular columnist for the American City Business Journals, Ms. Kinzey's editorials have appeared nationwide, addressing a wide variety of reputational topics such as corporate responsibility, trust, strategic communication, employee engagement, and developing planned relationships with government and nonprofit partners. Her corporate responsibility comments on sustainability and health and wellness issues in the grocery industry can be seen in her blogs on Supermarket News' ReFresh (www. whrefresh.com). She is a contributing writer to the U.S. Chamber's Business Civic Leadership Center and has helped select finalists for BCLC Corporate Citizenship Awards.

Always focused on strategically building the reputation of her employers, Ms. Kinzey's work captured: Progressive Grocer's Chief Marketing Officer (CMO) of the Year at two companies; Retailer of the Year; federal and state energy-related awards; International Association of Business Communicator awards; PR News Corporate Social Responsibility Environmental Communications recognition; National Association of Investors, Financial Analysts Federation, and Financial World awards for annual reports; and professional and industry recognition for employee communication.

She is the author of the book *Using Public Relations Strategies to Promote Your Nonprofit Organization* (1999).

Ms. Kinzey has a master's degree from University of Iowa in Journalism, with an emphasis on public relations. She is a magna cum laude and Phi Beta Kappa graduate of Coe College, where she earned a triple major in speech, English, and secondary education.

She is a member of the Public Relations Society of America, International Association of Business Communicators, The Communication Leadership Exchange, and Phi Kappa Phi. Ms. Kinzey serves on the College of Charleston's Communication Department Advisory Council. She also has chaired committees and served on boards of directors for multiple nonprofit organizations as well as been involved with fundraising.

Ms. Kinzey was named as one of the "Top 25 Women in Business" by the Charlotte Business Journal and is a Paul Harris Fellow of the Rotary International Foundation.

The Kinzey Company is headquartered in Salisbury, NC. The business is a member of A Billion + Change, which mobilizes skills-based and pro bono volunteer services to help build the capacity of nonprofit organization to meet community needs.

Acknowledgments

I never would have undertaken this project if Dr. Marcella DeVeaux, Assistant Professor in the Department of Journalism at California State University, Northridge, had not contacted me to locate copies of my first book, *Using Public Relations Strategies to Promote Your Nonprofit Organization* (1999). It was this email that inspired me to consider writing another book. It is my hope she will find this book to be as helpful to her in the classroom as my previous one.

Several professionals were willing to share their insights and practical experiences. For their dedication to and passion for the nonprofit sector as well as for their contribution to this book, I am deeply appreciative. These individuals are:

- Charlie Becker, Executive Director, Camp Courageous of Iowa
- Shelia Brown, FRSM, OBE, CEO, Newlife Foundation for Disabled Children
- Cheryl Carpenter, Managing Editor, *The Charlotte Observer*
- Michael Fanning, Director of Sustainable Development, Michelin Group
- Stephen Jordan, Executive Director, Business Civic Leadership Center; U.S. Chamber of Commerce
- Catherine (Kitty) Keller, Director of Communication & Outreach, Business Civic Leadership Center; U.S. Chamber of Commerce
- Jean Lupinacci, Chief, ENERGY STAR Commercial and Industrial Branch, U.S. Environmental Protection Agency
- Elaine Lyerly, CEO Lyerly Agency
- Kate Meier, Regional Communication Director, Carolina Piedmont Region, American Red Cross
- Dick Meisterling, Vice President for Advancement, Coe College
- Jane Meseck, Director of Citizenship & Public Affairs, Microsoft
- Michelle Nunn, CEO, Points of Light
- Katie Delahaye Paine, CEO KDPaine & Partners, LLC
- Dr. Karen Shumway, Associate Dean of the College of Business, Angelo State University

- Dave Stangis, Vice President, Public Affairs and Corporate Responsibility, Campbell Soup Company
- Stacy Wilson, President, Eloquer Consulting, Inc.

Several others helped by sharing resources, providing input, or facilitating research. These individuals deserve to be acknowledged as well:

- Larissa Allison, Events Coordinator and Director of Alumni Outreach, Communications Department, College of Charleston
- Dr. Bethany Crandell Goodier, Associate Professor and Chair of the Communications Department, College of Charleston
- Randall Hitt, Director of Marketing Development, Community Link
- Tom Murphy, Director of Corporate Communications, Citizenship & Community Affairs, Microsoft
- Hayes Roth, Chief Marketing Officer, Landor

Organizations

- European Union – Sustainable Production & Consumption, Ecolabel
- Forest Stewardship Council
- Marine Stewardship Council
- U.S. Environmental Protection Agency – Energy Star

Also, I wish to express my gratitude to all who offered encouragement and support throughout the research and writing process.

My husband, Joseph Elgin Gettys, deserves a very special "thank you." He was my greatest "cheerleader" in this endeavor. He urged me to take on this assignment and served as "chief motivator" throughout the entire process. For this, I am deeply grateful.

List of Models, Worksheets, and Boxes

Introduction

To set the tone, I thought it would be helpful to begin by hearing from three respected individuals who share unique perspectives on the non-profit world. Their thoughtful remarks serve as a foundation to many of the points made throughout the book and call attention to the not-for-profit ecosystem, which is affected by factors such as the economy, social media, shifts in commerce, and changing lifestyles.

The Nonprofit Landscape

Shelia Brown, FRSM, OBE, Newlife Foundation for Disabled Children

When I first joined a charity committee, I was told the "secrets of fund-raising." People have come up with hundreds of different versions of this in the intervening forty plus years, but I have applied these secrets consistently to my professional practice. And, they have proven to be true. The landscapes may change in the not-for-profit arena, but some truths hold firm. We just need to learn to adapt.

So, while I use the "three secrets" as a final test, the "mechanism" I now use to deliver the three fundraising secrets are very different from earlier years. Now, I consider how the "three secrets" can be achieved when trying to reach an increasingly sophisticated, rather sympathy weary, information-age-besieged potential supporter.

Here are the secrets. I was told there are only three reasons why people give:

1. They give because there is something in it for them.
2. They give because someone they respect or have a relationship with asked them to give.
3. They are or have been personally affected or fear being affected directly or that one of their family/friends will be affected.

Now, you may say this is a bit cynical, but if you examine this carefully, you will see the honesty of it.

Secret 1 is about raffles, lotteries, and theatre tickets as a result of making a donation, etc. You offer something they want—whether it's a ticket to a society ball or the lucky lottery ticket—and people will engage with you if you make it attractive and desirable, thereby raising funds.

It's about choosing to buy goods from low-priced charity shops. You don't need a lot of empathy as a donor to engage with this as it is self-rewarding.

However, you are more likely to make repeat or generous/multiple purchases, if Secrets 2 and/or 3 also apply to the offer.

The changing landscape has bought and will continue to bring fundraising delivered by technology and associated media communications. So, engaging in an online discount where you get a discount offer and the charity gets a donation for directing you to the site is still relevant to Secret 1.

The mechanisms have changed, and people's desires may be more sophisticated. For example, meeting a celebrity or attending a premiere may be more desirable than it was considered to be a few years ago. So, we must adapt to donor desires and the mechanisms we use. But the heart of Secret 1 remains: it's still about the offer and personal benefit.

I built a multi-million pound not-for-profit business based on giving the public something they wanted at the right price and letting them feel good about their purchase because they benefit and so does someone else. But, how do you sell the "something in it for them" offer?

Years ago, it was enough to stress that the "ask" was to "help a charity." Nowadays, the balance has changed. You must first stress the benefit and then follow up with how it helps the charity. This move toward "personal benefit" is key. Fundraising mechanisms must now be personalized to meet the donors' known or researched needs.

Recognizing donor needs is essential to using the "something in it for them." Forget offering young people a chance to win a ticket for dinner with a movie star, if the celebrity hasn't had a film in twenty years. However, if you target the age group who recognizes this person, they will be delighted. So, target benefits to donors and use a variety of mechanisms to succeed in this changing landscape.

Secret 2 is about "who" asks. In this networked world, whether corporate, family, close friends, or a Facebook group, we are all connected in some way.

We each receive so many "asks." We are assailed with requests by advertising, emails, street fundraising, and more. Wherever we go, someone wants something. How do we select who to respond to? In my experience, "word of mouth" is still the valued connection between people. Recommendations still work, even in this digital world. So, "who" asks us is vital.

Through the ages, we have seen a rise in celebrities doing the "ask," followed by leading business people appealing to donors to join them. Increasingly, governments deliver the "ask" as they face reduction in statutory funds to support welfare and services. Does this work? Probably, yes. And, some "asks" work better for some people than others.

Picking who asks on behalf of your charity is crucial. Should it be the latest TV star or a politician, the head of a multi-national, or a notable person of integrity (chair, minister, doctor)? The complexity of this is its undoing.

Strategically, not-for-profits have to use several people to deliver different asks. There is no point asking the head of a corporation to sell low-priced raffle tickets or getting a celebrity from an emerging pop group to ask via your direct email, as no one over forty (with disposable income) will recognize them. Using a "horses for courses" methodology, we see the personalization of asks being very different today than in the past.

I believe the transparency of the organization also will come into its own in the coming years. I see the trend of faceless charities coming to an end. People want to interact with people. In my organization, we are committed to this as a policy, sharing who does what in the organization and being very open on fund usage. People want to trust the charity they give to. If a staff member is asking, they are your ambassadors. So, they must be believable, credible, and knowledgeable about the whole organization.

Your "ask" may not come from the highly trained fundraiser, but from the pioneering doctors or dedicated nurse your funds support. The people-to-people connection is what will matter in an age when we can be very isolated as individuals, despite the noise that networking makes.

Secret 3 is about being personally affected. This is the most powerful one because it causes people to engage longer, give repeated gifts, volunteer, become passionate advocates and ambassadors, and effectively raise the most money. I have amended this secret to include "fear." I have added this because the world has changed.

Years ago, we didn't know we were at risk of developing all sorts of conditions or what risk factor we had, including falling foul of some misfortune, accident, or abuse. Today, we are assailed by this information, and fear is a big motivator. Whether it motivates you to go to the gym, drive more carefully, or fund research to help prevent something from happening, donors can be made to feel engaged by limiting their risks and reducing their fears.

Apart from the three Secrets, we, as not-for-profit organizations, have to understand what a charity is, if we are to survive and prosper. It's my view that giving to a charity is instinctive. To illustrate this, I often ask people to imagine walking along the street when a stranger next to them trips. The instinct of most people is to reach forward in that split second and grab them. It's a very human instinct to respond to a crisis. There are some who will lurch away rather than reach out, but they are in the minority. We understand it is instinctive to most humans to respond, when they see or are faced with a need. In the same way, if a charity reveals the needs of those it serves and does this in a honest and respectful way, allowing the donor to connect with improving a person's life and then goes on to reward them by showing how their gift has helped, the funding will be repeated and support will grow.

Personalization is the key to connecting. For example, we can no longer hope to issue one press release to carry a story. We have to reshape it for the tastes and interests of many readers in multiple media. While running in a sponsored race will appeal to some folks, knitting to raise funds will appeal to others. Now, more than ever, understanding the personality and needs of the supporters or potential supporters is critical. Only then, will the three secrets to increased giving levels really work.

In the not-for-profit world, we are very creative in trying to think of ways people can give, but I don't think we spend sufficient time asking ourselves what donors want to feel. It's not enough just making it easy for them to give. It's about giving them control. This means that charities should not just say they spent £1m on building a Community Center but should report the impact that the Community Center has on changing lives. This is increasingly important for developing a high level of trust. And, people must trust when listening to your message.

Years ago, people would make a donation. We would thank them and that was that. The next year, we would ask them again. They just trusted the organization to use the funds wisely. They surrendered control. Today, sophisticated people want control. They lack trust and want to know about impact. In my organization, 87 percent of donations come in with donor restrictions. They want to know that 100 percent of their gift has bought a bed or healed an animal (not a penny taken out for lighting or paperwork). Not only that, they want to know if the child or dog helped lives in their area and the child or dog's first name. We encourage this control. It's about detail and personalization. The detail matters.

Speed matters, too. If your "ask" says the need is dire, but you don't tell them how their gift helped for six weeks, it loses the impact in their heart and mind. We are living in a world of "instants." Everything is fast, and donors want quick satisfaction and service from organizations they support.

There is the "value for money" imperative that today's supporters' desire. They want to know the organization is efficient and effective. They want to know the charity is a good steward of funds. If they donate goods, they want to know the products are being sold for best value. When they buy from your shops or stalls, they want keen competitive prices; it's not enough to "be for a good cause." People have enormous choices about how they spend their money these days and want a bargain. Adding a premium to the price because it's for a charity just won't work long-term for most donors.

The changing landscape is driving charities to be more strategic, personalizing their "ask," highly targeting in their approach, delivering controls to the donor, and giving fast and effective feedback to feed the "feel good" factor. Regardless of location, human beings will by nature have a tendency to be loyal, but charities today and in the future will have to work harder and smarter to be the "chosen charity." We need to learn from industry and from one another what works. Jealousies and protectionism within the nonprofit sector often act as barriers to this.

The future will develop more speed, more effective information pathways, and clever mechanisms to engage donors. However, our charitable messages will be competing with a never-ending rise of "asks." Standing out from the crowd will be a challenge. Plus, it is likely we will continue to see a rise in the levels of "empathy fatigue," burn out, distrust, and cynicism. They must build relationship with donors more than ever before. Organizations need to be professional, but personality will matter. Organizations that have staff with personality who can personalize the "ask" and who are truly engaged with the culture and aims will succeed. This will differentiate their organization from the endless noise of other charities.

One final prediction is that there will be a greater threat from reputational damage. In the past and yet today, people tend to be generous in spirit. But the culture of complaining and the ability to spread a complaint virally, via the Internet and social media, is enormous. No doubt, we will see more of this. Organizations must deliver what the donor needs in a personalized way, must respond to prevent and manage issues, even saying "sorry" when this is needed. A complaint thirty years ago was an angry letter in red pen that stayed in the office. Now, the same letter can reach millions at the click of a mouse. I have been told you can't buy back reputation. It's truer for the not-for-profit sector than for the corporate sector, which can invest in marketing their way out of a reputational crisis.

I have explained why my tried and tested three secrets are strategically important and described opportunities and warnings about our changing landscape. I haven't mentioned governance and the many other things that haunt the day of a charity's CEO, but these are changing, too. Sometimes, it feels like not only are the rules to the game changing, but the goal posts have moved. Still, despite the frustrations, every day you work in our sector, you will be playing your part in making things better; and this can be personally rewarding.

Shelia Brown, FRSM, OBE, is the co-founder and CEO of Newlife Foundation for Disabled Children, the United Kingdom's leading children and family disability charity. Newlife has funded approximately £15 million of child health medical research.

Ms. Brown is a Fellow of the Royal Society of Medicine (FRSM). She was presented with the Order of the British Empire (OBE) by Her Majesty the Queen for services to child health in 2001.

In addition to being an advisor to trusts and organizations on numerous, not-for-profit subjects, including marketing and grant making, she also possesses a business background. Having operated a growing, multimillion pound business, she has received an Ernst and Young Social Entrepreneur Award.

Ms. Brown first served on a nonprofit committee at age thirteen. Two of her three grown sons suffered disabilities, so she her "passions are very personal."

A Marketer's Perspective

Elaine Lyerly, The Lyerly Agency

I understand the challenges that non-profit organizations face when it comes to engaging with volunteers and donors. Today, there is more competition for donated dollars, causing CEOs to strengthen their developmental staff and realign their boards. Because of this, effectively telling your story is more important than ever, but without an understanding of communications, it will be a struggle to connect with and retain members, donors, and volunteers.

What's essential is an understanding that communications and fundraising are the front and back of the same hand—and that all non-profit communications have fundraising as a goal. You must communicate in a way that reaches out and engages your audiences with your mission. This is where emotional branding comes into play. Donors need facts and figures to understand the impact of your organization (left brain), but they also need an emotional (right brain) connection because they make their decisions based on how they feel. By making an emotional connection, you retain and engage new audiences by acknowledging and appealing to their feelings. When you share stories that can be felt with the heart, you establish a perpetual bond and loyal donors.

Recent studies of donors prove several key points of difference that should be taken into consideration: men and women give differently—fundraising is not gender neutral; non-profits are more competitive today than ever before; and many organizations are experiencing donor bases "aging out."

The differences in how men and women give can be seen in the classic right brain, left brain scenario. Men tend to be left brain givers. They can be more analytical and look at an organization in terms of what it does, how it functions, and the impact the organization has made. They tend to write checks without developing a strong bond with the organization.

Women, on the other hand, are typically right brain givers. They want to know the organization is a good steward of their donation, and they also want to see the mission in action and hear the stories of those they have helped. The biggest difference is that women want to roll up their sleeves, get involved and get their friends involved, too. This is why there has been a tremendous growth in women's collective giving groups. Women are driving social change and finding ways to involve and engage within their communities.

While the importance of seeking donations from both men and women is obvious, heed this interesting bit of information: Women are responsible for or influence about 85 percent of all purchases and manage 83 percent of household income. Since we know women prefer to stay involved with the organizations they support, keeping women top of mind when constructing messages to attract donors is smart; they are key in making philanthropic decisions. Non-profit organizations are beginning to realize the value in speaking to women and how women have the power and desire to create consistent, long-term financial and volunteer support.

Another trend in the industry is the amount of competition surrounding non-profits. With more than 1.5 million non-profit organizations in the United States, keeping your mission recognized is a challenge, but the key to this is connecting your audience with your mission. Mission moments, or as I like to call them, your "five hanky stories," are a great tool to demonstrate the results of your organization's work. When donors can see their money in action through hearing the stories of people their donation has helped, this creates a connection that solidifies the opportunity of retaining current donors and recruiting new ones. It is one thing to hear a CEO talk about how contributions have helped the organization grow and touch lives, but it's another to see a mother cry tears of appreciation while telling her story of how the organization provided life-changing surgery for her child. Or, families recount their stories of being provided shelter and a new start after losing everything they had to a devastating tornado. These stories give life to an organization's mission and are the backbone of a successful program.

Finally, many non-profit organizations are experiencing their donor base aging out. The need to reach young donors is more important than ever to establish long-term support. Young adults are eager to contribute to causes they find worthy, however, the ability to make a donation must be streamlined and easy. In a fast-paced world of electronic information sharing, young adults don't want to pick up the phone and call in to make a donation or write a check; they want to text a donation or make a donation online—in seconds. Tailoring your communications to this audience will create a significant difference in your organization's success, but understanding what to say is crucial.

Promoting Nonprofit Organizations: A Reputation Management Approach is a must-have resource for non-profit organizations seeking help in understanding and communicating with potential members, volunteers and donors. The knowledge and experience Ruth Kinzey shares in this book are invaluable and can help you implement a successful non-profit communications program. This book offers key strategies and the knowledge needed to gain the attention of your audience and meet your organizational goals in the increasingly competitive non-profit arena.

Elaine Lyerly is president and CEO of Lyerly Agency, a marketing communications firm in North Carolina. She has more than thirty-five years of experience in strategic marketing, branding, and corporate communications.

Ms. Lyerly has served in numerous nonprofit leadership roles at the American Red Cross, including Vice Chair of the American Red Cross national Board of Governors, national Chair of Communications and Fundraising, national Vice Chair of Public Support. She also served as co-chair of a national task force to examine Red Cross' ability to raise non-episodic dollars. Ms. Lyerly served as national Chair of the American Red Cross Tiffany Circle, the most successful major gift program in the history of the American Red Cross. Having raised $44 million in six years, this women's giving group serves as a model for other donor engagement programs. In 2012, she received the highest Red Cross national award: the Harriman Award for Distinguished Volunteer Service.

Ms. Lyerly is a past Chair of the Women's Impact Fund and has received numerous leadership and business awards.

Collaboration with Business

Stephen Jordan, Business Civic Leadership Center

In this time of economic turmoil, civil society organizations, whether community groups, faith-based groups, or service-oriented non-profits, are more valuable than ever. Not just to the communities and the individuals they serve but to their partners in the business community. The past thirty years have brought about some significant transformations within the business sector. Businesses are expected to do more to give back to society, and at the same time, they are still supposed to take care of their employees, customers, and investors at or exceeding their previous levels of service. Most businesses will tell you that they would much rather stick to doing what they do best—hardware store owners would like to sell hardware, medical equipment manufacturers would like to focus on producing medical equipment, and so on; so, when it comes to engaging with community needs, they really rely on the experts—the non-profit sector.

This is why Ruth Kinzey has provided a valuable service in writing this book. It helps to promote understanding between the business community and the non-profit community. It helps all of us to understand each other better—our strengths and weaknesses, opportunities and challenges. In many ways, we are all on the same team, trying to make our own individual contributions to human progress according to our own lights. Books like this one start to provide insights about how our individual pieces might be able to work better together. This is the definition of social capital—that the whole can be greater than the sum of the parts, and isn't this what we all want in the end?

Stephen Jordan is the founder and executive director of the Business Civic Leadership Center (BCLC), the corporate citizenship affiliate of the U.S. Chamber of Commerce.

In addition to his work at BCLC, Mr. Jordan currently serves on the U.S. National Commission for the United Nations Educational, Scientific and Cultural Organization (UNESCO), the Board of Governors of the Corporate Responsibility Officers' (CRO) Association, and the New World Institute. He is a Caux Round Table fellow.

Previously, Mr. Jordan served as executive director of the Association of American Chambers of Commerce in Latin America from 1997 to 1999. He worked in the publishing industry and has a background in strategy, marketing, and new product development. Early in his career, he was a legislative assistant for the Senate Foreign Relations Committee.

Mr. Jordan holds an M.B.A. from Georgetown University and an M.A. in Political and Social Thought from the University of Virginia, with accompanying academic honors from both institutions. He is a member of Beta Gamma Sigma, the business honor society.

1 Welcome to the Not-for-Profit World

What I do, you cannot do; but what you do, I cannot do. The needs are great, and
none of us, including me, ever do great things. But we can all do small things, with
great love, and together we can do something wonderful.

(Mother Teresa of Calcutta)

What Is a Nonprofit?

Perhaps, jokingly. Perhaps, not. Companies sometimes say they are nonprofit because their business model just breaks even or, worse yet, their
current financial records show them as operating at a loss. But just because
a firm is not operating at a profitable level, does not qualify the business to
call itself a not-for-profit entity.

In fact, there are marked differences between a for-profit and a not-for-
profit. Some of these differences are:

Legally, a charity is required to serve its mission rather than to make a
profit.

Although a nonprofit can engage in selling products or paid-for services
and may compete with a company in this regard, its primary mission is to
raise funds to support its mission.

Typically, unpaid community leaders, members, or other such individuals volunteer time and expertise to serve on the board of directors of
the organization.

The nonprofit's board of directors is focused on meeting the needs of
the community, its members, or other key stakeholders rather than on
profit generation.

Any excess revenue generated through the sale of products or services is
plowed back into the institution. This is so the organization can continue
to serve its primary mission and ensures tax-exempt status is maintained.

Because the primary purpose of the nonprofit is to serve rather than
make money, it is not in a position to pay full costs for the services and
products it needs. Consequently, the organization may request nonprofit
discounts from for-profit businesses.

Unlike a for-profit business, nonprofit employees are never expected to be compensated at a "higher than reasonable rate" for salaries, hourly pay, and benefits. If this occurs, public outcry is common, producing reputational issues for the organization.

The nonprofit typically serves people and causes that cannot afford to pay at the usual fee-for-service rate, if at all.

In the United States, there are several types of organizations that qualify for tax-exempt status, falling primarily within the 501(c) category. (See Box 1.1: U.S. Tax-Exempt Organization Reference Chart for 501(c) Entities and Box 1.2: Other IRS Tax-Exempt Categories.)

At times, the term "NGO" is used interchangeably with "nonprofit." The acronym stands for "Non-Governmental Organizations." This organization is legally constituted to operate separately from the government and not as a for-profit business. Even if an NGO receives partial or total funding by a government entity, it maintains its non-governmental status by excluding any government representation in its membership or board.

Typically, the term "NGO" is used with a nonprofit that has a social aim with political aspects unrelated to political parties. An example is a not-for-profit that focuses on advocacy issues, such as the Nature Conservancy. Smaller groups, such as local nonprofits focused on improving a community or its ecosystem, would be considered NGOs, too.[1]

However, NGO is considered too broad of a name by some. These individuals prefer to use the term "private volunteer organization" or PVO.

The Status of the Nonprofit

The overriding purpose of a nonprofit is to meet a need or to solve a problem. Whether focusing on human services, saving the environment, improving the professionalism of an individual, or establishing a formal bond for those dedicated to a particular purpose or hobby, there is a common theme: the organization pursues a non-profit making mission. For this reason, donors and volunteers play a critical role in a nonprofit's ability to operate.

Volunteerism Today

According to the Corporation for National and Community Service, there were 62.8 million adults providing nearly 8.1 billion volunteer hours in 2010, with Generation X becoming a growing volunteer base and having devoted significantly more of their time to volunteerism than in the past.[2]

According to the U.S. Bureau of Labor Statistics, the volunteer rate rose 0.5 percent between September 2010 and 2011. This increase followed a decline of equal proportion in the previous 12-month period. While the overall percent was 26.8, the volunteer rate for women rose from 29.3 to 29.9 percent. Male volunteerism, which was at 23.5 percent, changed little. The volunteer rate for parents with children under 18 remained high

Box 1.1   U.S. Tax-Exempt Organization Reference Chart for 501(c) Entities

IRS Publication 557: http://www.irs.gov/pub/irs-pdf/p557.pdf

501(c)(1)	Corporations organized under Act of Congress, including federal credit unions
501(c)(2)	Title Holding Corporation for Exempt Organization
501(c)(3)	Religious, educational, charitable, scientific, literary, testing for public safety, to foster national or international amateur sports competition, or prevention of cruelty to children or animal organizations. Subclasses include private foundations and public charities
501(c)(4)	Civic leagues, social welfare organizations, and local associations of employees
501(c)(5)	Labor, agricultural, and horticultural organizations
501(c)(6)	Business leagues, chambers of commerce, real estate boards, and other organizations focused on the improvement of business conditions of one or more lines of business
501(c)(7)	Social and recreation clubs, including hobby clubs, dinner clubs, country clubs, college fraternities and sororities, alumni associations, amateur hunting, fishing, tennis and other sports clubs
501(c)(8)	Fraternal beneficiary societies and associations
501(c)(9)	Voluntary employees' beneficiary associations
501(c)(10)	Domestic fraternal societies and associations
501(c)(11)	Teachers' retirement fund associations
501(c)(12)	Benevolent life insurance associations, mutual ditch or irrigation companies, mutual or cooperative telephone companies, etc.
51(c)(13)	Cemetery companies
501(c)(14)	State chartered credit unions, mutual reserve funds
501(c)(15)	Mutual insurance companies or associations
501(c)(16)	Cooperative organizations to finance crop operations
501(c)(17)	Supplemental unemployment benefit trusts
501(c)(18)	Employee funded pension trust (created prior to June 25, 1959)
501(c)(19)	Post or organization of past or present members of the Armed Forces
501(c)(20)	Group legal services plan organizations
501(c)(21)	Black lung benefit trusts
501(c)(22)	Withdrawal liability payment fund
501(c)(23)	Veterans organization (created before 1880)
501(c)(25)	Title holding corporations or trusts with multiple parents
501(c)(26)	State-sponsored organization providing health coverage for high-risk individuals
501(c)(27)	State-sponsored workers' compensation reinsurance organization
501(c)(28)	National railroad retirement investment trust
501(c)(29)	Co-Op health insurance issuers

Box 1.2	Other IRS Tax-Exempt Categories
501(d)	Religious and apostolic associations
501(e)	Cooperative hospital service organizations
501(f)	Cooperative service organizations of operating educational organizations
501(k)	Child care organizations
501(n)	Charitable risk pools
501(q)	Credit Counseling Organizations
521(a)	Farmers' cooperative associations
527	Political organizations

at 33.7 percent. (This statistic obviously correlates closely with the increase in Gen X volunteerism.) And, individuals who possessed higher educational levels volunteered at a higher rate than those with less education.

The two most frequent volunteer activities are: fundraising and collecting, preparing, distributing, or serving food. Men and women volunteered in different ways. Men were more likely to volunteer time in general labor activities; then, coaching, refereeing, or supervising sports teams; and finally, fundraising. Women were more likely to fundraise. Collect, prepare, distribute or serve food was the second most popular form of volunteerism. Tutoring was the third most likely volunteer activity for women.[3]

But as the economic downturn continues, the question is will more individuals turn to volunteerism because of the positive and rewarding feeling it gives them and the skills and contacts it can provide, or, if weary from working multiple jobs and long-hours just to make ends meet for their families, will the pool of volunteers shrink?

The Status of Philanthropy

Globally, nonprofits made up the fastest-growing sector in 2008. There were more than 2 million nonprofits, and more than 1.5 million were in the United States. More than 161,000 were listed in Canada. In 1940, there were only 12,000 charities based in the United States, and, even as recently as 1998, only 733,790 not-for-profits were listed.[4]

According to Giving USA, 2011 charitable giving in the United States grew 4 percent over the previous year. When adjusted for inflation, this actually is a .9 percent increase. The organization also noted the impact of the significant recessionary period during 2010 and 2011 meant this rate of growth was the second slowest since 1971. The only time where charitable giving was even lower was the time frame following the attack on U.S. soil in 2001.

The Center on Philanthropy at Indiana University, which produces the Giving USA report, has tracked charitable giving for 57 years. Based on its recent findings, the organization states, "One truism ... is the importance of individual giving. Surprises include the fast growth of giving to international affairs over the last decade, thanks to both an explosion in the number of charities serving this arena and an increasing cognizance among Americans about needs beyond our borders."[5]

These two concepts—the important role of the individual and the increasing influence and recognition of worldwide affairs and issues, including the Global Village concept—have significantly impacted the conduct, fundraising capabilities, and mission of many not-for-profits.

In Competition with Business

Interestingly, those engaged in commerce may find themselves competing with nonprofits. When this is the case, criticism may be leveled against the nonprofit because of its advantageous tax-exempt status. But, nonprofits receive other financial benefits, too, such as reduced postage rates and use of office space, equipment, supplies, and even staff through government grants, foundations, and unrelated business enterprises. Of course, in-kind donations or other contributions to a nonprofit qualify for tax deduction status, thus making this type of commitment appealing to both individuals and companies.

Criticism of nonprofits' advantageous stature started to appear during the 1970s, when charities, NGOs, and other qualifying organization became increasingly sophisticated in their efforts to generate revenue. These not-for-profits ramped up revenue-generating tactics in the 1980s, when the U.S. government began cutting funding to many social services.[6]

Given today's economic slump and condition of the global economy, some nonprofits are seeing government support for their organizations wane. In addition, foundations may cutback or eliminate grants because of reduced budgets, which are linked to the stock market, banking institutions, or monetary contributions from individuals, community groups, or companies. Businesses, which made major monetary donations in the past, may reduce their giving level because of the decline in sales and profits, produced by this lengthy economic downturn.

It's clear the economic climate will always impact and many times challenge nonprofits. Consequently, these groups must focus on innovation to help with fundraising and volunteer recruitment. Currently, use of social media and an increased reliance on other tactics, such as cause-related marketing, are helping nonprofits fund their work. Operating at—what in some cases is a perilous level—these nonprofits will likely utilize the lessons learned during this recessionary period and continue to hone new communication, fundraising, and revenue-generating techniques well into the future.

In this Book

The purpose of the subsequent chapters is to provide a thoughtful dis-course on specific communication elements for the nonprofit of today that also has an eye on its future.

Similar to my first book, *Using Public Relations Strategies to Promote Your Nonprofit Organization,* each chapter takes an in-depth look at a particular communications element, which is of strategic importance to the not-for-profit world. At the conclusion of each chapter, insights related to the discussion will be shared by organizations. These comments add to the scope of this book's content and provide a real-life commentary on the subject.

2 Strategic Communications Planning

All men can see these tactics whereby I conquer, but what none can see is the strategy out of which victory is evolved.

(Sun Tzu, *The Art of War*)

The strategic planning function is a standard practice for for-profit and not-for-profit entities. It is an accepted process that enhances organizational credibility, reflects the degree of management's professionalism, and creates an operational roadmap—both financially and contextually. A pragmatic discipline, strategic planning fosters thinking and acting based on a well-researched analysis of the past and present; potential opportunities and threats; and organizational strengths, weaknesses, priorities, and competencies.

Strategic planning also frames resource deployment, while taking into consideration environmental interactions in a manner that will enable the achievement of superior performance.

This systematic approach, which focuses on shaping the future, creates a path to overcome obstacles by providing direction for management on a day-to-day basis and guidance in long-term problem solving and opportunity evaluation. A distinctive function, this effort aligns goals, priorities, competencies, and tactics with the mission and brand.

Business uses strategic planning because of its benefits as well as shareholders and/or government mandates. While the not-for-profit may not be legally or formally obligated to engage in this process, the astute nonprofit recognizes the value of a strategic plan and is committed to pursuing this proactive course of action on an annual basis to ensure:

- alignment of priorities and direction between board and staff, resulting in a clear understanding of and focus on the group's mission, purpose, goals, long-term vision, values, and cultural expectations;
- effective and efficient use of the limited staff and resources;
- a logical, problem-solving approach to shortcomings or issues management;
- risk and crisis avoidance;

- enhanced performance through well-planned and targeted effort within established time parameters;
- avoidance of seemingly excellent opportunities that would take the organization off its primary course and mission;
- a visionary and creative approach, which addresses "the big picture" through the development of a very specific plan of action;
- the framing of fundamental approaches to ensure the outcome will be the desired social reality; and
- a careful and deliberate selection and development of key external and internal stakeholder alliances to fully leverage all communication opportunities to maximize results.

But, isn't no strategic plan better than a poor one? In some ways, a poor strategic plan is the same as not having one. Characteristics of a poor plan include a lack of focus, permitting the organization to get off track. Lack of definition in or refinement of the various components of the strategic plan, such as insufficient direction, detail, or measurement, and not understanding the difference between strategy and goals create issues, too.

While few would argue the necessity of organizational strategic planning, it does not always occur in the communications department. Unfortunately, some nonprofits only talk about the importance of developing a solid strategic communication plan. Although the desire to undergo this process may be strong, these entities—particularly those of small or medium size—may find it difficult to keep up with the day-to-day requirements of the department, much less to commit the necessary time to develop this comprehensive document.

Many excuses may be offered for not undertaking this process, like "it won't fix everything so why bother," "we're still working from the one we designed a couple of years ago," or "we don't have time and everything is going okay." Yet, strategic communication planning must be a mainstream activity because by developing and adhering to a thoughtful strategy and plan, the department's efforts are more efficient, focused, and results-oriented. This contemplative preparation also helps ensure major communication barriers are uncovered sooner rather than in the midst of a campaign roll-out or during a crisis.

Consequently, rather than viewing strategic communication planning as a cumbersome burden for which there is no time, it must be seen as a function that complements the nonprofit's overarching strategic plan. There is only one reason why an organization should not routinely go through the strategic communication planning process: It lacks the resources or personnel with the skills and/or commitment to undertake this assignment and is unable to access assistance.

Communications Strategy

In today's fast-paced world of information overload, people find that determining which messages are important and why they should care is overwhelming. Therefore, it is extremely challenging for not-for-profits to cut through this chaotic bombardment and clutter of emotional appeals to connect with critical stakeholders. For that reason, it is worthwhile to tackle this arduous and challenging process by systematically analyzing the critical elements of a comprehensive and well-defined strategic communication plan and examining how these components interrelate.

Communication strategic planning is the process through which an organization identifies, agrees upon, and builds commitment among its important stakeholders for priorities essential to its mission. It also provides a broad and coordinated direction that enables the organization to respond to its environment as well as conceptually guides work and management, while staying within the parameters of allocated resources.

One thing is certain, strategic planning is not a smooth nor linear process. There are many challenges involved and numerous environmental influences must be taken into account, which make it necessary for any strategy to be reassessed and altered from time to time. Because influencing factors change, it even may be determined the original strategy is no longer viable and a more feasible approach must be adopted.

So, how does the development of communication strategy begin? In *Strategic Communications for Nonprofits*, the authors set the tone for this exercise with the following comment:

> The strategic communications programs that work best are firmly rooted in an organization's values and purpose. Your communication plan should support your organization's goals and mission statement. Communication is a tool, not an end in itself.[1]

At times, organizations treat departmental strategic plans as tasks to be checked off on a list, sometimes even before the nonprofit has finalized its long-term vision or operational plan. However, an effective communications plan must take its cue from the nonprofit itself. So, the chief communication officer must begin the strategic communications process by asking:

1. Does the nonprofit have a clearly articulated mission statement and purpose that guide all organizational efforts?
2. Does the nonprofit have a well-defined, long-term vision, which aligns with the organization's mission?
3. Has the nonprofit completed its strategic plan, including time frames and tactical components?

Armed with answers to these, it is possible to develop the communication department's strategy and plan, which fully leverages all of its available resources to support the organization's prime directive.

An important note: The outcome of the strategic communication planning process is never truly final. Instead, it is an evolution. Communication efforts must adjust constantly to the environment and adapt to changing priorities. This means the department's work must be assessed; a strategic plan developed and implemented; the work measured, analyzed, and reviewed to know if the goals and objectives were reached; and the assessment process started anew to identify what adjustments are now necessary to meet new challenges in the socio-economic environment (see Model 2.1).

People and relationship-building are at the heart of communications. For that reason, values and ethics should be incorporated into the strategic thought process. A time-tested adage about public relations supports this notion:

> The responsible organization is the organization that is responsible for the consequences it has on its publics. It does so by communicating symmetrically with those publics. Such communication effectively

Model 2.1 Strategic Planning Cycle.

builds good relationships for the organization. As a result, public relations and public responsibility become nearly synonymous terms.[2]

Erika Andersen, in *Being Strategic*, also suggests three features she considers foundational to strategic planning:

- Feasibility—Is it actually possible to achieve or make the effort?
- Impact—Will the proposed strategy be a good use of resources to make an impact?
- Timeliness—Is there a chance to do something within the time frame and can it be done in the necessary order.[3]

While the aforementioned may seem instinctive, it is necessary to give deliberate thought to the reality of what the department can deliver versus expectations. It is not uncommon for communications personnel to find themselves in awkward or seemingly impossible situations because the nonprofit's desired impact is unattainable due to lack of personnel, insufficient funding, or unrealistic time constraints.

Other complications may include:

- Underestimating the time necessary to develop a comprehensive plan;
- Not taking the department's current work load and available resources into account while planning is underway; and
- Derailment through lack of support or organizational barriers.

First Steps

At this point, the communication officer should have the following key organizational data:

- mission and ethics clearly articulated;
- culture and values understood;
- strategic plan finalized; and
- board and executive management's expectations of the nonprofit and the communications team.

It is now time to begin the homework necessary to create a strong strategic communications plan: research. This step enables the communication team to review where the organization has been and its current status in order to purposefully chart a course for the future. This work includes a strengths-weaknesses-opportunities-challenges (S.W.O.C.) analysis, a scan of environmental influences, a communication audit, a brand audit, and a stakeholder analysis. The data derived from these studies will prove invaluable in designing a targeted communication approach.

Strengths-Weaknesses-Opportunities-Challenges Analysis

The strengths-weaknesses-opportunities-threats (S.W.O.T.), threats-opportunities-weaknesses-strengths (T.O.W.S.), and the strengths-weaknesses-opportunities-challenges (S.W.O.C.) analyses represent time-tested tools. Frequently, organizations use this methodology to take an inventory of their current status, a particular problem, or an issue, followed by a gap analysis to help drive critical thinking to a desired shared vision (see Model 2.2).

Conducted during the initial phase of the strategic process, these models examine an organization's external environment and offer a reflection of the internal condition. The strengths and weaknesses are considered internal factors, while the opportunities and threats/challenges are considered external influences. While both S.W.O.T. and T.O.W.S. use a four-part matrix, they offer a different perspective because of the opposing emphasis. By changing the order of these components, the variation shifts the weight between the external and internal quadrants. Thus, with T.O.W.S., there is greater focus on opportunities and the improved management of threats.

A gap analysis scrutinizes each of the model's four components. Using agreed-upon criteria, a determination is made as to the level of functionality in each quadrant versus the desired performance. The "threats" quadrant typically is examined in terms of seriousness or probability of occurrence.

Results are compiled and recommendations made to correct any deficiencies while capitalizing on positive aspects. Even though this evaluation

Model 2.2 S.W.O.C.

tool can be subjective, it still renders useful data for strategic planning and development. Although business typically uses the S.W.O.T. or the T.O.W.S. approach, the nonprofit could use any of the three formats.

The board of directors should share the outcome of this analysis with the communication department as this insight will help the chief communications officer grasp what leadership believes is the current condition of the organization and the setting in which the nonprofit is operating.

It is recommended the communications team conduct a similar analysis for the department but employ S.W.O.C. methodology. This guidance is based on the possibility the communications team will have to face reputational challenges, which includes the likelihood of threats. As this matrix can identify influencing factors, such as organizational culture and stakeholder satisfaction, the heading of "challenges" addresses a broad range of issues.

The communications officer should probe deeply into each of these four quadrants. Once each category is fully addressed and the gap analysis completed, the outcome should produce a snapshot of reality for comparison to the desired situation.

With a more realistic view of capabilities and needs, it is easier to identify the reputational and operational gaps and thoughtfully determine how resources should be allocated to achieve the goals and objectives. Plus, with a better understanding of the opportunities and challenges as well as the strengths and weaknesses, it is feasible to see potential disconnections among projects, shortcomings in initiatives, or potential risks in planned environmental responses. An accurate assessment also makes it possible to determine the scope of a problem or the urgency of the opportunities and challenges. With this insight, priorities can be established.

For example, a weakness may be that the nonprofit does not have a sufficient social media presence. Therefore, the department is challenged to fully leverage this medium, which might be the most expedient and cost-effective way to reach teenage volunteers or to communicate quickly and directly to students during a crisis.

Likewise, if a board of director member is employed by a major public relations agency and this individual has not been asked to lend communication expertise and guidance to the communication department, there is a missed opportunity. Thus, realistic examinations of each of the four components, individually and how they fit together as a whole, influence both the communications strategy and plan. Worksheet 2.1 (Communications S.W.O.C. Analysis) acts as an initial step in this analysis.

A side benefit to conducting this research is learning how the nonprofit compares to its "competition." The "market" is filled with other nonprofits wanting monetary contributions, volunteer time, in-kind donations, corporate sponsorships, cause-related marketing opportunities, social media chatter, and positive media exposure. Therefore, it is helpful to think of the nonprofit in relation to how these other organizations are perceived.

Worksheet 2.1

Communications S.W.O.C. Analysis

1. List the nonprofit and communication department strengths, upon which the communication department can capitalize.

   1)

   2)

   3)

   4)

   5)

   6)

2. List the weaknesses or shortcomings of the nonprofit or the department that could cause issues or potentially prevent the organization from achieving its goals .

   1)

   2)

   3)

   4)

   5)

   6)

3. What opportunities are available to the organization or the communications department, which could be leveraged advantageously?

   1)

   2)

   3)

   4)

   5)

   6)

4. What communication challenges do the nonprofit and/or the department face?

   1)

   2)

   3)

   4)

   5)

   6)

5. Are there any barriers that would prevent the organization from fully leveraging the nonprofit's communication strengths?

6. Are there any particular risks resulting from the specified challenges that could impact communication?

Environmental Scan

While the S.W.O.C., T.O.W.S., or the S.W.O.T. reveals many things, it is essential to examine the environment in a broader sense. This is where researching trends in the technological, economic, political, regulatory, legal, and social arenas and analyzing their impact on the nonprofit and the department come in to play. The results of this study can reveal unique and compelling drivers affecting why, how, when, and if the organization should respond to its environment.

Technological

Many may say technology is one of—if not the single—most dramatic force shaping society and culture today, which is why it is paramount to monitor this area. With technology impacting how people work, live, and interact among themselves and the environment, it is particularly important this audit occurs at least annually.

An example of what was a trend less than a decade ago but which has significantly impacted marketing and public relations positioning of a nonprofit today is social media. Because this landscape continues to change at a rapid pace and influences a nonprofit's brand, social media is now a critical factor in the communication equation as opposed to a tangential element in the social and environmental landscape. This illustrates how what may be mainstream today may not be indicative of reality in just a few years. By taking these trends into account, it helps the nonprofit prepare for future survival.

The Competition

It is necessary to watch what other not-for-profits are doing. By noticing the marketing techniques, media-capturing tactics, and fundraising successes of others, the communications department can identify the most effective practices and avoid over-used tools or antiquated approaches.

Every nonprofit has a brand identity. Consequently, it is important to know what others are doing to learn if "brand confusion" could arise because of how two nonprofits similarly present their missions and efforts. Messaging distinctively is an essential part of the communications story and the positioning of the organization.

Economic

Nonprofits must watch the economy. A nationwide economic downturn or an individual community's depressed status can cause a budget shortfall or funding crisis for the not-for-profit. For that reason, the agile communications department recognizes this and adapts accordingly. The team may look at how it describes the institution's value to prove it is worthy of a contribution; the target audience may be adjusted to reach or market more likely to donate or volunteer; or a more cost-effective communication channel may be identified.

Political, Regulatory

The political and legislative arenas can influence how a nonprofit functions, too. That's why it is necessary to monitor pending regulation and government budgetary concerns. Changes in public policy or the economy ultimately can be reflected in the nonprofit's bottom line.

For example, since some associations rely extensively upon public funding, a decline in tax revenue could jeopardize the nonprofit's financial future. Even a potential threat, such as candidate's promise to cut monetary support, can impact the institution's strategic communications plan on multiple levels.

Another example is the passage of legislation affecting operations. As more privacy regulation is enacted, it is critical an organization watch for potential regulatory changes and lobby or share concerns accordingly. Otherwise, the nonprofit could be caught unaware and face non-budgeted items, services, or bureaucracy.

Sometimes local governments quietly impose taxes or fees on nonprofits, which can slip by those who aren't vigilant and produce financial hardship. In a survey conducted by Johns Hopkins Listening Post Project, 63 percent of the nonprofits responding to the survey said they were paying some type of local taxes or fees or making other voluntary payments in lieu of taxes. Furthermore, 14 percent said they were aware of state and local plans to impose additional taxes and fees, while 43 percent indicated concern local or state governments intended to adopt new fees or taxes during the next year.[4]

By staying in tune with the regulatory arena, the nonprofit is more likely to be prepared financially and organizationally to deal with legislative changes.

Legal

In this litigious society, the communication department constantly watches to see if another not-for-profit is facing a law suit, as there could always be implications—even if only perceptual—that result.

Another advantage is to learn from the mistakes of others. By studying the communications of organizations facing lawsuits, whether they be related to a personnel issue, a financial problem, or programming concern, it is possible to avoid a similar media faux pas; to create wording that distances the nonprofit from the other entity; and to be prepared with a response if the media asks for a reaction to the situation.

Social

A nonprofit is a social entity by its very nature. It depends upon people to fund its activities and volunteers or members to help it deliver its services. A social audit reviews relationships and perceptions, which reveal the pulse of the social scene and have tremendous implications for communication planning. Analyzing the social environment can identify losses such as:

- If a widespread belief persists that only people with money are likely to align with the nonprofit's mission or that only teenagers are interested in volunteering for the cause.
- If the public feels there is a community need, which is being addressed by the nonprofit, but few seem to be aware of the organization's efforts.
- If collaboration with business has raised the nonprofit's stance to that of a community leadership role.

In addition, this work makes it easier to see both trends and influencers, which could potentially affect the successful implementation of a strategic communication plan.

Other outcomes of the scan include:

- A better understanding of the competitive nonprofit scene
- Improvements in resource allocation
- Better strategic planning and decision-making
- Sensitization to the changing needs of constituents
- Social/economic/environmental sensitivity
- Potential strategic alliances and partnership opportunities
- Reputational insights

In summation, a scan beyond the organization's parameters is necessary, if the communications department intends to design effective communication. To assist with this research, see Worksheet 2.2: Environmental Scan Considerations.

Communication Audit

A communication audit is comprised of many facets, including the systematic examination of both the messages and the communication channels. While this research can be formal or informal, the audit captures a snapshot of communications capacity and performance.

Existing messages are evaluated for consistency with the nonprofit's mission, values, and goals. The channels used to communicate with stakeholders also are examined for effectiveness in reaching the targeted audiences and for cost-effectiveness and appropriateness of message conveyance.

Worksheet 2.2

Environmental Scan Considerations

Sample questions to pose when conducting an environmental scan.

Technological
1. How technologically savvy are your donors/members/students/volunteers?
2. How effective is your web presence as compared to other nonprofits?
3. What is the most recent social media innovation?
4. What public concerns are there about personal privacy and information sharing?
5. What changes are occurring in how people receive information and the type of information they want to access?

The "Competition"
1. How well known is the nonprofit within its geographic area of operation?
2. Are there other charitable entities, government agencies, professional or business associations, educational institutions, religious groups, or social organizations that offer the same services or serve the same purpose?
3. Are there any nonprofits experiencing reputational issues, which could impact your organization? (e.g. The parent organization? Not-for-profits with similar purposes or offering similar services? A shared board member whose integrity is being questioned?)
4. How successful are capital campaigns or other major fundraising initiatives in your "market"?
5. Are any nonprofits sharing resources or developing strategic alliances?

Economic
1. Have there been any layoffs in your area?
2. Are there any new businesses opening that could add to your donor base or provide major philanthropic support?
3. What changes in population are evident during the past one to two years?
4. What shifts occurring in household income?
5. Are there cutbacks in government services where you operate?

Political, Regulatory, Legal
1. Is there any pending legislation that would affect how you conduct your operations?
2. Do elected officials use your organization as an example of what is working efficiently? Or, criticize your spending and other fiscal affairs?
3. Are there law suits against your parent organization or another group with which you are affiliated?
4. Are there pending law suits against other nonprofits in the community, state, or geographic area in which you operate?
5. Are there any new laws about fiscal responsibility, which could impact how the public views your transparency and/or accounting?

Social
1. How are values or lifestyles changing?
2. What attitudinal shifts are occurring toward sustainability?
3. What generational trends are emerging?
4. What multi-cultural trends are emerging?
5. Are there changes occurring in how the family unit is perceived?

Delivery methodology and style are scrutinized. An example of this is observing how effectively an individual delivers a message during a small group session. And, is the communication highly structured, even institutionalized in appearance? Or, is it informally transmitted, almost in an ad hoc manner?

If the message is written, regardless of where it appears, it must be readable. Therefore, it is advantageous to examine the grade level on which the copy is written to ensure it is appropriate for the audience. Reading difficulty is determined by computing factors such as the average sentence length and average number of multi-syllabic words. There are many readability formulas that can assist with this endeavor, such as Gunnig-Fog (also known as the Fog Index), Flesch-Kinkaid, Dale-Chall, and SMOG.

The Flesch Reading Ease or the Flesch-Kinkaid grade level of a document can be checked very easily, if using a Microsoft Word program. When initiating work on the document, the author can go into the **Tools** menu, click on **Options**, and then **Proofing**. Under the grammar and spelling check box, there is a box referencing readability statistics. Whenever the author does a spell check, the readability information will be provided automatically, if this box is enabled.

Although the nonprofit can push a message out to its receiver, it doesn't mean the recipient hears or understands the message as intended. Listeners have many filters influenced by variables such as educational level, current socio-economic status, and family history. Consequently, it is helpful to gain insight into how the information is interpreted in addition to studying the message content and communication methodology. The goal is to have the message seen, interpreted, and remembered with the intended meaning. Interviews, surveys, and observation are all techniques used to ascertain the degree of comprehension and retention.

In addition to understanding the content, visual communication should be examined for format and appearance. For instance, is there strong brand design identity? Is logo style usage consistent? Is the web site easy to navigate?

The context provided through the communication audit enables practical decision-making, which leads to strengthening existing communication strategies, establishing new and appropriate approaches and channel selection, and leveraging cost-effective opportunities.

Brand Audit

The brand audit is connected to the marketing or development function but has implications for the communications professional as well. A comprehensive audit touches on a number of elements that relate to how the brand is perceived, from its positioning and attributes to its creative presentation and brand differentiators. This review examines both internal and external audiences as well as even how effectively the organizational brand represents its culture.

While the communications team may not find all of this data to be relevant, there are some elements that can assist the department in framing communication and aligning the organization's image with the brand. Rather than reviewing all of the characteristics of a brand audit, there are a few elements with which the communication officer should be familiar:

Brand Equity—This refers to the strength or value of the brand. This factor is framed by how familiar key stakeholders are with the nonprofit name, how favorable these audiences perceive the organization, and how distinctively these publics commit the institution's name and image to memory.

Positive brand equity can be particularly helpful to the nonprofit during a crisis because of the established credibility and degree of goodwill possessed.

Brand Personality—The term "personality" refers to distinguishing human characteristics. A brand personality, then, is a description of the nonprofit as if it were a person. For example, is the institution considered to be ethical? Caring? Friendly? Responsive? Just as is the case with human beings, the personality of the organization helps to differentiate it from the other nonprofits.

Possessing an understanding of branding qualities enables the communication team to emphasize these unique and desirable attributes in its messaging. If undesirable traits surface, the department can design "correction" messaging to reposition how the nonprofit is perceived.

Marketing Collateral Review—The study of the nonprofit's promotional materials shows key points emphasized by the development department and the consistency with which the institution's brand has been portrayed.

By tapping into this information, the communication team can identify topics to include in other communication vehicles, such as when further explanation is required about a particular subject; when a reminder needs to be issued about an upcoming event; when recognition or results should be reported; or when an alert promotes a soon-to-be-released announcement should be posted.

The timing of editorial coverage should be linked to marketing efforts as well. For example, if a capital campaign is scheduled, the communications team must determine when it should address this subject in its editorial copy.

These representative scenarios demonstrate much can be gleaned from a brand audit. If the organization's fundraising arm shares this marketing data with the communications team, messaging between the two departments will be better aligned, more fully leveraged, and effectively monitored.

Audience Analysis

The obvious first step in this process is to take an inventory of the non-profit's publics (See Model 2.3). This will provide answers to questions such as:

- With whom does the organization want to communicate?
- With which groups should the nonprofit communicate?
- Have critical audiences been overlooked?
- Due to challenges or opportunities, should more people receive communication through a structured venue?

When creating this list, it is best to use a format that will aid with the segmentation and prioritization of the audience, plus act as a springboard for the development of subsequent communication (see Worksheet 2.3: Audience Analysis Worksheet). With this insight, better message customization occurs, increasing the likelihood of achieving the desired behavior.

Demographic and psychographic data can help the nonprofit better know and understand its multiple audiences. This material can be collected through primary research like interviews, surveys, and focus groups

Model 2.3 Nonprofit Publics.

Worksheet 2.3

Audience Analysis

1. List all audiences of the nonprofit.
   1)
   2)
   3)
   4)
   5)
   6)
   7)
   8)
   9)
   10)
   11)
   12)
   13)
   14)
   15)

2. List criteria for determining primary and secondary audience status.

3. Prioritize audiences as primary or secondary, depending upon their relevancy as a stakeholder of the nonprofit.
   Primary:

   Secondary:

4. What insight do I have about each of my **primary** audience groups?
   Stakeholder Group:
   Demographic information:

   Psychographic information:

   Stakeholder Group:
   Demographic information:

Psychographic information:

Stakeholder Group:
Demographic information:

Psychographic information:

Stakeholder Group:
Demographic information:

Psychographic information:

Stakeholder Group:
Demographic information:

Psychographic information:

as well as from secondary research, such as recent census statistics, marketing studies, or Internet-based public opinion research.

What do the terms "demographics" and "psychographics" mean?

"Demographics" refers to facts like age, gender, education, income, and profession. Demographic information can be helpful in a number of ways. Examples are: knowing the educational level of an audience can help determine the level of message complexity; and knowing if the name "Bailey" or "Addison" refers to a male or female, can help personalize a direct mail letter with "Mr." or "Ms."

"Psychographics" provides insight into the attitude and behavior of the audience. It identifies what motivates people. Being aware of attitudes, lifestyles, beliefs, and opinions makes it easier to customize messages and to prepare appeals that will resonate best with donors. For instance, learning how an individual likes to receive information and the frequency with which updates are preferred can drive the communication channel used to initiate interaction and the frequency of engagement.

Thus, learning more about audience preferences can drive fundraising, public relations, and internal communication activities. This is why small and mid-sized nonprofits should conduct at least some level of research, even if they can't afford extensive or sophisticated forms of data collection. In fact, it is far better to at least informally and inexpensively gain a better understanding of critical audiences than to be planning without any insight.

Demographics are fairly easy to ascertain, if donors, opinion leaders, and government officials are local. If in a small town, it may even be possible even to observe professions, gender, and age. Free on-line tools, such as Survey Monkey and Zoomerang, provide a means whereby a nonprofit can design a questionnaire to obtain both demographics and psychographics.

As a Whole

There may be a reluctance to commit the time and resources necessary to conduct research before initiating strategy work. However, it is an investment worth making. Research can identify potential problem areas or issues, aid in avoiding mistakes or pitfalls, lead to sound decision-making, and ultimately save time and money. Research can help identify probable mechanisms to gain positive attention for the nonprofit's messages; uncover potential connections and strategic relationships; and enhance the understanding of key audiences and markets, which will result in improved and targeted communication. Plus, if a funding request is necessary, research can serve as documentation to substantiate the logic of the communication department's request.

Although one can find a vast amount of information on the World Wide Web or in printed form on a book shelf, it doesn't mean the research is quality. Therefore, if relying on secondary research, it is important to check its value by examining at least these three components:

- Is it formal, scientific, or quantitative research? If so, principles of scientific investigation should have been used, such as random sampling in surveys and the comparison of results against statistical standards. Reviewing the rigor in which the research principles were applied will provide an accurate picture as to the depth, breadth, and validity of the findings.
- How current is the data? If the research was conducted three, five, or ten years ago, the time frame may not be sufficiently current.
- How reliable is the source? Checking the credentials of the institution or individual conducting the research is necessary to ensure the data is unbiased and the source itself is qualified and reputable in the field.

While it may not be possible, particularly in a small or mid-sized non-profit, to gather all of the aforementioned data, it is apparent the more insight and understanding an organization has of its publics, the greater the likelihood an effective, efficient, and results-producing communication strategy will be developed and implemented.

The Strategy and Plan

As emphasized earlier, a ***strategy*** provides a coordinated direction to guide work and the organization's response to internal and external environments. Strategic formulation is the process of thinking, assessing, envisioning, and creating the future. Grounded in day-to-day operations with an eye on the long-term problems, opportunities, and possibilities of tomorrow, this approach lays the groundwork for the development of effective communication that contains appropriate messages for key publics through fitting tactics and channels with suitable regularity.

How does a nonprofit formulate this work into a written document? First, it should be remembered this document will serve as a roadmap for the department and as a vehicle to inform key stakeholders, including the board of directors and other staff members. This means detailed information is required to inform all interested parties, facilitate plan implementation, and keep everyone focused on the strategic goals and objectives.

The document should begin with an overview in the form of an ***executive summary***, which is typically one to two pages in length and highlights the contents. It should be written sufficiently simple so even an "outsider" can grasp the salient points and how department strategies, goals, and objectives support the organization. This section also should mention the alignment between the strategic communication plan and the nonprofit's mission, overarching goals, and culture. If it is highly likely unusual circumstances will arise, these should be referenced.

It is advisable to share this section—once approved—with the nonprofit's board of directors, volunteer communication committee members, and other departments within the organization. This action is recommended because it will set the tone for updates throughout the year and raise the department's level of visibility within the organization.

A ***communication situation analysis*** is next. This clearly articulates the nonprofit's current environment. A realistic assessment, it takes into account research findings, the gap analysis, and the nonprofit's short- and long-term goals. Possible content for this section includes:

• Are there significant gaps that will affect achieving the desired outcomes?
• Directionally, is the nonprofit positioned to achieve its goals?
• Are there organizational mandates influencing how communication must be approached?

- Are resources being requested to ensure the tactical components can be fully executed?
- What internal and external forces are noteworthy because of their significant influence on the plan's successful implementation?
- Are critical issues being faced upon which the future of the nonprofit hinges?

Goals and objectives are found here, too. The role of each should be understood because these are essential building blocks in communication planning.

Goals outline the desired result, the aspirational outcome. They can be operational in nature, impacting the structure of the communication channels and tactics. They can be reputational, such as wanting to improve the image or credibility of the nonprofit. They can be behavioral, such as desiring to improve employee engagement.

Objectives are measurable statements that represent attainable outcomes. Communication objectives can be informational, motivational, or behavioral. They are very specific, may be assigned to ensure accountability, and many times have established time frames for completion.

NOTE: Some organizations assign the same meaning to the words "goals" and "objectives" because of its overall approach to strategic planning. If this is the case, it is advisable to select one of the two and to use that term consistently to avoid confusion.

With goals and objectives defined, work priorities are clearer. Assigned responsibility permits even better coordination of work, can serve as a motivator, and makes it easier to evaluate staff. Because time periods, numbers, or other measurable factors are included in objectives, it makes the task of judging communication effectiveness and accountability easier, too.

With a clear picture as to where the nonprofit has been, its current status, and where it intends to go, it is necessary to determine the best way to leverage the past and present to chart a specific future course.

One of the first steps in this next phase is framing key messages. *Key messages* are the salient points; the information the nonprofit wants its audiences to remember recorded in concise and jargon-free language.

Typically, an organization has three to four key messages and no more than five. Providing more makes it too difficult for the average person to retain. These statements are theme-based and convey critical elements of the organization's platform, such as why the organization does what it does, why the work matters, and why anyone should care.

Key messages are used internally and externally because these statements offer a clear line of sight for message recipients. Listeners are able to understand what the connection between what the nonprofit is fundamentally about and its actions, stances, and requests. These statements are mission-driven and action-oriented.

Key messages may be reworded for different purposes and audiences, but their essence is consistent. They should align with and support the nonprofit's primary directive and culture. They are, in fact, like a good commercial. Through repetition, they become associated with the non-profit and help shape the organization's reputation.

When customizing these key statements, both evidence and emotion should be leveraged to ensure message effectiveness. To aid in creating more persuasive messaging, Aristotle's three appeals can be utilized: logos, pathos, and ethos.

Logos is the appeal to logic. Use of dates, statistics, validated trends, and proven facts help to reinforce the logic of a point or a request. The authenticity and provability of the evidence makes the information credible. Most people like to think of themselves as well reasoned and capable of making deliberate, logical decisions. So, a rational person wants to review evidence and examine content.

Content is more likely to be memorable and engage the audience, if it is audience-oriented. This is why key messages may have to be re-framed slightly to foster an improved understanding of the nonprofit's mission and work and to connect more solidly and build rapport with the specific audience target.

Pathos touches the listener's emotions. Wording can evoke a feeling of compassion, generosity, reverence, pride, or disdain. A personal success story as to how someone turned their life around or an illustration as to how a team accomplished a significant goal can bring an audience to tears, rally them to their feet, or have them swiping their credit cards to make donations.

If the audience makes a strong connection with the example, the appeal is likely to increase the relevancy of the message for the listener, result-ing in a more timely response or even creating a change of mind that is of greater benefit to the nonprofit. In fact, the more a message links to listeners' values, experiences, and opinions, the more likely the message will motivate the audience to action.

Ethos is linked to speaker or organizational credibility. The character or competence of a person influences the degree to which the listener is likely to believe message content. So, although two speakers may use both logi-cal and emotional appeals, the person with stronger ethos is more likely to be successful in persuading the audience to take a specific action or to behave in a certain way. If the nonprofit has a stellar reputation, the information it provides is more likely to be accepted without question. Therefore, the ethos of the organization or the person delivering the mes-sage influences believability.

The key messages, along with the nonprofit's mission and values state-ments, combine to create a ***communication platform*** that can be lever-aged for wording and messaging in many ways.

This is not to say everyone needs to be exposed to all dimensions of the platform. A case in point is where an organization interacts with children. A brownie in Girl Scouts or a cub scout in Boy Scouts may not need to know the organization's key messages, vision, or mission. This may be a situation where too much information is even confusing for the message recipient. So understanding the relevancy of the messaging to the audience is of the utmost importance in determining what to say to whom.

The Communication Matrix

It is now time to combine many of these elements into the tactical communication matrix. The communication activities, whether spurred by a need to provide information, solicit donations, motivate volunteerism, or adhere to board of director mandates, must be purposeful and aligned with the goals and objectives. And, these actions also must be appropriate for the targeted audience. The research conducted during the preparatory stage of the strategic planning process will be immensely helpful in selecting what to say, how to say it, when to convey the message, and the correct method to do so, all within budget parameters (see Worksheet 2.4: Communications Planning Matrix). In addition to being a critical component of the plan, this matrix will serve as a working document for the department.

The first step in the development of the communication matrix is recording communication goals. Then, those objectives supporting the overarching goal are noted.

Communication Tactics and Initiatives

The most effective communication does not solely flow in one direction. In today's world, dialogue is expected. Stakeholders anticipate engaging in conversation with an organization. If this invitation is not extended through formal means, these individuals will make themselves heard. They may blog their complaints; they may stage a protest capturing media attention and grabbing headlines; they may post videos on YouTube; or they may establish a competing association, educational institution, charitable organization, or private-public agency. Therefore, adherence to the principles of two-way communication can contribute to the protection of organizational reputation.

Basic two-way communication starts with a message, which originates from a sender. This could be verbal, written, or even nonverbal in form. The message is communicated through a channel, such as in a one-on-one meeting, town hall gathering, direct mail solicitation, or DVD (see Model 2.4: Simple Communications Model).

Before the message recipient actually receives, processes, and reacts to the message, there are many filters through which the message must

Worksheet 2.4

Communication Planning Matrix

GOAL:

Objectives	Communication Tactic	Audience(s)	Timing	Point Person	Budget
Objective 1:					
Objective 2:					
Objective 3:					
Objective 4:					

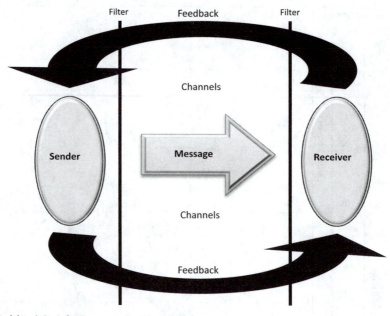

Model 2.4 Simple Communications Model.

travel. There could be environmental distractions, such as excessive noise, that detract from or interfere with the message distribution. Once the message arrives at the target, more filters are encountered. The recipient's current state of mind, past experiences, educational background, and socio-economic status will influence how the message is perceived.

In turn, the recipient will react. Even a non-response is a response. This feedback will guide the original message sender on how to reply. For example, does the target recipient need more information? Or, did the message fail to break through the noise or physical barriers, thus making it necessary to resend the content?

This two-way model, then, captures the ongoing communication cycle that occurs between the nonprofit and its audiences and should be taken into account during the tactical selection process.

Tactics contribute toward bringing the strategy to fruition. They are what enable the nonprofit to communicate in a targeted and appropriate manner to audiences with the expressed purpose of sharing information, shaping opinions, modeling behavior, and producing communication goals and objectives within an established time frame.

The savvy communications officer has an arsenal of communication channels and tactics. The challenge is selecting the correct ones for the audience and situation while avoiding any implementation barriers and resource limitations.

The tactical choice list can be used as a "thought starter" and is not all-inclusive (see Table 2.1).

Table 2.1 Tactical Ideas

There are many options from which to choose, when selecting a communication tactic. But in determining which vehicle is the best, it is necessary to make sure the choice is appropriate for the audience, is an effective means for clear message communication, stays within budget parameters, can occur within the specified time frame, and can be implemented with the resources available.

In some instances, advertising and techniques more likely to be development-oriented in nature must be combined with public relations activities. Because both are leveraged by strategic communications plans, those tactics found in both categories are listed.

While the following list is by no means comprehensive, it does identify many communication possibilities from which to choose. It also should be emphasized that many times it is important to use a combination of these for an effective campaign, rather than simply relying upon a single tactic.

Advertising	News release
Annual meeting	One-on-one-meetings
Annual report	Pamphlets
Awards or other recognition	Panel discussion
Billboards	Photos
Blogging	Posters
Briefings	Press conference
Brochures	Press kit/media kit
Cable programming	Public Service Announcements
Cause-related marketing	Question & Answer
Celebrity spokesperson	Radio news story
Community Panels	Radio talk show
Conferences	Rally
Conference calls	Seminar
Direct mail campaign	Signs
Displays	Speaker's bureau/presentations
DVDs	Special events
Editorial	Special reports
Email blasts	Specialty items
E-newsletter	Sponsored communication
Exhibits	Sustainable citizenship report
Facebook page	Teleconference
Fact sheets	Telephone campaign/telephone tree
Feature stories	Telephone hot line
Interviews	Town meeting
Issue briefs	Training material
Issue surveys & results	TV appearance
Letters	Tweeting
LinkedIn	Videos/video streaming
Magazine	Video news release/B-roll
Meetings	Webinar/web-based interaction
Magazines	Web site
Message boards	White paper/working paper
Newsletter	

Audience

Much has already been said about audience identification, segmentation, and prioritization. Using the results of the completed Audience Analysis worksheet, the audience(s) should be noted in relationship to each of the objectives and tactics. It is not uncommon to identify multiple audiences per tactic, such as may be the case for a quarterly publication or weekly email. Likewise, a key audience may receive multiple forms of communication from the agency or association.

Timing, Accountability

When and how frequently should communication occur? Unfortunately, some nonprofits only become concerned about messaging when there is a crisis. A funding shortfall or an individual or group attacking the integrity of the organization causes the department to spring into action by suddenly expanding its quantity and quality of communication.

While it is critical to share nonprofit's "side of the story," the institution should have been proactively sharing its accomplishments on a timely basis; regularly helping stakeholders see the connection between the organization's mission and the work being performed; strengthening trusting relationships through transparent, informative communication prior to the development of the sensitive situation; routinely reminding critical audiences why they should be supportive of the nonprofit and its endeavors; and reinforcing relations through value-based dialogue.

Frankly, there is a strong case for conducting some degree of ongoing and timely messaging with all audiences. The matrix can log communication distribution in a manner such as "Q1" (first quarter), summer, or even August–November. This box also can be used to note communication frequency, such as quarterly or monthly. By customizing this simple format, work flow and audience connectivity can be mapped and tracked.

Next, an individual should be assigned to monitor the tactic or initiative. By holding someone accountable, there is less likelihood deadlines will be missed and a greater chance issues or problems will be managed in a timely manner. This team member can be held responsible for providing progress reports and tracking budget discrepancies.

The financial requirements of each initiative or particular tactic should be estimated as closely as possible to ensure, when these figures roll up into the department budget, all figures are realistic, and will fall within monetary and resource parameters.

The Budget

Following the tactical communication matrix, the department's annual budget should be inserted. Given the financial limitations of nonprofits, in general, and small and mid-sized organizations, in particular, constructing a thorough and realistic financial plan for the department is imperative. The budget should estimate the communications expenses and income for the nonprofit's fiscal year. If money can be leveraged from the previous year's budget, it should be reflected.

Government grants for a communication program? Earmarked contributions from a donor to support a particular initiative? The need to add a staff member or to supplement communication work with a freelancer because of additional department responsibilities? Using an agency to conduct interviews or focus groups for measuring public opinion? All should be noted in addition to routine expenses. It may even be necessary to obtain preliminary bids or estimates for some of these items, so department costs can be projected more realistically.

Why so much detail? Even though the budget may never be requested by anyone outside of the department, this thoughtful preparation safeguards the department from exceeding its financial limits. If a project must be added or if the department's budget must be cut mid-year, the communications officer is aware of what this will mean and can make proactive adjustments to ensure department fiscal responsibility.

There is another very important reason why having financial detail readily accessible is wise. The Sarbanes-Oxley Act of 2002 has significantly impacted both the level of documentation and the degree of transparency required of U.S. commerce. Businesses have experienced reputational crises when failing to meet these higher standards of documentation and transparency. Currently, there is even an outcry for greater financial transparency.

Nonprofits must recognize they, too, can be asked to provide greater financial detail, be more transparent in their dealings, and meet a higher standard of reporting than in the past.

If another nonprofit in the same sector or within the same geographic market has failed to be fiscally responsible, all area nonprofits may be find their integrity questioned and need to proactively demonstrate accountability.

Since the communications department is responsible for the organization's reputation, its budget should set the standard for financial documentation and transparency.

While these actions may seem overly cautious, one can look at the Senate Finance Committee's investigation into Quadriga Art, one of the world's largest direct mail providers for charities and nonprofits, and CNN's coverage of how nonprofits paid millions to this company. The Disabled Veterans National Foundation was one such charity. This nonprofit paid more than $60 million in fees for the $56 million collected. The National Veterans Foundation raised more than $22 million over three years but spent approximately $18.2 million doing so. And, SPCA International owed Quadriga Art, LLC, and its affiliated company, Brickmill

Marketing Services $8.4 million for what a spokesperson from Quadriga Art referred to as an "aggressive strategy" as well as a "successful strategy.[5]

When communication materials and donor outreach is more expensive than what is left to pursue the nonprofit's mission or to serve its purpose, the organization can be faced with more than negative press. The institution also can be downgraded by independent groups, such as Charity-Watch, which is a charity rating and evaluation service.[6]

In addition to the reputational damage caused by the negative press and a downgraded rating, the nonprofit may discover donor outrage over such news is even more devastating to the organization.

Editorial Calendar

With the communication matrix completed, there is another helpful planning tool: the **editorial calendar.** This "content planner" charts key messages, the purpose of the communication, the target audience, the tactics used to distribute the content, the frequency of the distribution, the distribution date, and the author or editor (see Worksheet 2.5: Editorial Calendar). Depending upon the breadth and depth of the nonprofit's communication tools, a master editorial calendar may not be sufficient. A separate editorial calendar for specific communication like blogs, e-newsletters, and capital campaigns may be necessary.

Excel spreadsheets are very effective for constructing and updating an editorial grid, but one also can be developed in Word. If developing a tactic-specific editorial calendar, it may already be created. For example, WordPress and Google offer editorial calendars for blogs.

The advantages of a master editorial calendar are many. By creating a complete record of what messages are going to whom, when they are to arrive, how they are to arrive, and who is getting them there, it is possible to:

- Ascertain if all critical audiences are being touched;
- Determine if certain stakeholders are experiencing information overload;
- Ensure multiple venues are used to create variety and increase the likelihood of "being heard";
- Release information on a timely basis;
- Control publication of content across multiple channels; and
- Incorporate additional steps, such as a review of content by the legal team, if applicable.

While the editorial calendar helps plan delivery timing and content of the communication being used, it is also beneficial to know the department is effectively and efficiently reaching out to its many stakeholders in a prioritized fashion. The Audience/Message Planning Aid can assist with

Worksheet 2.5

Editorial Calendar

Due Date	Vehicle	Frequency	Purpose	Key Message/Content	Audience	Editor

this endeavor. By completing this worksheet, the communication officer can ascertain if insufficient time is being spent communicating with a key stakeholder or if too much of the department's time is dedicated to communicating with noncritical audiences. While not a requirement of the formal plan, this planning aid presents another view of where and how key messages are distributed, thereby providing a "double check" that resources are being utilized strategically (see Worksheet 2.6: Audience/Message Planning Aid).

Strategy Termination

With all of the time and effort put into the development of a strategic plan, it is difficult to think—in the midst of implementation—the strategy may have to be terminated. However, given the rapid pace with which change occurs on societal, economic, and environmental levels, it may be necessary to abort the plan and make a significant strategic shift. For example, due to financial difficulties, a nonprofit may be forced to cut programs, reduce staff, or merge with another entity. Consequently, a forward-thinking communications department has an exit strategy, even if only in outline form.

While strategy termination must be customized, just as is the strategic plan itself, there are considerations, regardless of the situation, that can guide the thought process at this difficult juncture. During this decision-making process, the nonprofit should consider the following:

- Are the performance issues/outcomes of the existing plan sufficiently off base to require a significant strategy shift?
- What would constitute the "right" change?
- What are key stakeholder groups, public officials, and important opinion-leaders saying? Is there support for shift?
- Will the new approach more properly position and emphasize the mission, vision, and values of the nonprofit?
- What is the best long-term decision?
- What communications issues will be encountered, such as barriers to transparency, morale issues, and reputational concerns, if a strategic shift occurs?
- How can this change be measured to determine the degree of movement?

While examining the aforementioned issues won't make a strategic directional shift any easier, it will help to ensure the decision was made thoughtfully and an implementation process designed to create as smooth of a transition as possible to the new course of action. Consequently, it is advisable to include strategy termination procedures in the plan, so they are available.

Worksheet 2.6

Audience/Message Planning Aid

Audience	Priority 1-5 1 = Very important 5 = Not important	Key Messages	Communication Channels	Frequency of Communication	Measurement
Bloggers					
Board of Directors					
Business					
Community					
Donors					
Elected Officials					
Federal Regulators					
Foundations					
Local Regulators					
Other Not-for-Profits					
Service Recipients/Members					
Special Interest Groups					
Staff					
State Regulators					
Traditional Media					
Volunteers					

Next Steps

Evaluating the Plan

With the comprehensive communication plan completed, it is time to review the written document. After checking to see all relevant information is contained, the plan should be examined for its strengths and weaknesses to determine if any modifications are necessary.

In fact, this may be the ideal time to test a new program, tactic, or distribution channel. That way, if there are any technological challenges, wording issues, or funding problems, they can be identified. The insights gained from this are well timed because they can be incorporated into the final version of the plan.

To create the best strategic plan possible, the evaluation process should include feedback from other key stakeholders, such as the executive director, appropriate members of the board, and communication team members. Input originating from multiple points of view can help prevent the possibility of missing plan defects or vulnerabilities and build "buy-in" support from these stakeholders through the adoption of their recommendations.

Soliciting thoughts prior to finalizing the strategy and plan also can uncover a potential lack of support or concerns. By communicating the plan to select leadership at this juncture, the department can outline the strategic framework and provide context for what is driving the work plan. By taking this precaution prior to finalizing the plan, it is feasible to obtain alignment with the organization's opinion leaders. In essence, the proverbial "meeting of the minds" occurs, which will increase the likelihood of a smooth approval process for the adoption of the communication strategy and plan.

Routine Updates

In addition to distributing the finalized executive summary to key stakeholders, individuals critical to the performance and success of the communication efforts or those whose ongoing support is beneficial, should be updated routinely. If barriers to goal achievement arise, these individuals are made aware. They may be able to provide material assistance, professional guidance, additional contacts, or other relevant forms of support, which could divert a potentially negative outcome.

Or, if the department is working hard to reach a stretch goal, providing progress reports along the way can motivate staff and volunteers. By celebrating the achievement of smaller goals along the way, these "mini-wins" can keep morale positive and help the group remain focused on the ultimate goal. At times, these updates can serve as a quick clarification of facts or offer additional explanation to keep an initiative headed toward successful completion. Plus, regular progress reports raises the department's profile.

Measurement

In addition to ongoing communication monitoring, formal measurement is important. As the public relations and communication professions have evolved, there has been a greater demand for results. Gone are the days when the chief communication officer can use the elusive claim of "people will feel better about us" as an outcome of a project. Boards and senior leadership want to know what type of return on investment resulted from spending time and money on the development and execution of a communication program. They want to know what opinions or behavioral changes were produced. But in addition to the requests for proof of effectiveness that are generated from outside of the department, the communication professional values measurement for the following reasons:

- Manages time and resources;
- Demonstrates success;
- Clarifies what has and hasn't worked in the past;
- Contributes to the strategic planning process by providing a form of research content;
- Aligns the team and the organization around the work;
- Helps to specify the audience target and the communication purpose and needs; and
- Reflects the actual impact.

Measurement development, however, is not easy. A research-based discipline, evaluation can be designed to measure short- or long-term goals. But, it is situational. The environment in which the target audience operates and in which the communication tactics are performed is complex and context-filled. Because evaluation is multi-faceted, it is necessary to study the goal or the objective to ensure the correct technique is selected for obtaining viable results.[7] Remembering objectives can be informational, motivational, or behavioral, it is necessary to design a research approach that will generate a statistically correct evaluation of the degree of success or failure in meeting the desired outcome.

In all of these instances, the communicator is trying to determine what type of relationship, if any, has been established by the delivery of the messages to the recipients. Has this targeted public simply been exposed to the nonprofit name and important elements of its communication platform? Or, have recipients been able to retain the message and possibly even alter their behavior to support the message request?

Because an audience can say one thing but act very differently—or even not act at all—measurement design must be carefully crafted. For example, a spectacular redesign of the nonprofit's Facebook page can be posted. The number of "likes" can increase one hundredfold. But if the objective was to gain more donors—not simply to gain positive visibility of the nonprofit name—then measuring the effectiveness of the redesign by the number of people who clicked "like" is not be a good performance indicator.

To guide the development of the evaluation process, there are a few principles to consider:

- Selecting the best metrics to determine the degree of goal/objective achievement;
- confirming communication reach;
- assessing if the desired informational, attitudinal, or behavioral response is occurring; and
- juxtaposing communication budget and resources against performance to identify the department's return on investment.[8]

Plus, the performance measurement system must be realistic and pragmatic because restrictions, such as funding or resource limitations, can impede the process. It is necessary to consider what cost-effective or even nontraditional methodology could be used to measure the change in behavior or attitudes.

Scott M. Cutlip, Allen H. Center, and Glen M. Broom, in their evaluation model, recognize there are different levels and types of evaluation for differing demands. In their tiered approach, they demonstrate how communication measurement can range from simply counting the number of news releases distributed to the media to determining the number of individuals who favorably change their opinions about the organization.[9]

While statistics and scientifically collected data may offer extensive proof a return on investment occurred, it is recognized a nonprofit may not be able afford this level of measurement sophistication due to any number of reasons. Limited by time, money, and personnel, counting the number of attendees at the nonprofit's annual meeting or the number of registrants participating in a fundraising walk/race may be the best the nonprofit can afford. But, this is a start. And, gathering such statistics will at least establish a benchmark from which the organization can evaluate its performance.

What is ***benchmarking***? This technique identifies best practices, which presents an opportunity for the nonprofit to look at how it performs compared to its peer group or how it performs to its previous record.

For example, how successful is the nonprofit's new member campaign as compared to its previous year? Or, how does its recruiting efforts compare to similar organizations?

Thus, benchmarking provides relevant context for the measurement process by comparing the standard of excellence or past performance in relationship to what is currently being measured.

While no measurement plan is perfect, it is necessary to remember monitoring and formal evaluation help to ensure an opportunity is created for continuous communication improvement.

Evaluation Tools

Sampling surveys can be a quick and easy way for an organization to collect and measure data. Surveys can be a simple, one-page form distributed to volunteers at the conclusion of a training session; a printed, multiple-page questionnaire mailed to members about possible association policy changes; or an online survey leads participants through a series of questions depending upon their responses.

While there are free survey tools available, there also are a myriad of paid, online options, such as the ones offered by Constant Contact. In selecting which one to use, it is extremely important the nonprofit weighs cost against the quality and timeliness of the data generated.

Focus groups or one-on-one ***interviews*** can help reveal attitudes and values, too. Focus groups use a trained moderator who presents the information and leads the session. Participants can discuss issues important to the nonprofit and share their thoughts and ideas through the exchange. Through these methods it can be learned if key messages are understood, communication techniques need to be reformulated, or how critical an audience might be of a change in strategy before it occurs. In fact, observing nonverbal signs and listening to vocal tones and inflections throughout the session can reveal the participants' passion for a subject or strength of conviction about an issue. One-on-one interviews can offer similar insights into audience behavior and values. Nevertheless, it should be cautioned the results cannot be extrapolated and applied to a larger population.

A ***media trend analyses*** is a particularly beneficial form of measurement. Rather than simply counting the number of articles appearing in the paper or the number of media outlets mentioning a campaign, other factors should be studied. Which media is airing or printing the story and who is the author? Some news outlets carry more credibility than others, and some reporters are more influential than others. So, appearing in smaller, more select media or being covered by a highly recognized journalist may be much more important than the mere quantity of media hits.

As K.D. Paine, a well-known public relations measurement expert, told the membership of the Minneapolis, Minnesota, chapter of the American Society of Association Executives: "You don't have to analyze the world, just those publications or media sources that are most important to your audience."[10]

Tone and content is considered in this analysis, too. Are key messages included in coverage? Does the tone project organizational sentiment? Is an emotional appeal presented strongly enough to motivate someone to donate, to join, or to volunteer? And, is the information positive, negative, or neutral in nature?

Therefore, it isn't just the quantity of coverage with which the communications team should be concerned. It is also important to look at the quality of the exposure.

In the past, *clipping services* relied solely on manual labor. A pile of newspapers and magazines were scanned for a nonprofit's name, stories about the organization were cut from publications, and clips were sent through the mail, showing up in the communications department days if not weeks later than the actual publication date. Notebooks were filled with mounted clips, and content indexes were prepared in an attempt to make locating a single clip easier.

Today's automated process locates clips quickly and delivers them via email, along with an analysis. This electronic format permits the nonprofit to be apprised of breaking news about the organization; to search blogs, broadcasts, podcasts, and international online news sources; and to assemble news stories into electronic clip books for easy storage. Software and services, provided by companies like Vocus, will even deliver results to mobile devices, keeping the communication officer constantly updated.

While there are many clip options available, such as Luce Online, MediaClipping, LEXIS-NEXIS clip tracker, and Webclipping.com, this may be significantly more than is needed by a religious nonprofit serving a small community. And, given the budget size of such an organization, a college intern may be the "search engine" collecting the clips with the communication director reviewing them one by one.

The point is that it is necessary to track the public image projected by the media regardless of the size of the organization. As the Institute for Public Relations points out, "Media coverage can serve as a proxy for public perception and is relatively inexpensive and accessible."[11] Therefore, studying media's perceptions of a nonprofit can reveal information that will assist with the reputational management function.

The world of social media has changed the communications landscape in many ways, too. But, measuring impressions, "likes," and the number of Twitter followers does not necessarily identify actual influence. Influence connects to individuals who will act as a positive and compelling force for the nonprofit. So rather than having a large e-newsletter distribution list, it may be much more important to know the percentage of recipients who clicked from the e-newsletter to the nonprofit's web site or made an on-line donation.

Clearly, *Internet management* is crucial to protecting and enhancing the organization's reputation as well as ensuring key messages are communicated and both the nonprofit and the department's goals and objectives are achieved. It is important to know:

- which online communications are effective and which are not;
- your communication is reaching the intended audience;
- what people are saying about the nonprofit;
- key messages are communicated positively;
- when to join the online conversation; and
- how to strategically manage all of this in a cost-effective manner.

One way to do so is to pay close attention to online metrics.

What is a metric? A metric is an accepted unit of measurement. Tracking, measuring, and comparing online metrics can help the nonprofit determine its degree of progress in achieving online communication goals and objectives.

Specific nomenclature is used when discussing online metrics. Two basic terms used in audience measurement are ***reach*** and ***engagement***. In the past, the communications professional had to go through channels, such as journalists at professional publications, TV stations, or newspapers to connect with desired audiences. Sometimes, a story or key message was reported. Sometimes, it wasn't.

With the Internet, traditional media outlets no longer reign as the only communication channels supplying information. Instead, if people have access to the Internet, there is the possibility the nonprofit's message can reach them. Information can be shared directly, such as through e-marketing techniques, or stories can be picked up through search engines. An online network of followers, connections, and fans can retweet, forward, or like the messaging and encourage others to do so the same. Thus, the nonprofit can push out the message and even reach beyond targeted recipients.[12]

Engagement refers to action-taking. When a web site visitor does something—such as making a donation, downloading a document, volunteering to participate in a fundraiser, or retweeting information—beyond merely viewing a web page or reading a blog, this behavior is identified as "engagement." While the tool used to measure engagement varies according to the media outlet, this metric helps to determine if an actual connection is made with key audiences and how the relationship between the nonprofit and its stakeholder is developing. Because the ultimate goal for a nonprofit is to achieve a societal or cultural change and to gain a committed following willing to assist in this endeavor, determining the level and type of engagement is very beneficial to the communication planning process.

Consequently, it is beneficial to know the meaning of these additional terms in relationship to Internet communication channels:

Media	Terminology
Web Site	*Hits:* A hit occurs when a visitor goes to a web site and requests a page be loaded. As every page consists of multiple files, the hit is registered for the page, all images on the page, and every file. As some of these files are hidden, the statistic can be distorted. Thus, by one user visiting a single page, numerous hits could be generated, creating a large number. Therefore, a hit may not be the best form of measurement when looking at web site statistics.

Page Views: Views refer to the loading of a single web page. This occurs either when a visitor is directed to the page by a link or when the URL is entered. This metric can reveal the frequency with which a visitor goes to a specific content page and can be helpful in looking at which are the "favored" pages in a web site. It should be noted, however, that sometimes multiple pages are framed and loaded as part of a single page. Nevertheless, page views can be a pertinent measurement metric, particularly if looking for trends in web site visits.

Unique Visitors: Views occur when a visitor looks at a web site from the same computer or device over a particular time frame. "Unique visitors" is the name used to differentiate new versus repeat visitors to the site. Unique visitors are tracked by cookies or other scripting techniques. Tracking can be skewed as computers may block or delete the cookies

Social Media   *Likes:* If a nonprofit has a Facebook page, it can create the opportunity for users to "like" it. Although counting the number of "likes" provides a metric, this does not necessarily translate into action or a behavioral change.

Followers: With Twitter reported to have reached 500 million accounts by February 2012, there is a potential audience. But unless the nonprofit is proactive, it is unlikely anyone will know it exists. Providing interesting and relevant content is necessary. Engagement metrics, such as retweets, clicks to links, and answers to posed questions, offer more relevant metrics than simply counting followers.

Emails/   *Deliverability Rate:* When tracking an email marketing campaign or
E-Newsletters   e-newsletters, this metric refers to the arrival of material. Is the email bouncing back because the address is invalid? Has the recipient unsubscribed from receiving the monthly mailing or blocked the communication? Is the recipient's mailbox full? If the email doesn't reach the intended audience, then it can never be opened and no action will occur. Unfortunately, not all Internet service providers (IPS) report email delivery with such detail.

Open Rate: This term refers to the number of emails actually opened. However, this tracking method is not always accurate. A plain text reader using a mobile device could ignore the message and preview panes can be "read" as opened, when the recipient didn't really interact with the message. Nevertheless, this can be a helpful metric when trying to determine the time of day emails are most frequently read as well as to test subject lines and other messaging.

Click-Through Rate: When an individual clicks on a link in an email, e-newsletter, online document, or web page, this is known as a click-through. The metric, also known as a "CTR," pertains to the percentage of links clicked by an individual. In most cases, email tools permit the ability to see both the number of link clicks as well as the per-click detail.

Web analytics can help a nonprofit track online activity. How many individuals are visiting the web site? What percentage of the site visitors click through to the on-line donation form and actually contribute? Is your web site geared to accommodate the level of traffic it receives?

For the cash-strapped nonprofit, free analytical tools are very helpful in obtaining this relevant statistical information. Google Analytics has a robust web analytic offering and is easy to use. Statistical information— the number of visitors, where the visitors are coming from, how long they visit the site, how frequently they return, how and where do they click through the site, and what the average length of the visit is—can help the communications professional improve the navigability of the nonprofit's web site, identify message content needs, and capture the level of site engagement.

Listening is a key relationship-building ingredient. Regardless if it occurs by monitoring Facebook communication or retweets, valuable data is discovered through listening. While it takes considerable skill and time to sift through this information, these conversations can be mined, sentiment determined, key influencers identified, and the communication landscape mapped. Monitoring conversations on a regular basis can even enable the nonprofit to develop a real-time response to a crisis or to rapidly adjust a public relations campaign.

For the Internet metrics novice, *Internet for Nonprofits Management*[13] may be particularly helpful. This book delves into topics ranging from communication metrics to online fundraising and volunteer recruitment measurement strategies.

Once all measurement results are gathered, a careful analysis aids communications personnel in determining the degree of success in meeting goals and objectives, guides the department's next steps, and identifies necessary adjustments to enhance the strategic communication plan.

But, an over-simplification of data can misrepresent reality, produce misinformation for those designing strategy and tactical improvements, and negatively influence key stakeholders who receive progress reports. Recognizing the significant role measurement plays, it is critical evaluation results are studied meticulously, an accurate representation of results prepared, and the correct context provided.

The Final Pieces

While the strategic planning focus in this chapter has been on developing a comprehensive communication strategy and action plan that will help the nonprofit achieve its overarching strategy and goals, two additional components must be taken into consideration: crisis communication preparedness and sustainable citizenship communication. In the course of the day-to-day operation and even in long-range planning considerations, these may not be top of mind. However, chapters 3 and 4 will delve into both of these and emphasize the necessity of addressing these subjects during communication strategy development to ensure proactive reputational protection and enhancement mechanisms also are in place.

Thoughts on the Subject

Jean Lupinacci
Chief, ENERGY STAR Commercial and Industrial Branch, U.S. Environmental Protection Agency, Washington, DC

Q: How has strategic communication planning contributed to the success of the EPA's ENERGY STAR Program?

A: In 1992, the U.S. Environmental Protection Agency (EPA) created the ENERGY STAR program to overcome market barriers to energy efficiency and create a healthier climate for all Americans. Twenty years later, ENERGY STAR has grown to include nearly 20,000 organizations from every sector of the economy and has become one of the most recognized environmental brands in the world.

Over the years, ENERGY STAR has traveled a carefully planned journey, considering each step with deliberate and thoughtful examination. At the heart of this journey was an understanding that to succeed, ENERGY STAR needed to be more than a mark of efficiency but a symbol of trust, quality, and responsible stewardship of the environment. This understanding of its identity has guided the strategic communications planning efforts of the ENERGY STAR program for the past two decades. The program's long-standing achievements are the result of well-crafted strategies, market-defined insights, and a commitment to ongoing improvement.

In order to inspire an action-oriented ethos around protecting the environment through energy efficiency, greater awareness and changes in behavior are necessary. Consumers and companies trying to navigate increasingly complex environmental and economic decisions need to be able to rely on ENERGY STAR to help them make informed choices that lead to cost-effective energy savings. Integrated communications strategies and tactics are designed to achieve this vision and to create a connection with consumers and businesses that inspires change. At the center of the

ENERGY STAR communications planning efforts are several core principles: simplify decision-making for consumers and businesses, represent an assurance of quality, and offer a relevant and credible choice among competing offerings.

Strategic communications planning is an essential component of effective social marketing and advocacy programs and has been instrumental in the success of EPA's ENERGY STAR program. Strategies applied by the ENERGY STAR program include: defining short- and long-term goals; developing measurable objectives; crafting a range of complementary tactics that together create momentum and progress toward goals; conducting regular research on market trends and attitudes; targeting messages to market sectors based upon research findings and understanding of key business drivers; leveraging partnerships to raise awareness and drive demand; using incentives, particularly recognition, to motivate and sustain change; and conducting ongoing evaluations of progress and results.

EPA's integrated efforts to engage, educate, and inspire consumers and businesses are transforming how America uses energy. Over the past twenty years, American families and businesses have saved nearly $230 billion on utility bills and prevented more than 1.7 billion metric tons of greenhouse gas emissions, with help from ENERGY STAR. More than 80 percent of Americans recognize the ENERGY STAR label, and awareness continues to grow each year. It is a well-recognized brand with two decades of results that show ENERGY STAR continues to deliver on its promise to America of cost-effective, relevant, and high-quality energy efficiency solutions.

Katie Delahaye Paine
CEO
KDPaine & Partners, LLC, Berlin, NH

Q: Why is measurement an important element in a strategic plan?

A: Not every element in your strategy is going to be equally effective. Without building measurement into the plan, you have no idea which programs are effective and which are not. And, if they aren't effective, without detailed measurement, you won't know how to fix them.

People confuse measurement with "justifying your budget"; in reality, no responsible organization should fund a measurement program just to justify the existence of a PR program. But if done correctly, you will save enough from eliminating ineffective programs to expand efforts that are working.

Put it this way, sooner or later your boss will come in and say the equivalent of: "Congratulations you're kicking butt" or "damn, we're getting our butt kicked." Without a measurement system backed into your program, you'll have no idea what "kicking butt" means and no way to respond.

Something to Think About

1. How could key messages be introduced to audiences unfamiliar with the nonprofit?
2. How can a communication strategy help to garner support for the nonprofit's long-range plans?
3. Why could a mid-year communication program check be helpful?
4. What are cost-effective research and measurement tools a small or mid-sized nonprofit could use?
5. How will social media trends impact channel selection?

3 Sustainable Citizenship

It's a question of discipline, the Little Prince told me later on. 'When you've finished washing and dressing each morning, you must tend your planet.'

(Antoine de Saint-Exupéry, *The Little Prince*)

Terms, such as "citizenship," "sustainability," "corporate stewardship," "social responsibility," and "corporate social responsibility" (CSR) are associated with business. Commercial enterprises have discovered adherence to corporate social responsibility principles granted them benefits such as customer, societal, government, and investor approval to operate; employee engagement and retention; recruiting advantages; cost savings; marketing opportunities; and enhanced brand image. The reality is that with growing demands for transparency, increasing calls for accountability, decreasing natural resources, and growing societal expectations of companies, all of which are publicized significantly in this era of social media, the very underpinnings of the go-to-business model has been reshaped.

The societal revolution surrounding business conduct is affecting the not-for-profit world as well. NGOs and nonprofits can expect to see requirements similar to those experienced by business from donors, the community, government, employees, and individuals who receive or use their services. Savvy charitable organizations will take the cue from their for-profit counterparts and recognize formally incorporating sustainable citizenship into an organization is beneficial on several levels.

Setting Context

Before examining the concept of sustainable citizenship in a nonprofit context, it is important to take a step back and reflect on how the principles of social responsibility evolved in a for-profit setting. Early records on this subject can be seen in ancient Chinese, Egyptian, and Sumerian writings describing rules of trade and commerce in relation to public interest.[1]

Social activism, in response to business decisions, also has been witnessed throughout history. In the 1790s, for example, a large-scale consumer boycott occurred in England because of slave-harvested sugar.[2]

One also could suggest the concept of the "company town," which appeared in the United States during the early 19th to early 20th centuries, represented another stage in the corporate social responsibility journey. Companies supplied housing for workers and provided parks and other community services and facilities for their workers. The problem, however, was such arrangements were not always beneficial to the employees. Instead of practicing social responsibility in the purest sense, there were times these civic contributions came with a price, such as evicting strikers from their homes and leveraging the monopoly status of a company store to increase prices.[3]

In 1906, U.S. business could be seen responding to disasters, when, for example, Johnson & Johnson sent trainloads of bandages and first-aid kits to San Francisco to treat the thousands who were wounded in the 7.9-magnitued earthquake that rocked the city. This in-kind donation evolved into one of the company's core competencies and business operations.[4] Then in the 1940s and 1950s, corporate America responded to World War II and increased its philanthropic efforts to aid in the recovery from the incredible destruction.

When the 1960s and 1970s arrived, social action movements influenced many corporate practices.[5] In fact, the decade of the 1960s was a time of cultural revolution. This period saw increasing affluence in the middle class, a rising education level for the average citizen, significant technological advancements, and a heightened awareness of the world. Such factors prompted a transformation, which proved foundational to the corporate social charter.[6]

With the corporate world shifting its values, an evolutional sequence was started, according to Ian Wilson, which caused a cascade of policy instruments. These appeared in the form of a written code of conduct; disclosure policy; well-defined corporate policies; greater attention to the details of corporate philanthropy; sensitivity and training in conjunction with diversity and public policy matters; increased emphasis on environmental and health and wellness issues; and an intensified concern for product quality, safety, and truth in advertising.[7]

Once the 1980s arrived, companies became more strategic with their philanthropic efforts. The likelihood lessened of a corporate donation being given exclusively because it was the CEO's pet project or the favorite charity of a spouse. At the same time, social responsibility gained popularity because of a growing belief that CSR added to the bottom line.[8]

It was in this time frame The Brundtland Commission, an outgrowth of the United Nations' World Commission on Environment and Development, was formed. Established in 1983, the Commission was named after its chair, Prime Minister Gro Harlem Brundtland of Norway. The

Commission released a report in October 1987, which identified two global imperatives: meeting the basic needs of all human beings with the elimination of poverty and recognizing the finite resources of nature requires limits on development.

Optimistic, but not without contradictions and challenges, the document suggested there was a moral responsibility to future generations to undertake these two priorities.[9] And while it did not overlook the importance of meeting current needs, it clearly stressed the future welfare of subsequent generations should not be compromised.[10]

In the mid-1990s, John Elkington developed the triple bottom line (TBL). The purpose of this framework was to help corporate America measure its performance beyond profits, shareholder value, and return on investment. This more comprehensive approach added social and environmental components to the financial dimension. The triple bottom line, also referred to as "People, Planet and Profits," is so popular it is used by many organizations.

In addition, the triple bottom line helped corporate America understand business had a larger constituency than just shareholders. Extensive attentiveness to accountability surfaced. This keen interest was further driven by an increasing social awareness in commercial decisions, practices, products, and services, particularly on environmental issues. But, there was still a challenge: Establishing an agreed-upon, consistent form of measurement, indexing and reporting.[11]

Because of the emphasis on environmental sustainability, companies quickly scrambled to market themselves as "green." The problem? Not all of them were. This trend became so prevalent that New York environmentalist Jay Westerveld dubbed this attempt to mislead the public with unsubstantiated, positive environmental claims as "greenwashing." Although Westerveld introduced the term in his 1986 essay regarding the hotel industry's use of placing "save the environment" placards in rooms to promote the reuse of towels, its use spread quickly. The terminology is used when a company misrepresents, overpromises, or overcommits the reality of their environmentally-friendly actions.

In *Green to Gold*, Daniel Esty and Andrew Winston discuss how some companies were so eager to catch the "Green Wave," they promoted their environmentally-friendly work before taking action. At times, the products or procedures were not even close to materializing before the marketing buzz started.[12]

Consequently, it wasn't surprising the Global Reporting Initiative (GRI) Sustainability Reporting Framework and Guidelines emerged in 1999. In many ways, GRI's criteria have become the de facto standard for sustainability reporting. Its independent board and universally applicable elements of measurement are widely endorsed on a global basis. Many businesses, governments, and even nonprofits have turned to GRI for guidance on reporting because multi-stakeholder input went into the framework.[13]

Whether relying upon GRI's reporting standards or becoming certified on environmental aspects of the business, including the Blue Angel in Germany, The White Swan in Nordic countries, the European Eco-Label in the European Union, the Energy Star label in the United States, or the global Marine Stewardship Council and Forest Stewardship labels, business recognizes the trust placed in third-party criteria and leverages various forms of affiliation with these organizations to substantiate claims, aid marketing efforts, and enhance its brand image (see Figure 3.1).

To further prove a commitment to the environment, some firms pursued Leadership in Energy and Environmental Design certification for their properties. Frequently referred to as LEED, the system was developed by the United States Green Building Council (USGBC) in 2000. Through a committee process, a rating system was developed and an independent third-party verification process established to rate a building, home, or community in key areas of environmental and human health.

| European Union's Ecolabel | U.S. EPA Energy Star Label |
| Forest Stewardship Council International Certification | Marine Stewardship Certified Sustainable Seafood Logo |

Business relies on third-party certifications to validate sustainability efforts.

Figure 3.1 Examples of Certification.

Water savings, energy efficiency, indoor environmental quality, and material selection are a few of the key areas examined for excellence in green building design, constructions, and maintenance solutions.

The business case for certification can be found in outcomes, such as energy and water conservation, lower operating costs, and qualifying tax rebates. But, companies with LEED certification have discovered there are reputational advantages as well.

The results of Landor Associates' 2011 ImagePower Green Brands Survey attests to the continued focus on the environment by the public. The research, which captured opinions from more than 9,000 consumers in eight countries, found there was an increased desire to buy "green," with consumers even scrutinizing the environmental friendliness of product packaging. The report stated green practices are of interest to consumers around the world.[14]

While focusing on the environmental component, business was becoming more aware of stakeholder relations and the need to connect substantially to the responsibilities of global citizenry and risk management issues.[15] With several egregious corporate scandals beginning to grab the headlines in the late 1990s and early 21st century, a monumental focus on corporate accountability and transparency emerged. One result of this was the passage of the Sarbanes-Oxley Act of 2002, which offered some of the most sweeping legislation since the Great Depression by increasing regulation in an attempt to restore the public's trust in corporate financial reporting and company executives.

Business was mandated to comply with all 11 sections of the Act, which addressed accountability, transparency, and fairness—all considered to be underpinnings of corporate governance and key elements of business responsibility. By building additional accountability into U.S. laws, it was hoped to influence other governments similarly. This focus on accountability and corporate governance continues to represent an influential social movement, signifying the importance of protecting shareholders and the public from fraudulent activity.[16]

Although ethical standards, fiscal accountability, and stringent reporting requirements were elements of Sarbanes-Oxley, U.S. business suffered a similar reputational crisis less than a decade later. Wall Street was criticized for excessive profits, disproportionate executive pay scales, and misleading the public in matters ranging from retirement investments to home mortgage lending techniques.

The public's trust in business and attitude toward for-profit corporations deteriorated. The Occupy Wall Street movement emerged in 2011, demonstrating against corporate greed, social and economic inequities, corruption in business, and the excessive influence of Wall Street on the government, particularly in the financial sector.

The public's disappointment was clearly noted in the 2012 Edelman Trust Barometer, which emphasized the wide trust gap between public expectation of business and how companies were perceived. Sampling over 30,000 respondents from 25 countries, the study showed there was a mistrust of business institutions around the world. Trust in corporations fell globally from 56 to 53 percent. Some Eurozone countries, such as France, saw a double-digit dip in business trust. CEO credibility declined as well, with respondents saying they were more likely to believe the news shared by a peer than delivered by a company officer. Given the scandals rocking Wall Street, it wasn't surprising banking and financial services were ranked as having the least amount of credibility.[17]

Since this was a time of growing negativity toward business and diminishing belief in the integrity of the corporate environment, business refocused its efforts, updating its socially responsible model to improve its image and regain public trust.

In the 2012 RepTrak Pulse Study, 150 U.S. companies were rated by a sampling of 10,198 consumers, based on factors such as performance, leadership, citizenship, governance, workplace, innovation and products/services. These drivers were linked to the emotional connection consumers have for business: esteem, admiration, trust, and feeling. In the study, products/services, governance, and citizenship were the top three factors in this reputation equation, representing 47.3 percent of the rating system. But, it is important to note the data showed 91 percent of these organizations either stayed the same or experienced a decline in their reputational score over the previous year, rather than seeing their brand image improve.[18] It is interesting to examine this finding in relation to two other studies.

The 2011 CSR Index, researched by the Boston College Center for Corporate Citizenship and the Reputation institute, identified a correlation between an organization's long-term commitment to corporate responsibility matters and how positively the company was perceived. A total of 32,946 ratings were reviewed, based on a list of the 285 companies. The data captured public perception about corporate citizenship, governance, and workplace practices, all of which contribute to how a brand is viewed positively or negatively. Polling U.S. online consumers in January and February 2011 to identify corporations the public distinguished as leaders in the corporate social responsibility field, corporations whose brands were historically linked to corporate social responsibility initiatives, such as Publix Super Markets, Google, UPS, Kellogg's, Campbell Soup Company, FedEx and 3M, topped the list.[19]

And, the 2012 Global Corporate Reputation Index showed many companies underinvest in their citizenship platform and that this action limits the ability to build a corporate reputation in areas such as quality and innovation. According to the index results, the lack in citizenship investment actually drags down the brand and can even place honesty and trustworthiness in doubt.[20]

It is clear the image of commerce is fluid. The corporate responsibility journey is a never-ending response by business to the world in which it operates. In the past 200 plus years, societal expectations have evolved, bringing us to today's definition of "acceptable corporate behavior." Company performance is now judged on a shared value platform with society, which broadens and underscores responsibility in the social, moral, legal, economic, and even political arenas.

In Wayne Visser's book, *The Age of Responsibility*, he contends the new DNA of business is found in CSR 2.0. He believes corporate social responsibility can be seen in the four intertwined strands of

- value creation,
- good governance,
- societal contribution, and
- environmental integrity.

Visser explains CSR 2.0 actually represents both responsibility and sustainability.[21]

As globalization increases and the corporate responsibility journey continues, another triple bottom line viewpoint emerged. According to Vanita Shastri and Preeta M. Banerjee, business increasingly operates in an "economically, socially, and environmentally sustainable manner." They also see business leaders, acting as change agents, who are caretakers of the planet, assuming a holistic perspective, and who are capable of impacting multiple locations in multiple ways simultaneously. In their book, *Social Responsibility and Environmental Sustainability in Business*, the pair identified a number of examples where the global village concept appears to be shifting to what they have identified as the next level of CSR: global social entrepreneurship (GSE).[22]

Meanwhile, business increasingly recognized the branding benefits of "doing good." Through behavioral psychology, marketers have learned a company's image is linked to consumers' emotions and personality. Customers and employees reinforce their own beliefs by aligning themselves with companies reflecting their values. This reputational aspect has become an important factor in the marketing equation of many organizations and has resulted in corporate linkage to environmental, social, and philanthropic platforms.

In his book, *Firms of Endearment*, Professor Raj Sisodia identifies several companies succeeding in the marketplace because they worked to gain a share of consumers' hearts, not just their wallets. He calls this business transformation "Conscious Capitalism" because a company fundamentally realigns itself to ensure a "good" consciousness frames its capitalism.[23]

Jim Stengel builds on this idea with the introduction of the "brand ideal." According to Stengel, this principle provides a framework for the goal of improving lives. The ideal is, in essence, the reason for "business being." It is a call to a higher order in which the only sustainable way to recruit, unite, and inspire all stakeholders is through a commitment to improving people's lives. In his book, *Grow,* he emphasizes "brand" and "business" are interchangeable because: "A brand is what a business is all about in the hearts and minds of the people most important to its future."[24]

Such branding discussions indicate both employees and customers' opinions of a company's socially and environmentally responsible approach can help retain and recruit employees, while driving business. However, the enhanced intangible value produced by the perception of an organization believed to be CSR-oriented can diminish quickly, if the company is exposed for not doing what it said or acting contrary to its stated socially responsibility and sustainability mission.

There are investor implications to good corporate stewardship, too. In the December 2011 *McKinsey Quarterly,* the report asserts that with stakeholders paying closer attention to both the social and environmental footprints of for-profit business, corporate responsibility has moved into "uncharted management territory." It stressed the critical role of re-engineering to become "greener," support more social causes, initiate employee volunteer programs, and lobby for human rights.[25]

Another increasingly popular trend impacting business is socially responsible investing. In this portfolio strategy, investors seek investments consistent with their values. They will even forego investing in an entire industry sector, if it represents values that are incongruent with theirs. This isn't to say socially responsible investors don't pay attention to finances. Instead, these individuals scrutinize business decisions and conduct to ensure the company is transparent, ethical, and a good steward of the environment and the community in addition to being financially sound.[26]

Whether a for-profit business finds itself embedding a more socially responsible approach into its day-to-day conduct because of moral implications, ethical considerations, marketing advantage, regulatory issues, investor ultimatums, or legal demands, the corporate world understands it must employ corporate responsibility and sustainability principles to be successful. As Richard Barrett states in *Building a Values-Driven Organization,* "cultural capital is the new frontier of competitive advantage—it is the key differentiator between a good company and a great company, and between a success and a failure."[27]

The Case for Nonprofit Sustainable Citizenship

Just as business cannot operate in a vacuum, neither can a not-for-profit organization. Charities, associations, and NGOs are compelled to respond to the demands, influences, changes, and opinions of society for many reasons. Most certainly, if they want to continue to attract dollars from individuals, businesses, or members, they must conduct themselves in a manner meeting or exceeding donor expectations. And, just as a positive public perception of a business can produce significant credibility and trustworthiness, desirable affiliations, favorable legislation, and public support during a crisis, so, too, can a nonprofit have a brand that attracts the backing of business and individual donors, excellent media exposure, and complimentary regulatory measures.

In reality, nonprofits have an advantage over business. There is a level of trust granted to them automatically. Phrases such as "charitable organization," "professional association," and "NGO" carry a connotation that the organization has a cohesive organizational identify based on an unwavering commitment to a "higher cause;" to develop personal or professional skills, attributes, or talents; to improve the quality of life in a far-reaching manner; or to be committed to advancing a particular cause that significantly impacts society or the environment. This is unlike the word "business," which can carry a negative connotation because of association with terms potentially seen as opportunistic or self-serving, including "profit" or "personal gain." Hence, the nonprofit has an established level of "trustworthiness" that can motivate an individual or corporation to "invest" time, talent, money, or in-kind contributions, without even seeing a financial statement or receiving any proof of socially responsible behavior.

Unfortunately, the potential exists for the not-for-profit to disappoint, especially when information materializes undermining this deeply seated trust. The donor or volunteer can become disillusioned by news of a flaw in accountability, the misuse of funds or resources, or leadership integrity issues. Consequently, a not-for-profit can fall from grace in the same manner as a for-profit. But because the nonprofit was so highly esteemed, this "fall" can be deeper and, quite frankly, recovery can take longer. This is because those who invested time, talent, or resources now feel betrayed and even foolish for having placed trust in the organization. With beliefs and confidence dashed, these supporters lose both the positive emotional connection with the nonprofit and the self-esteem boost created by affiliation with "doing something good."

Any number of examples can be cited where a nonprofit has tarnished its reputation through a misstep, causing stakeholders to lose trust. From the Susan G. Komen Foundation's controversial and politically-linked decision to withdraw Planned Parenthood funding for cancer screenings[28] to the United Way of the Central Carolina's controversial CEO compensation package including a divisive discrimination lawsuit by the former CEO[29] to Invisible Children, Inc.'s financial issues and breakdown of its director in conjunction with the Kony 2012 campaign[30] to the publicly-funded North Carolina League of Municipalities refusal to disclose salary information,[31] nonprofits can be met quickly with great public outcry, substantial loss of support, and future skepticism; a situation magnified by this world of instantaneous communication.

In addition, when a nonprofit's reputation has been tarnished, it has the ability to affect the image of other not-for-profits, particularly in that sector. So like business, NGOs—as a category—have experienced a decline in trust. According to Edelman's 2012 Trust Barometer, trust in NGOs entities fell 5 percent to its 2007 level. Nevertheless, the goodwill automatically granted to nonprofits resulted in this category continuing to reign as the most trusted institution globally. In fact, the level of public trust in NGOs actually surged in China and India.[32] So, it is clear non-profits still have an advantage over business, as the public naturally places greater trust in these groups than in corporations.

Nonprofit Responsible Behavior

A nonprofit can impact its "brand" and derive benefits—similar to those experienced by business—through the incorporation of socially and environmentally responsible behavior beyond its stated mission. While the advantages are many, the following list identifies a few:

- reinforce trustworthiness in the minds and hearts of donors;
- establish clearly its critical role in the welfare of society and this planet;
- proactively protect its good name by fortifying its already stellar image;
- improve a tarnished reputation;
- capture reputational opportunities by aligning itself with the increasing interest in environmental and socially responsible conduct;
- assert a leadership role by incorporating additional social and eco-friendly principles in its operation and programming, creating a "value-add" proposition;
- make a conscious effort to positively impact its social and environmental footprint, while potentially improving efficiency and reducing costs;
- magnify its existing reputation for honesty and doing the right thing by expanding its positive social and ecological footprint through updated policies, procedures, and practices;
- guide others to aspire to demonstrate principles of good stewardship and exemplary conduct; and
- inspire and engage multiple stakeholders to support it in the form of currency, volunteerism, in-kind donations, and other forms of patronage because the incorporation of supplemental social and environmental responsibility elements into its mission and operating platform.

With so many reasons why—not if—a nonprofit should reach beyond the confines of its basic charter, additional questions, such as "What would you call this effort?" and "How can it become an active influence in the organization's day-to-day operation?" logically follow.

In tackling the first of these two questions, the world of commerce does not bring clarity to the naming rights of this concept, as there is much confusion surrounding the words and phrases attributed to the many social and environmental activities and strategies. Should the phrase "socially responsible" be used or is "steward of our world" better suited to describe such actions? For purposes of this discussion, the phrase "sustainable citizenship" is recommended. The truth is that there is nothing magical about this term. There is, however, logic for it.

In examining the first word in this expression, there are several reasons why the term "sustainable" is applicable.

In consulting *Webster's Encyclopedic Unabridged Dictionary*, the word "sustain" has several definitions, including:

- to keep up or keep going, as an action or process;
- to supply with food, drink, and other necessities of life;
- to provide for by furnishing means or funds;
- to support as aid or approval;
- to uphold as valid, just, or correct;
- to keep from giving away, as under trial or affliction.[33]

This term easily can be used in reference to the ongoing action or process of improving the quality of life on both social and environmental levels in a self-sustaining manner. This, then, is a journey without an end, extending beyond the time parameters of a defined long-term vision.

If you consider the word in the context of life-giving properties, there is the application of feeding people and the planet as well as providing the type of furnishings and aid necessary for a quality of life that focuses on the elimination of poverty and treasures natural resources, as outlined by the Brundtland Commission. Since in many cases, nonprofits, including NGOs, are viewed as safety nets for economic, educational, social, and environmental challenges and opportunities, the concept of "keeping from giving away" and of enduring, even when under trial or affliction, carries relevant implications.

In *Working Toward Sustainability*, the book's authors set context by explaining there are at least 70 documented definitions just for the phrase "sustainable development."[34] This provides further support there is a lack of agreement on the use of terminology. But as Simon Bell and Stephen Morse point out, *Sustainability Indicators*, despite the lack of a concrete and universally understood definition of the term "sustainability," it still represents an enormously popular concept.[35] Why? Because at its core, a condition is described that uses a societal-environmental lens to commit to a self-sustaining paradigm of environmental, social, and economic well-being.[36]

In consulting the dictionary for a definition of the word "citizenship," the following can be found:

- the state of being vested with the rights, privileges, and duties of a citizen;
- the character of an individual viewed as a member of society;
- behavior in terms of duties, obligations, and functions of a citizen.[37]

As members of society and citizens of the world, not-for-profit organizations, regardless of their mission or organizational structure, have rights and privileges. It already has been established nonprofits automatically have public trust and credibility. Tax advantages, reimbursements, grants, or deferments of some nature may be allotted, providing beneficial financial outcomes. And even when countries are at odds, nonprofits may be exempt of the feud and able to conduct their programs, operating freely within the warring nations and even functioning internationally without interruption.

But, duties also are associated with citizenship. Whether a charity, professional association, educational institution, or NGO, rules of conduct in the areas of governance, transparency, ethics, and diversity must be exemplified.

Another inferred citizenship responsibility is to act as a role model for business and individuals, leveraging the not-for-profit's sphere of influence to motivate others to enhance quality of life. In many ways, the not-for-profit entity functions as an intersection for nature, values, and civilization with the ultimate goal to improve the quality of life on this planet.

While the definition may sound lofty, there is a practical side, which requires an operational component to make sustainable citizenship come to life. To make this a reality, the nonprofit must have:

- a charter, vision, and mission aligned with and capable of adopting and evaluating the long-term implications of this concept;
- values-based processes and protocols, which demonstrate a commitment to quality of life improvement through social, economic, or environmental indicators—regardless of how incremental they might be; and
- the ability to educate and guide others to aspire to these principles.

Carrying the Lessons Forward

Just as confusion surrounds the language, there is much ambiguity as to what protocols, processes, tactics, and measurement should be associated with sustainable citizenship work. Drawing from this broad-based definition and framework, numerous elements may be selected for an organization's citizenship profile. However, before identifying components and designing a strategic plan, the nonprofit must determine its readiness level to embrace this thinking.

First and foremost, the board must endorse the ideology and clear the way for employees, volunteers, and donors to engage in the sustainable citizenship platform and practices. This governing body is responsible for establishing the correct infrastructure to facilitate consensus-building and the representation of diverse social and environmental viewpoints. And, this framework must allow for capacity building as adjustments will be necessary, especially if the nonprofit approaches citizenship work as a journey rather than as having an end point. Such a structure should encourage the dialogue necessary for building trust, ascertaining changing societal expectations and priorities, uncovering nuances in specific situations, and establishing two-way communication between the board and its multiple stakeholders.

In addition, the leadership group should serve as a sounding board, ensuring the nonprofit meets its prime directive while displaying sustainable citizenship qualities. The board is, after all, ultimately accountable for oversight. Through it all, directors must conduct themselves in an exemplary manner, demonstrating rules of good governance – such as transparency, fiscal responsibility, legal compliance, diversity, integrity, and ethics.

It is equally critical for the executive management team to embrace sustainable citizenship because this group must develop, execute, and communicate the attributes and outcomes of this work. In fact, the executive director and senior staff must consider what social and environmental drivers can be incorporated into the day-to-day operation to embed sustainable citizenship and add value even beyond operational efficiency, branding opportunities, and alignment with the nonprofit's mission. This includes:

- sharing leadership responsibilities with the board of directors;
- serving as a "role model for staff and volunteers by emulating sustainable citizenship principles;
- gathering intelligence on cultural and political trends that could influence the group's social and environmental strategies;
- examining conventional processes and providing recommendations for improvements in the linkage between the nonprofit's mission and sustainable citizenship;
- implementing sustainable citizenship tactics, without losing site of the not-for-profit's primary purpose;
- monitoring performance and adjusting strategies and standards;
- assessing potential risks that could possibly materialize from sustainable citizenship efforts;
- reporting the results of this work to appropriate stakeholders; and
- adhering to all legal, ethical, and fiscal duties.

One could say, then, the executive team "owns" sustainable citizenship because it ultimately implements and is responsible for all strategy and tactics.

Once full support is gained from both groups, the nonprofit can begin developing a customized strategy and plan aligned with and complementary of its mission, culture, and brand.

A natural first step in this design process is to take an inventory of the organization's strengths and weaknesses in relation to current environmental and societal needs. Just as companies have learned the approach to corporate social and environmental responsibility must support the business case, mantra, and culture so, too, must the not-for-profit select the sustainable citizenship components that align with its own mission, ideals, and organizational beliefs.

Although books and various publications are available that delve into the details of strategy and plan development, and focus on the measurement and reporting of social and environmental factors (see Bibliography), this discussion is limited to a few basic considerations and principles involved with creating a nonprofit sustainable citizenship plan.

Development Principles and Considerations

To gain an understanding of the breadth of this topic, it is essential to highlight the many factors representing sustainable citizenship. These include: transparency, ethical behavior, diversity, legal compliance, environmental components, health commitment, and societal contributions (see Table 3.1).

The nonprofit should overlay these broadly defined categories on its mission, strategy, tactical plan, and daily operation. Then, evaluate how the organization performs in each of these areas. During this step, the not-for-profit's strengths and weaknesses must be scrutinized to gather valuable data, which could identify potential areas of improvement and core competencies likely leading to sustainable citizenship opportunities. It also is necessary to analyze how the entity can raise its performance standard by identifying and implementing actions that magnify its societal and environmental contributions. While seemingly a tall order, management must realize even incremental improvements, over time, will increase the impact it makes.

For example, do the organization's financial reporting procedures comply with all legal requirements and adhere to sound fiscal policies, including the timely and transparent presentation of accounting data? Is this information shared openly with donors and easy to access, demonstrating a commitment to transparency?

From an ethical standpoint, do organizational policies respect employee work-life balance, matters of personal privacy, and human rights?

Do the board of directors and executive management team represent a diverse cross-section of the population the nonprofit serves, with which it interacts, and of the community?

Table 3.1 Sustainable Citizenship Components

Transparency	Relates to full disclosure of operating practices and financial records
Ethical Behavior	Encourages the consistent adherence to global, organizational, and personal values reflecting a social and ecological focus that commits to a long-term, quality of life improvement and is represented by the adherence to globally accepted standards, as outlined by the commonly referenced mantra of "doing good" and laws exemplifying socially-accepted governance; equality and respect for human rights, worker rights, and animal rights; integrity in day-to-day conduct
Diversity	Reflects representation and respect of cultural, gender, religious, and ethnic backgrounds; opportunities to engage a broad range of talent and experience
Legal Compliance	Refers to the fulfillment of local, state, national, and international regulatory guidelines and rules that protect human rights and the environment as well as statutes that specify acceptable operational conduct and fiduciary responsibility
Environmental Components	Includes reducing consumption of natural resources; reusing assets possessed by the organization and reusing donated new or used items that can be utilized by the nonprofit; providing a second life for the item while saving money for the not-for-profit; recycling materials for which there is no longer need through donation to others; product stewardship protocols that examine the environmental friendliness of a product or action; the pursuit of efficiencies that limit usage of natural resources while balancing human needs; avoidance of activities that pollute or contaminate the environment; natural resource sharing through collaboration and partnership
Health Commitment	Considers the health of employees, stakeholders, the community, and society as a whole; employee work-life balance
Societal Contributions	Emphasizes education to enhance the quality of life, whether this is on a single issue, raising awareness on a cultural, societal, or environmental level, or building a network of collaboration and partnering devoted to sociological or ecological problem solving; developing and encouraging collaborative behavior to tackle and solve societal and environmental issues; community outreach that positively touches others beyond the defined scope of the organization's mission

Has the group committed to reducing waste through recycling or re-use?

Is there a social or environmental issue, related to the organization's core focus, that the nonprofit should undertake to strengthen its contribution to creating a better community, adding value to its commitment to be a "good steward," or to alleviating a problem?

While the aforementioned simply offers a sampling of the types of queries to be posed, no question should be considered too detailed or insignificant.

Likewise, careful attention should be paid to possible weaknesses. By recognizing current limitations or faults, the nonprofit has the opportunity to shore up areas where the organization falls below public expectation or the perception of acceptable behavior.

Finally, if the organization is truly committed to "making a difference," it should scrutinize its strengths-and-weaknesses in terms of its long-term vision and aspirational goals. This examination can lead the nonprofit to leveraging fully its core competencies and to raising the standard of other key organizational drivers. Since this is a "personal" journey, the not-for-profit must consider the prospect of enhancing its brand by imprinting its name on an issue or cause.

Once the strengths-and-weaknesses analysis is completed, the question arises as to what should be done with the findings. This can be a conundrum for the organization. Does it tackle everything or part of what it identified? If it involves a change in operation, can the budget accommodate the additional expenses? What type of time frame is required to accomplish various undertakings?

A pragmatic approach is best to use when working through this phase. It is necessary to look at the socio-economic, cultural, and environmental issues and how the individual weaknesses and strengths can be logically grouped for leverage, refinement, and implementation. It is likely a number of options will appear (see Worksheet 3.1). Because the organization won't have sufficient resources to tackle them all, prioritization must occur.

Sustainable citizenship components cannot simply be tacked onto the nonprofit's mission, divert resources of its central purpose, or be viewed as a separate plan for a simple initiative. Instead, it is critical to see how the identified attributes align with the nonprofit's charter and fit into the overarching strategy as these will assist in determining what to address first.

Other thoughts that can aid in the prioritization of these elements include:

- Would work in this area help the organization address a current shortcoming or problem, such as a transparency issue or accounting matter?
- Does the effort represent "low hanging fruit" because it can be assimilated quickly with minimal resource investment, such as a recycling program?
- Will this element reinforce the work to which the nonprofit is already committed?
- Is this area of particular interest to foundations or business, such as governance policies?
- Can this particular work benefit one or more stakeholders?
- Does it have the capacity to engage multiple audiences?

Worksheet 3.1

Sustainable Citizenship Project Ideas

Potential Project (Environmental)	Yes	No	Maybe
Recycle aluminum cans			
Recycle plastic			
Recycle ink and toner cartridges			
Recycle/reuse paper			
Recycle batteries			
Recycle or/reuse cardboard			
Use of solar panels, wind, or other alternate energy sources			
Use of energy-efficient light bulbs			
Use of motion detectors for lighting			
Use of temperature-regulated thermostats			
Switch to water- and/or energy-efficient appliances and equipment			
Reuse office equipment and other materials, giving a "second life," or donate to another institution that can provide additional use rather than taking to the landfill			
Install bike racks to encourage biking, rather than driving a car to work			
Use "green" cleaning products			
If own the building, caulk, insulate or incorporate other energy-saving techniques			
Volunteer (staff/members/students) to keep a roadway, park, waterway, or other public area clean			
Use soy-based ink in the printing process			
Potential Projects (Social)			
Volunteer (staff/members/students) to provide training (professional, reading, tutoring, etc.) at another not-for-profit or NGO			
Participate (staff/members/students) in a fundraiser (such as a run or walk) for another cause			
Ensure healthy choices are available in vending machines			
Initiate staff involvement in disaster relief collections			
Institute and communication a clear diversity policy			
Use local talent and services, if possible			
Offer training for staff to improve skill level and career opportunities			
Improve physical working conditions for staff			

- Could it provide a quick or big win?
- Will it save money for the nonprofit?

Once the "to do" list is identified and prioritized, a determination can be made as to if these items should be part of the current operational plan or included in the long-term vision.

Having given focus to the sustainable citizenship efforts, greater definition must be provided by succinctly articulating the desired outcome of this work, establishing parameters to guide the effort, developing goals, and identifying criteria for success to support measurement. The vocalization of these four areas provides an opportunity to ensure they complement and compliment the organization's existing mission, vision, and brand. In addition, the public affirmation that the board of directors and executive team are aligned fully on these matters conveys a level of involvement and accountability by both groups. Thus, the nonprofit is well positioned to undertake this expanded sustainable citizenship role.

Ready to begin constructing its roadmap, complete with goals, strategic guidelines, time frames, and policies and based on the agreed-upon sustainable citizenship components, the organization must take a holistic view to design a model that serves the overarching the needs of society yet is customized to fit seamlessly into the organization's infrastructure and achieving the desired outcomes. To do so, it is necessary to establish a strong linkage between its planned environmental and socio-economic efforts, on the one hand, and its mission and brand, on the other.

To ensure a crisis in confidence does not occur along the way, this roadmap must be comprehensive, with thought given to associated risks and potential implementation barriers. Goals and measurement are necessary, as the ability to judge performance and assign accountability are essential to establishing credibility and will demonstrate the intent to deliver on promises.

A Brief Word about Measurement

Armed with the knowledge from the strengths and weaknesses inventory, the organization can create a baseline from which it can grow. Using this foundational information, along with its aspirational goals and objectives, the nonprofit now must determine the most appropriate methodology to record both its short- and long-term achievements. The selected form of measurement should have qualities representing the character of the organization and concentrate on the sustainable citizenship aspects most relevant to it.

Other important measurement characteristics are:

- Legitimacy, reflecting believable and mutually agreed-upon metrics by key stakeholders;

- Verifiability and reliability to ensure credibility;
- Understandability to enhance the qualities of communication between the nonprofit and its stakeholders as well as to support transparency efforts;
- Comprehensiveness of content, including fiscal responsibility and socio-economic, cultural, and environmental impact factors; and
- Accountability to ensure an individual, department, or group will be held responsible for the success or failure of the particular effort.

Another essential metric feature is the ability to adjust or modify the measurement tool. By including this accommodation in the design, the nonprofit will be able to adapt the measuring device to changes in programming and resources, shifting societal interest and trends, and any record-keeping refinements. Finally, the dashboard or scorecard should be set up to capture both small and large opportunities and wins as well as establish the timing of the measurement cycle, which should include a completion date for each initiative listed. The scorecard design should track performance of the sustainable citizenship initiatives and measure this against the goals.

Provisions should be made for routine audits. This practice demonstrates a solid management approach and, quite frankly, is common sense. Whether financial or social in nature, this process helps to certify the integrity of the entire measurement and reporting process (see Model 3.1.).

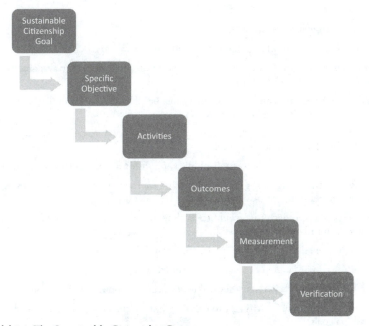

Model 3.1 The Sustainable Citizenship Process.

An independent social audit demonstrates initiative on the part of the nonprofit and provides valuable, verified information that keeps the organization focused on its socio-economic, cultural, environmental, and even governance commitments. Although the social audit is not required and the actual impact of the sustainable citizenship efforts may be very difficult to prove because of the complexity and ubiquitousness of the concept, it is still recommended as it can act as a trust-building mechanism.

At this point, tactical direction, outlining how the organization specifically intends to achieve the championed sustainable citizenship assets, is the next stop on the roadmap. To select the most appropriate tactics, the nonprofit must take several factors into consideration. To assist in this process, there are a series of questions that can be posed (see Table 3.2).

Sharing the Journey

Even if a nonprofit has embedded a sustainable citizenship platform into the organization, that is not enough. The not-for-profit must communicate this work and routinely report progress to its multiple stakeholders, if it intends to benefit from its socially responsible and environmentally-friendly

Table 3.2 Tactical Consideration Query

Will the board of directors support this initiative?
How does this initiative align with the organization's mission, values, and culture?
What is the implementation time frame?
What approach will be the most?
Will collaboration with other groups or individuals be necessary?
What resources will be required for initiative execution and how readily available are they?
Are there any budgetary considerations that must be addressed before proceeding with this project or adopting this course of action?
Is there an infrastructure, including the management function, to assign tasks and establish direct lines of accountability?
How easy will it be to gain donor/staff/public support for the particular tasks involved?
Can this work be leveraged or grouped with other tactical work to gain maximum sustainable citizenship results with minimum investment?
Is there a specific approach that would streamline the initiative's implementation process and contribute to its success?
Are there barriers that will impede implementation?
How will success or failure be evaluated, measured, and reported?
Which key communication messages will be leveraged to communicate this initiative?
How will this particular activity or project contribute to the nonprofit's sustainable citizenship's goals?

actions. In fact, with the escalating interest in this type of responsible behavior, it could be noticed if an organization is not advancing a social and environmental platform. Thus, it behooves the astute nonprofit to tell the story of how it adds to the quality of life of a community, a nation, or the world through sustainable citizenship.

To reap the aforementioned benefits, strategically planned communication is essential. The sustainable citizenship communication should be incorporated into the organization's overarching communications strategy and plan (see Chapter 2). There are, however, noteworthy practices critical to the effective conveyance of information on this topic. These include:

Establish a strong connection between the nonprofit "brand" and mission and the sustainable citizenship work underway.

Whether communicating issues related to transparency, how employees are participating in a recycle and reuse effort, or how collaboration with another nonprofit is increasing the degree of societal impact, this work must exemplify sustainable citizenship, while at the same time link to the nonprofit's mission and brand identity. In fact, communication should emphasize how these of "doing good" reflects the character of the nonprofit, in general, and enhances its ability to fulfill its prime directive.

Communicate with and engage critical stakeholders in the sustainable citizenship work.

Although the board has announced support of this platform, its involvement is paramount. For example, if the nonprofit is trying to be more eco-friendly and undertakes an Earth Day activity or adopts a highway or park for cleanup, the board should participate with staff.

Employee engagement is essential, too. Without their commitment and involvement, the opportunity to convey total support and organizational progress is less than stellar. Why? Because employees act as citizenship ambassadors. Their performance must instill belief in the nonprofit's commitment to this platform. Therefore, they serve as role models to inspire others to make similar contributions.

Government representatives are a key audience, too. Because these individuals have the ability to influence everything from the passage of legislation supporting the organization's advocacy work to nabbing government funds financing specific citizenship programs, this group of stakeholders should be kept updated.

Actually, visibility to opinion leaders, other nonprofits, special interest groups, individual and corporate donors, and even the public-at-large is essential, if the nonprofit is going to make this platform sustainable as people must be aware before they can develop supportive opinions and become engaged (see Model 3.2).

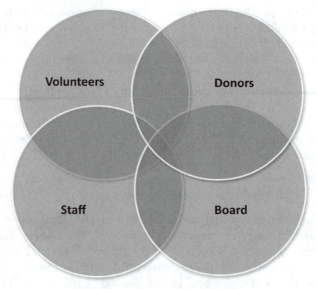

Model 3.2 Ideal Sustainable Citizenship Engagement. Ideally, the nonprofit can identify sustainable citizenship activities that engage staff, board of directors, donors, and volunteers in order to achieve maximum effectiveness of this concept.

Ensure two-way communication mechanisms are in place to create a feedback loop and encourage interaction.

Communication, especially two-way methodology, is crucial to engage other interested parties in the nonprofit's good corporate citizenship practices. By incorporating consistent, two-way communication, there is the chance to learn the point of view of the not-for-profit's many audiences. Are key stakeholders aware of the operational improvements and dedication to making additional valuable contributions to society and the environment? Do they support the work being performed or do they believe the nonprofit's sustainable citizenship journey should follow a different path? The two-way process provides opportunities for listening, dialogue, and setting the stage for participation.

Demonstrate transparency.

Open and honest communication about the additional measures a nonprofit takes to ensure it is executing its agency's mission to the fullest extent by incorporating other sustainable and socially responsible practices into its program presents a well-rounded, efficient, and caring picture of the organization. Such actions exemplify integrity and lead to a relationship of mutual trust with stakeholders. In fact, the willingness to share information and knowledge can even solidify the group's leadership position.

Transparency also permits the introduction of ideas, subjects, and processes in a manner that is informative and encourages two-way communication. When stakeholders are kept abreast of the sustainable citizenship journey, an opening for questions and an opinion exchange are created. Such a process can help flag issues before they become a problem and even enlist stakeholders in the development of a solution. When infrastructural weaknesses, organizational flaws, or barriers to progress are identified, the forthcoming style of the not-for-profit can actually lead to enhanced credibility.

Deliver valuable content.

In today's world of information overload, carefully selected, appropriate information is welcome. But, what exactly does this look like? Concise, clear, jargon-free writing is essential. In plain language, the nonprofit should describe the relevancy and challenges of sustainable citizenship, along with its unique approach to add value.

Plus, it is necessary to establish the direction of the sustainable citizenship platform and link the activity or tactic to the organization's overarching strategy, creating a clear line of site for the audience. This will ensure the work is viewed as an extension of the prime directive.

Statistical data and examples should not be so complex as to be confusing. Instead, the additional proof and support should aid understanding.

Features that make reading faster and easier, such as an executive summary or a photograph, are appreciated by time-crunched readers. Unique examples can provide additional insight into a subject and make it more memorable.

Use storytelling techniques.

Storytelling presents a perfect opportunity to emotionally connect with readers. Case studies can bring dry, statistical reports to life through a vibrant and compelling account of the organization's progress, impact on the community, or life-changing influence on a member, student, or beneficiary of the services. It also gives the sustainable citizenship platform a more personal feel, making this concept more relatable.

As a writing device, storytelling is extremely effective in conveying the progress. Therefore, it is ideal to use this technique to convey the citizenship journey.

In Closing

Business recognizes the importance of social and environmental responsibility and has reaped numerous reputational benefits on multiple levels from such actions. As additional CSR demands are placed on the world of commerce, through the expectations of customers, employees, investors, vendors, special interest groups, the government, and the public-at-large, it is obvious a socially and environmentally responsible approach has become a standard for doing business. And, data suggests public expectations will continue to rise.

Up to now, it has not been presumed not-for-profits would broaden their impact beyond their charter. However, as the public becomes more aware of the additional contributions these entities could make and as nonprofits recognize the reputational benefits of adopting a sustainable citizenship platform, they will be obliged to "leverage their halo" and build additional goodwill by assuming a greater responsibility to society and the environment. This, in turn, will intensify the demand for non-profits to act as change agents in areas outside of the scope of their defined mission and to contribute to the transformational change necessary to sustain communities and nations.

In the future, these entities will be expected to drive the level of environmental, social, ethical, and cultural conscience. Their passion and dedication present new possibilities, along with more fully leveraging their core competencies, and can broaden the scope of their social responsiveness. Consequently, rather than being singularly focused, the nonprofit of tomorrow should represent a multi-faceted, sustainable citizenship ideology.

As these entities begin their sustainable citizenship journey, they will be wise to review corporate social responsibility successes and failures. This will enable them to travel the sustainability journey more smoothly as they can avoid pitfalls and crises while emulating the successes.

Thoughts on the Subject

Michael Fanning
Director of Sustainable Development
Michelin Group, Clermont-Ferrand, France

Q: Companies understand the importance of sustainability in the equation for "good" citizenship. Why should nonprofits, although already "doing good," incorporate sustainability in their efforts?

A: Today, more and more companies have sustainability on their agenda, and those that are truly leading edge have made it a cornerstone of their business strategy. But what of the world of nonprofits? Haven't they traditionally been focused on sustainability, or citizenship as it has been commonly termed? Well, the answer is "yes," but the challenges of the future might call for a different approach. Let's examine the issue.

First, it's necessary to define what is meant by sustainability. A commonly used term is that of the U.N. Brundtland Commission, which in 1983 stated that "Sustainable development is development that meets the needs of the present without compromising the ability of future generations to meet their own needs."

With the world on a path toward 9 billion people by 2050, compared with 7 billion people today, most reasonable people concur that the current trajectory of resource consumption is not feasible. In addition, a sustainable world encompasses the notion of all people living well, which implies universal access to healthcare, education, employment, a safe environment, and other life essentials. Finally, under the mantle of people, planet and profits, sustainability calls for a balanced approach.

When it comes to the arc of the sustainability agenda, most companies have moved from a purely environmental approach—less harm to nature and resource conservation—to one that also encompasses a good corporate citizenship approach—philanthropic donations and volunteerism.

And now more enlightened companies look at a shared-value approach with society: Companies provide solutions to societal problems—eco-efficient car engines and technical resources for small- and medium-sized farmers, as examples—and, in turn, they are rewarded with reasonable profits and a sustainable enterprise.

Turning to nonprofits, one would think that sustainability and citizenship have been traditionally embedded in their missions. After all, nonprofits were created to address areas where society's inequities needed to be addressed, whether in healthcare, disease prevention and eradication, cultural and arts promotion, environmental advocacy, etc. Today, I would posit that nonprofits need to move to a truly multi-stakeholder approach that concentrates on sustainable solutions for a given community.

Let's take an example: A good start would be to convene businesses, governments, and nonprofits in a study of a community's needs over a specified period of time. From that vantage point, a slate of sustainable solutions should be identified. When that has taken place, each nonprofit would assess its mission against the greater needs of the community. It's likely that the missions of some nonprofits would overlap those of others and that certain critical community needs would rank higher than those of others. A sustainable approach would be to examine carefully how nonprofits might re-align themselves to better serve the entire community rather than how individual nonprofits currently serve a specific population. There might be some tough choices, with possible mergers, alliances and possibly even closures to achieve the greater good. But in a world with countless needs, declining funding sources and overlapping missions, a greater alignment of resources against existing problems could be the future of nonprofit sustainability.

For further thoughts on this approach, please visit the website of Greenville (S.C.) Forward at http://greenvilleforward.com.

Dr. Karen Shumway
Associate Dean of the College of Business
Angelo State University, Department of Management and Marketing, San Angelo, TX

Q: Companies have recognized the benefits of good citizenship through better transparency, promoting sustainability, and social responsibility. Why is it important that nonprofits demonstrate a similar focus?

A: Nonprofits are held accountable by a wide variety of stakeholders, including but not limited to their own boards of directors; clients or users of their services; organizational members; the general public/communities served; individual donors; funding foundations; funding corporations; federal, state, and local government bodies/agencies; as well as employees and volunteers. Nonprofits are also faced with highly challenging and dynamic environments due to increased demands for services and shrinking resources in traditional funding sources. To make matters worse, recent widely publicized scandals regarding unethical behaviors in some well-known nonprofits have undermined public trust of nonprofit leadership.

Citizenship is a holistically accountable position with regard to all aspects of the organization's relationship with society and stakeholders. It is a fundamental ideology or value system, embedded in the organization's strategies and coordinated throughout every aspect of the organization's activities. Citizenship should not be viewed as a stable, secure condition, but rather an active and continuous pursuit to align the organization with its societal or external environment and deploy resources to support that alignment internally. Attention to building good citizenship may create distinctive and exceptional organizational capabilities including:

- strong trust-based collaborative relationships with key stakeholders;
- robust organizational knowledge and learning based on understanding the effectiveness of past interactions with societal stakeholders and subsequent effects on the future; and
- on-going development of innovative approaches to providing high quality services.

Something to Think About

1. Sometimes people assign very separate meanings to the terms "values" and "ethics." In the not-for-profit world, do you see these as interchangeable or different? Why or why not?
2. Briefly discuss the moral, rational, and ethical arguments for nonprofit sustainable citizenship.
3. Do you think the size and type of nonprofit affects how it approaches sustainable citizenship?
4. Select a not-for profit for discussion purposes. What type of sustainable citizenship messages could be used with the organization's primary stakeholders?
5. Initiating an employee soft drink recycling program is an easy add for organizations not already focused on environmentally responsible actions. What are other examples of socially or environmentally responsible efforts, which could be easily added into an organizations daily operation?

4 Crisis Communication

In life, unlike chess, the game continues after checkmate.

(Isaac Asimov)

Before discussing crisis communication planning, management, and follow-up, it is necessary to establish context. Obviously, crises have occurred throughout history. But, the science and practice of crisis preparedness and management as a documented field is much more recent. There are many theories related to crisis causality; models mapping the anatomy of a crisis; prototypes for risk assessments; issues management templates; and research documenting the reputational impact of "good" versus "bad" crisis communication. These theories, models, collective research, and case studies are extremely relevant and useful in the crisis communication planning and management process. However, it is the nonprofit's actions during a crisis that ultimately impacts its future operation and reputation. Therefore, it is advisable to put as much thought and time as possible into proactively preparing a crisis communication plan and routinely conducting simulations. That way, the nonprofit will better handle a catastrophic and reputationally devastating event.

Media as a Key Story Influencer

Traditional and social media play an incredibly influential role in shaping the crisis story and impacting an organization's reputation. In fact, "the media has the power to transform an issue over time by framing it in a new light."[1] Therefore, understanding how media works, the importance of interacting with this key influencer, and becoming familiar with basic media relations principles can be particularly helpful.

Some forms of traditional and social media are viewed as relatively unbiased, so the public is likely to assign a certain degree of credibility to these reports. And, although a nonprofit may have direct access to key stakeholders through a wide variety of technologies, those formally and informally reporting on the crisis have the same communication vehicles available to them and potentially benefit from the added factor of greater believability.

Because of the gatekeeping role, others have the ability to determine what and if the nonprofit can use vehicles such as broadcasts, newspapers, and government reports. This means the nonprofit actually has fewer communication tools available than do these other sources. With the understanding other sources may have more news outlets and greater credibility, it is clear media's influence during a crisis cannot be underestimated and relations should be carefully orchestrated.

What Is News?

When a crisis strikes, a journalist looks for the facts that will tell the story: who, what, when, where, why, and how. While these are essential elements, there also are aspects a reporter, editor, or producer relies upon to determine newsworthiness.

When any of the following components are present individually or together, news coverage is frequently generated:

- *Timeliness*: Is it happening now, in the near future, or occurred fairly recently?
- *Proximity*: Is it happening "close to home"? The more nearby, the more likely an event will draw attention.
- *Consequences*: If an event, problem, arrest, or issue occurred, how was it handled, managed, or solved?
- *Prominence*: Are high profile people involved? This can be relative to the location of the news outlet.
- *Drama*: Examples include homeowners being displaced by a flood or fire and animals in peril due to an environmental disaster.
- *Progress*: Regulatory, social, or technological advancements represent this category; a new court ruling to save the wet lands and block a development becomes a crisis for business progress while it is viewed as a progressive step toward sustainability for the environmentalist.
- *Emotion*: A starving child, an injured puppy, or a homeless veteran may offer an emotional connection.
- *Sex*: Examples include affairs, divorce, and sexual misconduct.
- *Conflict*: Wars, feuds, fighting, disagreements, lawsuits, and stand-offs are prime examples.
- *Oddity*: It is not so unusual for a dog to bite a man. It is unusual for the man to bite the dog.

By recognizing and understanding how these angles can pique the interest of both traditional and social media outlets, the communications officer will better predict what will be asked and the probable story line. If multiple angles are of significant interest to readers or viewers, a high degree of coverage is expected, and it is anticipated the level of reporting will quickly escalate, the story is said to have "legs." Because it is not uncommon for a crisis to quickly "run away" from an organization, crisis coverage typically falls into this category.

Media Manners

There are many good journalists who want to produce a balanced account of a crisis. But, as with any profession, there may be those who are out for personal gain. So, it is possible to encounter individuals who sensationalize or editorialize. Regardless of the reporter's style or motivation, professionalism on the part of the communications officer is mandatory.

It is advisable to make the initial media contact during a "time of normalcy." During this interaction, the spokesperson should share contact information, promise to be available for media inquiries, ask about the preferred news gathering method, and check on deadline timing.

This rapport-building process provides an opportunity to familiarize the journalist or blogger with the not-for-profit. Fact sheets, the organization's history, a list of board of director members, and similar materials can be offered. By conducting this educational process during the pre-crisis stage, the organization has a chance to establish its reputation as a well-managed and purposeful group. The spokesperson has the chance to build credibility through open and honest communication and a responsive attitude.

After the initial meeting, whether virtual, in person, or over the phone, the relationship should be cultivated. Recognizing the competitive pressures of news reporting and the issues caused by shrinking staffs can help the public relations practitioner better understand media behavior. As smaller news teams are asked to do more with less, the communications officer will find it helpful to rely on the following tips, which demonstrate respect for a journalist's goals of conveying the story quickly and informing and educating the public with noteworthy information (see Box 4.1: Basic Media Relations Principles).

AP style should be used when writing releases. This well-known and journalistically respected writing style is valued by news outlets as it likely means less editing will be necessary. Given time sensitivity and news staff size, well-written releases make it easier for reporters and can help ensure wording will more closely resemble what the nonprofit released.

Social Media's Influence on News

Being anti-social during a crisis can create a crisis in itself. Social media significantly shapes the reporting landscape. A story may make headlines, but once the story goes into cyberspace, the news can go viral through tweets, postings, "likes," wikis, and emails, taking control out of the

---

Box 4.1   Basic Media Relations Principles

DO:

Respect deadlines
Act ethically and honestly
Stay on message
Get back to reporters as promised
Release accurate information and statistics
Write concisely and use AP style
Prove "quotable" answers
Offer graphics and visuals to help tell the story
Give appropriate access to subject matter experts
Listen carefully to questions before responding

DON'T:

Send releases not applicable to the reporter's area of coverage
Beg or threaten to go to an editor or publisher to receive coverage
Promote an adversarial relationship by becoming irritated
Play favorites among the media
Use company or industry jargon
Go "off the record"

---

hands of the nonprofit. Consequently, closely monitoring this spontaneous form of communication is beneficial in identifying escalating interest and the circulation of misinformation.

As media can tell and show a crisis, it's advisable to think like a television producer. By doing so, the communication team can better anticipate what will be said and what visuals shown. Plus, it can help the spokesperson as well as determine what photos, graphics, and videos will complement the nonprofit's news releases, updates, press conferences, and other communication.

Crisis Characteristics

A crisis is unpredictable in form and timing; yet, the concept of a crisis occurrence isn't unexpected. Instead, the question is never "if" but "when" a negative or catastrophic situation will occur.

It's also important to remember crises *are steeped in public perception.* A scenario may not conform to what a logical person would label as a crisis; yet when set in a specific context, the public may perceive it as such. Thus, a nonissue can erupt into hostile public opinion and negative press. This is particularly true, if the organization does not respond in a manner consistent with public expectation.

For example, if accusations arise that a pedophile works at a homeless shelter for families or at a church school, the public expects the individual to be relieved of duties until a thorough investigation into the matter is conducted. If the organization opts to ignore the reports or permits the individual to continue to work while the investigation is underway, the nonprofit's seeming denial of the seriousness of the situation will certainly draw ire from the community.

Crises *impact stakeholder reputation*. Whether it is staff, donors, the board of directors, volunteers, or recipients of the service provided by the nonprofit, those closest to the nonprofit are touched in some manner by the crisis. Through their affiliation with the organization, these individuals can have personal credibility and competency questioned; be considered unemployable; receive pity from others; be acknowledged through kudos and awards; or even be hurled into the public spotlight.

Those connected in a tangential way may find themselves affected, too. For instance, a journalist reporting inaccurate information, which was provided by the nonprofit, experiences reputational damage. An elected official who fought for legislation to help a charity, which is later discovered to be fraudulently using funds, may find his or her credibility questioned. For this reason, an improperly handled crisis can take its toll on affiliated stakeholders, making them "collateral damage."

An extremely *condensed time frame* is another characteristic of a crisis. The nonprofit must be ready to act with speed because an immediate response will be demanded. There is no time to hold focus groups to test messaging, no chance go on vacation before responding to the media, no opportunity to begin developing a checklist of materials for a crisis response center.

Uncertainty becomes the *new organizational norm*: the organization's operation is interrupted in some way, removing it from its status quo; and the nonprofit's reputation is impacted, likely tarnished, unless the challenge is turned into opportunity.

While it seems odd to think about capitalizing on a negative, it's possible the crisis could provide an opportunity for the nonprofit to justify its existence or, better yet, prove its value. This can be seen in a weather-related crisis where a charity provides much needed support following a hurricane or tornado, even though it is dealing with catastrophic storm damage, too. Its exemplary performance could be cited for best practices, positioning the group as a leader within its particular nonprofit sector.

The purpose of crisis planning is to prepare so the nonprofit can manage the crisis in such a manner that its operation is returned to some degree of normalcy or balance as quickly as possible and its reputation fully restored or enhanced.

According to Robert Ulmer, Timothy Sellnow, and Matthew Seeger, in their book *Effective Crisis Communication*, there are two types of crises: unintentional and intentional. Unintentional crises instigators range from natural disasters to an economic downturn to a disease outbreak. Intentional crises are connected to an individual or group responsible for events, such as sabotage, unethical leadership, and workplace violence, in which a purposeful action is taken.[2]

But, a third crisis category seems to have emerged because of the power of technology. This is when an event, which would normally be considered a nonissue, is magnified to crisis proportion because of the "environment" surrounding it.

For instance, an innocently but poorly made decision by a nonprofit's board of directors occurs simultaneously with a similar decision made by a board with less scrupulous purposes. When the second organization makes headlines, captures the attention of bloggers, piques the interest of investigative journalists, and becomes a trending topic on Twitter, the first organization may be catapulted into the spotlight, too. Due to the timing of its naively made decision, the first nonprofit is compared to that of the other board. When this comparative analysis is reported, the situation could become negative very quickly.

Another example is a community-based charity experiencing a crisis that is picked up by social media. Although only a small geographic area may be affected, the nonprofit's name and situation could go viral, reaching a much larger audience.

Three Stage Approach

Preparing, managing, and recovering from a crisis is a complex and challenging task. To simplify the discussion, communication planning and executional work flow will be categorized into the three stages referenced by many crisis management experts: pre-crisis, crisis event, and post-crisis.[3]

Pre-Crisis

First, it is virtually impossible to be overly prepared. Thoughtfully considered plan development and simulations offer the opportunity to uncover vulnerabilities, provide "real life" scenarios to see how effectively both people and processes stand up to pressure, and test component design for flexibility and efficacy.

When a crisis occurs, it is likely there will be some unforeseen angle or unanticipated but influential event. Through rigorous planning, it is feasible to have a plan design that is applicable to the majority of situations and the basic components adaptable to manage similar scenarios. Such preplanning helps minimize the amount of reputational damage and operational disruption or possibly avoid the crisis altogether.

Fortunately, some of the work completed during the nonprofit's strategic planning process can contribute to this crisis communication activity. The department should refer to its strengths-weaknesses-opportunities-challenges (S.W.O.C.) analysis, environmental scan, key messages, and audience analysis to kick start this effort.

Issues and Risk Management

"The essence of risk is not that it *is* happening, but that it *might* be happening."[4]

The nonprofit's S.W.O.C. analysis uncovered risks and vulnerabilities, which potentially could escalate into a crisis. These known issues should become focal points where the institution dedicates time and resources. The reason is that issue resolution and improved risk management techniques can lead to crisis avoidance, a logical first step in crisis management and one that provides many rewards.

The results of the environmental scan can be extremely helpful in vulnerability identification, too. Public concerns and opinions should be examined to learn trends and subjects of interest and distress. A look at the social landscape in which the organization functions reveals likely risks that could be triggered by other individuals or factors and over which the NGO has no direct control. The nonprofit should be sensitive to the possibility of this occurrence.

Observing mainstream and nontraditional media are part of this scan. Both should be tracked, a trend line developed, and an educated projection made as to how emerging news topics could be linked to the nonprofit. It should be noted there is a secondary benefit to this type of review. By analyzing media coverage, there is an opportunity to learn from the mistakes of others. Witnessing how another organization has turned a situation into a crisis because of poor media management or a faux pas can help the nonprofit circumvent a similar reputational fate.

Issues and problems that surfaced through the analysis and scan are areas of risk. Ideally, risks are managed proactively, resulting in crisis avoidance. However, that cannot always happen. The nonprofit should prioritize the issues based upon the likelihood of occurrence in the next one to five years, rank them in terms of severity, and categorize them by their degree of controllability. By taking this proactive and systematic approach, there is time to tackle the most critical problems, develop action plans, and build messaging around the areas of concern.

To stay abreast with developments that could affect the emergence of issues and risks, a simple log can assist with this early detection process. (See Worksheet 4.1: Issues Template.) To ascertain greater predictability, Pamela Walaski's risk assessment matrix applies weighted values to help determine both the probability and the severity of potential crisis.[5]

Since *rumors* represent the oldest form of media, it is essential to listen carefully for this form of information sharing and speculation. Rumors can over-emphasize previously unnoticed or unessential details, distribute speculative information, re-surge floating urban myths, exaggerate or misinterpret facts, and even manipulate responses. Therefore, their power should not be minimized or underestimated.[6] Because of their innuendos and half-truths, this communication can be extremely damaging to staff, volunteer, and board morale.

Worksheet 4.1

Issues Template

Issue:
Nature of threat:
Stakeholders impacted:
Likelihood of risk:
High   Medium   Low
Warning signs:
Target resolution:
Issue:
Nature of threat:
Stakeholders impacted:
Likelihood of risk:
High   Medium   Low
Warning signs:
Target resolution:

Contact Lists

Up-to-date, comprehensive, and specialized *media directories* should already be in place for the department's day-to-day operation, but they become critical during a crisis. These lists should include the contact's name and title; media outlet name; contact details (email address, business and cell phone numbers); and any deadlines. Subgrouping media may be appropriate as well. For example, it may be helpful to have a list containing only bloggers or television news outlets.

An *emergency contact list* should be developed and updated routinely. Business, cell, and home phone numbers; email address(es); and even home addresses should be compiled for employees, volunteers, and board members.

Calling protocols should be designed and accompany the emergency contact list. These guidelines establish who is to call whom and for what. This way, time is not wasted by having multiple people notify the board president.

The communication department may need to compile other contact lists, as it could be helpful to have relationships with spokespersons at the fire and police departments, other nonprofits that would collaborate in an emergency, and vendors or suppliers. If the nonprofit is a chapter within a regional, national, or international charity, NGO, or professional group, contacts from the parent group should be kept on file. These contacts can offer valuable support with monitoring and responding to media during a crisis.

As in life, it's important to know who your friends are. The communications team should develop a strategic network comprised of individuals or groups that can serve as *third-party collaborators*, such as: government agencies, other nonprofits, special interest groups, businesses, community leaders, donors, volunteers, board members, and social and sector-specific experts. Their validation, expert testimony, investigative acumen, established credibility, and personal experience will help validate and support the nonprofit's position. Through their affiliation with the nonprofit, these individuals and groups can endorse both the good name and the work of the institution.

An example of this is a small chapter of a national or international charity. Questions may arise, such as issues pertaining to pending, sector-specific legislation or concerns over dismissal protocol, both of which may be more appropriate for the parent organization to address. Plus, this technique can help deflect some of the negative focus from the local group.

It's also conceivable an executive director's salary or benefits package could be challenged or a clinic's treatment protocols questioned. In such instances, it is helpful to have a knowledgeable, third-party expert who is willing to be interviewed by the press or, at the very least, to issue a statement or quote on the subject, substantiating the nonprofit's actions.

Identifying these third-party entities and developing relationships in advance save time and offer support when needed the most. A valuable resource that should be built is a file of letters and other written documentation, attesting to the nonprofit's past exemplary behavior, record-breaking performance, and ethical conduct. These statements, certifications, awards, compliments, and acknowledgements can be used later in a news release or advertorial, if proper approval is on file.

It should be noted that *texting* plays an increasingly important role in reaching key audiences during times of crisis. Students may need to be warned about a threat on a school campus. Hospital employees may need to be asked to report to work immediately to deal with a community tragedy. Volunteers may need to gather at a specific location and time to help sandbag for a flood. Donations may be needed as quickly as possible to provide essential relief to victims of a manmade or a natural disaster. All of these scenarios have one thing in common: the speed with which communication must be achieved.

Texts can be sent easily and reach intended audience quickly. Nonprofits should prepare and test routinely both its text and voice mail emergency contact lists, rather than waiting for a crisis simulation. This will help to ensure critical audiences can be reached as effectively and efficiently as possible.

A list of *assigned communication responsibilities* should be in the plan, too. Duties, such as who is responsible for answering telephones, emails, tweets, and web site inquiries and who is acting as the spokesperson, must be assigned prior to the crisis.

A small or mid-sized charity or association may have only one full-time person in the communications department. As one person cannot manage all of the communication necessary during a major crisis, identifying potential crisis support personnel, delegating responsibilities, and providing training in advance of a crisis are paramount. Individuals can be recruited from the board of directors or volunteer base or they could be a hired freelancer or public relations agency account executive.

Whether large or small, the nonprofit may have to rely upon the paid help of an agency or consultancy. It is less than ideal timing to have to research and hire this type of assistance in the middle of a significantly sensitive situation or catastrophic event; worse yet would be a report that the nonprofit was busy hiring a public relations firm rather than dealing with the crisis. This could make headlines, causing additional speculation that the problem was so big "hired guns" were required and criticism that the nonprofit's focus was not where it needed to be. Consequently, researching where back-up support can originate and developing an agreement with consultants in the pre-crisis period ensure professional support will be available quickly.

Never had to hire a consultant before? Ideally, a formal request for proposal (RFP) can be issued. But if unable to guarantee work, many firms may be unwilling to participate in this time-consuming and formal process. In addition, department time to develop an RFP may be lacking. If either is the case, the nonprofit may find itself employing a less formal decision-making process, such as relying on telephone conversations, meetings, and email exchanges with potential PR and crisis communication agencies. If this less-structured route is followed, the public relations firm should supply this basic information:

- Company description, including mission and values statements;
- Experience in the nonprofit arena and crisis communications;
- Account executive who would manage the account and this individual's experience;
- Fee structure, including any nonprofit discounts;
- Explanation of the agency's crisis communication media support offerings; and
- Disclosure of any potential conflicts of interest.

Spokesperson Selection

When assigning roles, considerable thought should be put into who will serve as the chief spokesperson. It is also prudent to have more than one spokesperson, even though someone should be selected as the primary representative. The logic for this is twofold. First, if a crisis is lengthy or around the clock, the primary spokesperson will tire and not be able to function at the high performance level required for this demanding position. Therefore, back-up is essential. Plus, what happens if the primary spokesperson is simply unavailable? It doesn't matter if the person is out of the country or in the hospital. Either way, the person would be unable to perform the spokesperson duties.

It is important to acknowledge there may be times when someone else is better suited to act as spokesperson. For example, if the executive director must be terminated, the board president may be more appropriate to release certain statements than the primary spokesperson.

Spokespersons should have crisis media training. Just because the person delivers excellent presentations, is a wonderful public speaker, or interviews well for feature stories, doesn't mean he or she will perform in an exemplary manner during news conference, when bright television lights are glaring and questions are being shouted from all sides.

While one could argue appearance shouldn't matter, it does. Spokespersons must be coached on details such as what to wear and which nonverbal techniques to employ or avoid. Word choice, response length, the importance of not speculating, the need to demonstrate an appropriate level of concern and compassion represent just a few of the modules that should be addressed during media training.

Holding Statements

When a crisis strikes, it's important to remember: There is no second chance. That's why it's essential to have something to say, which positions the nonprofit in control and pictures the spokesperson as calm and knowledgeable. Since crises are unpredictable, the ability to respond immediately with a crisis-specific response may be next to impossible. This is why holding statements are a necessity.

This statement professionally acknowledges the journalist inquiry or blogger's posting, recognizes the scenario is emerging, and offers reassurance the situation is being researched or managed. This approach is more comforting to any audience than "no comment," which many times connotes guilt or is perceived as such.

The advantage of holding statements is that they can be prepared in advance, receive approval from key stakeholders, and be sufficiently generic to use in a broad spectrum of situations. The key messages, developed during the communication department's strategic planning process, should be incorporated into these holding responses to emphasize the organization's mission and brand.

Example: One key message of an NGO focused on sustainability could be:

> *"We are committed to creating a toxic-free world by emphasizing safer alternatives to hazardous chemical use and processes." What if an investigative reporter discovers the charity's headquarters has failed to use eco-friendly cleaning compounds? The holding statement can begin by emphasizing the not-for-profit's dedication to creating a world free of toxic chemicals and then be followed with a promise the allegation will be investigated and handled appropriately, so the organization can continue to serve as a role model for others.*

Risks, issues, and vulnerabilities identified during the S.W.O.C. highlighted situations that could develop into crises. It is wise to develop holding statements for those scenarios rated as having the greatest likelihood of escalating to a crisis.

Also, the executive team might believe it never could be accused of fund mismanagement, embezzlement, discrimination, or sexual harassment; yet, it is important to remember the organization could be accused of such, even if totally blameless. This is why holding statements for generic possibilities in addition to nonprofit-specific risks should be developed. Perhaps, these statements may never be needed; but should the situation arise, it will be extremely beneficial to have them.

It is advisable to have all holding statements reviewed by the board, the executive leadership, and an attorney, so there are no surprises to anyone when these comments appear in public. Finalized statements should be maintained in the crisis communication plan. Some spokespersons even memorize them, recognizing the possibility of ambush interviews.

Additional tips for developing holding statements:

- Jargon-free and easy to understand;
- Brief and "packaged" in easy-to-use quotes or sound bites; and
- Sufficiently generic to act as a springboard for later commentary or to which specifics can be added.

Although holding statements are very helpful at the onset of the crisis, they will only "buy" a little time. It is during these critical first minutes and hours that the communications officer must be collecting facts and gaining an understanding as to what has actually occurred because the media will expect a case-specific response before long (see Box 4.2: Examples of Holding Statements).

Box 4.2   Examples of Holding Statements

Serious injury accident on grounds, office:
"The accident, which occurred in (on) our (cite location), is deeply troubling and unfortunate. Our primary concern is for the injured party(ies). We are working closely with authorities (cite authority) to provide them with the information and support they need. As soon as we know more about the nature and cause of the incident, we will share it with you."

Shooting of Employee, Board, or Volunteer on property/at activity:
"(Nonprofit name) is deeply saddened by today's (yesterday's) tragic events. Our thoughts (and prayers) are with those families affected by this needless violence. We ask the media to respect the privacy of our employees (and volunteers) at this time. All questions about these grievous actions and the continuing investigation should be directed to the local law enforcement officials (or supply name of investigating agency)."

Security issues following an incident at a school, camp, treatment center, battered women's shelter, or other similar facility:
"(Nonprofit name) does not share security details, so as not to compromise this investigation. We also do not discuss security details in order to better protect our (members, clients, campers, patients, families, employees). It is our concern that, if we make such details public, we could create a security risk by providing information to those individuals who committed these criminal acts.
"Please know that as part of our debriefing process, we review our security efforts and constantly look for ways to improve our existing program to better protect our (members, clients, campers, patients, families, employees)."

Rumors about changes in board membership, executive leadership, program changes, etc.:
"(Nonprofit name) does not comment on rumors concerning (fill in event). Because we are committed to (fill in appropriate key message regarding transparency or values), we announce any such changes in (leadership, programming, etc.) should they occur."

Templates

Just as holding statements are very helpful during this condensed time frame, so, too, are news release templates. Partially completed news releases can be drafted for issues or risks with a high likelihood of escalating into a crisis. This saves a significant amount of time during the actual emergency.

Plus, when rushing to write a time-sensitive release, there is always the possibility critical information will be left out. Having a prepared form with blanks for customization helps to ensure all salient points will be covered.

Timely responses are essential to promoting an image of transparency. A *media log* can help avoid an inquiry being overlooked. This record also can serve as a means to monitor and analyze the types of questions posed. Whether simple or sophisticated in nature, the log can be designed in advance and available in both paper and electronic formats (see Worksheet 4.2: Media Log).

Some *frequently asked questions documents* can be prepared prior to a crisis. When working on FAQs, it is advisable to go through this exercise: Think of the five most embarrassing and challenging questions that the organization never wants to be asked about an issue or subject. Prepare responses for these. This portion of the Q-and-A may be kept confidential with only a few people, such as the executive director, board president, communications department, and legal counsel, having access. Prepared responses to tough questions will ensure the media relations person is not as likely to be blindsided or unprepared to reply to an extremely embarrassing or significantly reputationally damaging question.

Having identified catastrophic events that could have a high likelihood of occurring, the charity should consider creating a *dark site.*

During the 9-11 tragedy, business discovered the critical need for communicating with employees and their families. Telephone and cell phone service was interrupted due to volume. Traditional media outlets were carrying the "big picture" story. The result? A recognition that organizations needed an outlet to communicate during such emergencies.

A dark site can be comprised of a single page or multiple web pages, which do not post until needed. Typically, this is not a separate web site. Links can be inserted on the home page directing the visitor to a location with crisis-specific information. Or, the content could temporarily replace the home page.

Content is audience-based. Key crisis messaging would be the same. But, content-rich pages would be a source for audiences to find what they need quickly and conveniently. Depending upon the purpose of the page and its design, a compassionate, personal message from the executive director could appear. Temporary instructions could be posted and routinely updated. News about the crisis could be shared with up-to-the-minute

Worksheet 4.2
Media Log

Today's Date: _____   Time: _____ a.m./p.m.

Your Name: _____

Name of Journalist: _____

Media Outlet: _____

E-mail Address: _____   Phone: _____

Deadline: _____

Proposed air, publication, and/or post date: _____

Requested interview topic or angle of story?

What do you know about this issue/crisis now?

Will anyone else be interviewed? If so, who?

Which media team member is handling the inquiry? _____

Note date and time handled: _____

Is follow-up required?

details or announcements. Telephone numbers, critical contacts, and even links to other sites could be included, if helpful to those seeking direction or support.

Dark site pages can be designed for the intranet, so staff can access information without making the content available to the general public. Depending upon the crisis, benefit-related materials, such as health coverage details or directions on how to obtain grief counseling, may be posted, so employees have the personal support they need. This action helps staff members deal with individual issues in an expedited manner and enables them to get back to their roles of assisting with the crisis.

As this content is prepared in advance, there is time for thoughtful consideration of what should appear and how it should be worded as well as page navigability. By having pages ready to post after only a few modifications, critical information can be disseminated quickly via Internet and intranet.

Telephone scripting and basic Internet responses can be developed in advance, too. Since it is likely there will be a deluge of inquiries, the persons answering the phones should have a standardized script and directions as to how inquiries are recorded. This way, questions can be answered properly and in a timely manner. As an immediate response to each email inquiry would be extremely difficult, an automatic response acknowledging the contact and containing a commitment to respond as quickly as possible should be prepared for use as needed.

Depending upon the situation, a telephone hot line may be essential. Research of and the arrangement for a hotline should be conducted in advance. Cost, the ability of a system to handle a large volume of calls, and other relevant aspects should be explored. Script development can be outlined, if not completely written, for specific scenarios.

Gathering Materials, Identifying Meeting Places

What happens if the office is flooded, yet the agency needs to serve constituents, or, if the crisis requires the communication team to go into the field and work from a remote location? Trying to determine what equipment and supplies are needed at the last minute can create problems.

It is best to develop a *checklist* in advance to avoid a last-minute scramble. Extra batteries, cell phones, lap top computers, a portable lectern, and paper are just a few of the necessary items. Some supplies can be compiled and stored for later use. In other cases, materials must be purchased from a vendor at the exact time of need. In these situations, advance arrangements should be made to ensure the purchase or rental can be executed quickly and flawlessly.

Computer files should be backed up at an off-site location to guarantee they will be available remotely and important files are not destroyed. File back-ups can be done manually or through the parent organization's IT network. If these options aren't workable, various firms offer are paid solutions, such as Carbonite, which automatically backs up computer files.

A potential work location should be selected and the communications team made aware of the alternative spot. If the office serves as the crisis management location, a "war room" should be created. This room must be equipped with everything from extra electrical outlets to ensure sufficient available power for lap tops and cell phones to white boards for planning to extra landline telephones.

Crisis Communication Plan

The crisis communication plan packages procedures, guidelines, templates, and reference materials into an easy-to-use reference tool, which helps save time and work in the midst of a crisis. While some plans are more elaborate than others, there are recommended components for any basic crisis communication plan:

- *Brief introduction* to explain the manual's design and how it works in case those unfamiliar with the plan need to reference it.
- *Crisis communications objectives and guiding principles*, which should cover subjects such as reputation protection and enhancement, ethics, and transparency.
- *Issue and risk identification research, including log templates*, so concerns likely to escalate to the magnitude of a crisis are identified, recorded, and monitored.
- *Initial response protocols and checklists*, including the particulars for everything from the hot line implementation process to dark sites "go live" directions to the internal communications notification procedure to the assigned responsibilities checklist.

  Pertinent organizational and department policies should be in the manual, such as the next-of-kin notification process, staff dismissal procedures, and employee safety codes.
- *Media relations materials*, including holding statements, news release templates, media logs, the standard news release boiler plate, and media directories.
- *Directories* can be broken into an individual section or included under specific headings. Regardless of where these appear, essential contact lists are: staff and board of director contacts; media directories; and third-party collaborators.

  Although not mentioned thus far, a vendor directory should appear in the plan, too. This catalogues companies providing essential communication services or support, such as PR Newswire, Carbonite, and the selected public relations agency.

  A list with contact details for regulatory agencies, elected officials, and advisory groups is particularly important for some nonprofits, such as a chamber of commerce.
- *Public relations materials.* Copies of fact sheets, the mission statement, board of director listing, brochures, organizational history, and other information should be available both electronically and in print copy formats as a course of conducting the day-to-day operation. These same public relations materials may be needed during a crisis, so they should be available for easy reference and use. These documents also should be referenced for language and positioning

before writing crisis-specific communication to ensure consistency with previous organizational messaging.

Since visuals are critical to supporting written communication and can, at times, better illustrate a point or convey a concept than the written word, these resources should be convenient as well. Careful consideration should be given to how visuals, like photographs, videos, charts, graphs, jpegs, and other graphics, can contribute to the communication process.

- *Paper or Electronic?* Should the plan be printed or maintained electronically? The answer is "both." As a crisis is unpredictable by its very nature, the plan should available in both formats. The printed document should be kept in a tabbed notebook. The three-ring binder approach will make it easy to update. Plus, the communications team may want others, who would not have access to the department's electronic files, to have copies of the document. The executive director and the board of directors' president are potential recipients.

A worst case scenario would be that the communication team's paper and electronic versions of the crisis communication plan are destroyed. If proper file back-up precautions were taken, this may create a slight delay in accessing materials but will ensure the planning work is not destroyed.

Simulations

Crisis simulations take time. So, it is not uncommon to hear excuses why one is not conducted during the pre-crisis phase. However, it should be noted that the simulation experience is beneficial for many reasons in addition to the practice it provides. Complications or flaws in the organizational and communication crisis plans can be discovered by testing. Other benefits to practice sessions are:

- Helping everyone understand the pressures and demands on staff during a crisis;
- Training everyone on individual crisis roles;
- Raising awareness as to how various responsibilities inter-relate in the crisis management process;
- Building team confidence; and
- Providing an opportunity to assess contingency measures.

Crisis communication plans should be workable, easily understood, and familiar to those who need to implement them on a moment's notice. The best way to ensure this is through practice sessions with the enactment of a representative scenario and staff role playing assigned tasks.

While the mock-crisis is ideal, the preparation, cost, and time may be more than a nonprofit, particularly a small or mid-sized charity, can afford. If this is the case, a table-top exercise should be conducted. This format would at least open discussion as to how the agency or NGO would respond to a crisis. An outside facilitator can guide the team through the drill to ensure all salient components of the plans are reviewed and analyzed for performance, cost, and resource allocation.

During the Crisis

How do you know when an issue or problem has crossed the "magical threshold" to become a crisis? The reality is that crises are subjective and in some ways symbolic. A crisis to one charity may be a little more than a blip on the radar screen for another. When the nonprofit finds routine is disrupted and the flow of events escalated to the point of losing control of a situation while at the same time facing mounting media interest, it is likely the situation has been transformed into a crisis. Faced with adversity and instability, the nonprofit finds it is impacted on one or several of these levels: social, economic, political, reputational, or operational.

When faced with the immediate demands of a crisis, it is essential to:

- ensure staff and/or family members are supported;
- cooperate fully with investigating authorities or regulatory bodies;
- pinpoint potential liability claims or lawsuits that could erupt into public discussion;
- help the crisis task force contain the situation; and
- manage the reputational situation.

And while all of this is going on, it is important to listen to: what the media is reporting; what those affected are saying; how staff and volunteers are describing the event; and how community leaders are weighing in. In fact, the value of listening during a crisis cannot be underestimated. By monitoring what traditional and social media outlets are saying, the communications team can identify any inaccuracies and better anticipate additional questions.

Capturing minute-to-minute coverage as a crisis unfolds can be a daunting task. Small agencies, associations, or NGOs may not be in a position to pay for this service. That's why an RSS feed can be helpful and cost-effective. An RSS reader is software that grabs fresh content appearing on the Internet. Twitter mentions, blog posts, news headlines, YouTube videos, and web sites are examples of the media scanned. The resulting content is syndicated automatically and delivered directly to an individual in his or her RSS feed.

RSS, which stands for Really Simple Syndication, is available free of charge from some sources. However, when volume is high, making it difficult to monitor both the number of mentions as well as analyze the sentiment of the conversation, it is advisable to use professional services and tools. Radian6, BuzzLogic, Trackur, and Filtrbox are examples of these.[7]

If misinformation is being reported about the crisis, it is essential the media relations person moves quickly. Otherwise, the inaccuracies will be picked up and repeated by other outlets. In addition to notifying and sending the correct facts to those distributing the misinformation, the nonprofit can leverage technology to make the correct information public. Material can be posted on the web site and tweets sent. If the organization has a blog or Facebook page, these can be used for notification purposes, too.

Correcting misinformation is more important than ever in this world of instant reporting and Internet archives. When newspapers and magazines were the only news outlets, inaccurate information had a limited audience. Later access to the content was limited to what one could find in archives. In cyberspace, that same incorrect information could go viral, spanning the globe in a matter of hours, and continue to appear in Internet searches for years. Only by real-time monitoring can errors be caught and damage control initiated.

Monitoring helps identify emerging topics of media interest. Responses should be developed to address these new subjects, as it is much better to be prepared for a tough question and never have to use the response than to be caught unaware and unable to answer.

While these questions will not pertain to all crises, the communications professional can use the following to begin constructing answers:

- What happened?
- What caused the crisis?
- Any injuries, deaths, property damage, rescues, impact to others?
- What are the legal and financial implications?
- What are related areas of vulnerability for the nonprofit?

Response development takes into account the ultimate audience. Just as citizens in a community, members of an association, recipients of a charity's services, or supporters of an educational institution are curious and want to know what happened, they also want to know what it means to them. How are they affected? What will change for them? That's why answers must include details such as if the nonprofit will continue to operate its regular office hours or if services are being limited or added.

Comments should be structured to present the organization as confident, competent, and responsive. This helps reassure critical audiences the nonprofit has maintained a degree of situational control. Brand attributes can present the nonprofit's "human side." It is particularly important for organizational messaging to demonstrate characteristics of compassion, concern, and empathy for those hurt or affected by this catastrophic event.

The old axiom that "silence is golden" is not applicable to crises. Even though it may not be feasible to release all information immediately, the communications department must be available and have some response other than "no comment." Why is the phrase "no comment" a poor way to respond? Quite simply, it isn't strategic. These two words have come to be associated with an organization hiding something from the public. When news outlets report "no one could be reached for comment" or the spokesperson responded with "no comment," it typically is assumed there is a degree of guilt or that there is a cover-up. It is much wiser to structure a simple reply transmitting a similar meaning but carrying at least one of the nonprofit's key messages (see Box 4.3: "No Comment" Substitute Statements).

When needing to direct the questioner to another source, such as investigating authorities, the hospital, fire department, or a government regulatory body, a better answer than "no comment" is: "The individual (or group) better suited to provide you with that information is ..." And, then supply accurate contact information.

A reporter will accept an answer such as, "I don't have that information right now, but I will find out and get back to you." In this case, personal

---

Box 4.3 "No Comment" Substitute Statements

The following examples can help you avoid saying "no comment." Some even provide you with an opportunity to bridge back to your key message.

"It would violate the law to reveal that information, but what I can tell you is ..."

"In order to protect the privacy of our employees, our policy has always been ... We can, however, provide you with ..."

"We do not know at this time, but we hope to find out as quickly as possible."

"Because of the impending litigation, we are not allowed to make any statements about the issue. When it is possible, we will be glad to answer that question."

"In deference to the families that have yet to be notified, we are not releasing the names of the injured. However, once all parties involved have been apprised, we will provide that information."

"I don't know the answer to that question, but what I can tell you is ..."

"Rather than speculating on the future, I'd like to share the following facts with you ..."

"The best way I know to discuss potential outcomes is to discuss the current situation ..."

"It is too early to predict that outcome, but we do know that ..."

credibility is on the line, so it is important to follow up with the requested data.

Other "dos and don'ts" for crisis media management:

- Don't speculate.
- Don't try to minimize the problem or blame someone else.
- Don't "dribble out" the story.
- Don't over-confess by turning a press conference into a therapy session.
- Don't promise too much too soon to avoid needing to renege on a commitment.
- Don't let media drive the communication strategy.
- Do stay focused on your communication goals.
- Do accept responsibility rather than blaming, if you are at fault.
- Do keep staff, leadership, and board members on script.

Properly framing messages can be as important as their content. The communication officer should design a credible response framework for conveying relevant information and positively positioning the nonprofit.

When should media communication be initiated? There are four times when it is logical to proactively communicate:

- Immediate acknowledgement of the controversy or incident.
- When an initial assessment of the situation is available.
- When significant discoveries or updates are available.
- When the crisis is over.[8]

(See Worksheet 4.3: Interview Prep and Box 4.4: Crisis Video Tip Sheet.)

Apologies

There are times when an apology is required. Perhaps, the agency wasn't seen as responding quickly enough to a natural disaster; an educational institution was blamed for not providing timely notification of a rapist or shooter on campus; or an NGO fired its executive director for misuse of funds. Although the aforementioned represent uniquely different situations, all could require some form of apology.

As W. Timothy Coombs explains: "Apology is the most complex and perhaps controversial of the crisis response strategies. It is critical to differentiate between full and partial responses. A full apology must acknowledge the crisis, accept responsibility, include a promise not to repeat the crisis, and express concern and regret. A partial apology is typically just an expression of concern and regret. Why the split? The answer is legal liability."[9]

Worksheet 4.3

Interview Prep

Individual handling interview, if not spokesperson: _____

Date and time of interview: _____

How or where interview will be conducted: _____

Interviewing journalist: _____

News outlet(s): _____

Interview topic and likely angle?

Primary audience(s) of the media?

If others are being interviewed for this subject, who are they?

What key messages should be delivered?

What examples/anecdotes will reinforce these messages?

Most difficult or obvious questions that will be asked?

Question: Answer:

Question: Answer:

Question: Answer:

Question: Answer:

Are there any visuals (video, charts, tables, models, etc.) that will help illustrate our points and messages?

To be completed after the interview:

Were any materials promised that must be provided prior to deadline? If so, what?

What updates or follow-up contact is required?

In her 2006 *Harvard Business Review* article, Barbara Kellerman addresses what she refers to as the "Framework for Apologies" in which she poses five questions:

- "What function would a public apology serve?
- Who would benefit from the apology?
- Why would the apology matter?
- What happens if you apologize publicly?
- Will your refusal to apologize (or your refusal to do so promptly) make a bad situation worse?"[10]

In addition to the litigious elements cited by Coombs, Kellerman's query can help test the need for and type of apology required. But as she

---

Box 4.4   Crisis Video Tip Sheet

- Always accompany a videographer, producer, and photographer. Do not permit unrestricted filming, videography, or photo-taking on your property/at your event. Supervision is recommended to ensure scenarios are not taken out of context; an investigation is not compromised; sensitive, confidential, or personnel-related information is not divulged; or a crisis story is not reframed improperly.
- When providing photos or videos or when permitting these to be taken, scrutinize where and when the organization's logo appears. There are times that it is not advantageous to have your logo appear; while at other times, you will want it to be seen clearly.
- If planning to conduct a news conference, carefully select the environment where it will be held. You may want volunteers to be shown helping or video taken at the crisis site to emphasize the magnitude of the situation. Conversely, you may need to seal off the site or limit access to the location for any number of reasons. In this case, strategically selecting an alternate site for this media event is appropriate.
- The film, videos, or photos taken on your location by others will remain in the archives of the news outlets. These materials could be pulled and used later by the media. Because the visuals would be used at the discretion of the individual outlet, your visuals could be shown again, when a similar crisis occurs for another organization. If a negative scenario was conveyed by the particular visual, the negative is repeated. If a positive situation was shown (such as demonstrating a best practice), this image is reinforced through the additional appearance(s).
- If you have permitted/encouraged news outlets to take photos or videos in the past, these visuals will be in archives. If you opt not to permit the media to record or take pictures of the current crisis, they could pull old visuals from the files and use them to support the current crisis news report.
- If another organization is experiencing a crisis and you permit B-roll footage to be taken at your location in order to build your relationship with the news outlet by helping it, be sure to monitor for the appearance of your logo or other recognizable characteristics of your organization. Be judicious and strategic in determining if these should appear (or not) as well as how their appearance could visually link the crisis to your nonprofit.
- **Note:** Any employee, volunteer, or bystander can take pictures or capture video with a smart phone and then post them. Take precautions to control this situation as much as possible.

and other point out, an apology should never be taken lightly. It must be sincere.

Attention to Audiences

It is imperative that the communications department serves as a focal review point to ensure message consistency and that information is released according to a carefully orchestrated schedule. Therefore, even if communication is developed by another area, such as government relations, communications personnel should review the content and language to ensure no inconsistent information is released and no opportunities are missed to reinforce key organizational messages.

Employees are a primary crisis communication audience. As brand ambassadors, staff members can be a huge asset because of the credibility they offer and the human face they provide the organization. Consequently, employees should be alerted to important information prior to its release to the media. They should be updated with pertinent details to keep them abreast of the situation in a manner that enables them to perform jobs in an exemplary manner and to help avoid the possibility of an employee making a derogatory remark about being uninformed.

For example, staff should be instructed as to how and where to direct questions. He or she should be able to provide the proper contact for a reporter or be able to pass along the inquiry to the nonprofit's spokesperson. Likewise, if a member or constituent has a question about services, staff should be able to direct the individual to a functioning department for assistance. If volunteers want to know how to help, the employee should be able to direct these persons to the appropriate colleague. After all, if a nonprofit wants to reassure "outside" audiences the organization is managing the crisis promptly and professionally, these brand ambassadors must appear positive, knowledgeable, and capable. This is only feasible, if employees are well informed.

Equipped with this information, employees will feel more "in control" of this unusual and uncomfortable situation. In fact, when the communications team prepares question-and-answer documents for the web site and the media, a version should be prepared specifically for employees.

It is important to note that any written documentation provided to a staff member could appear in a blog or news story or on a Facebook page. This is why carefully worded language is essential. And, the need to closely hold confidential information during the fact verification process is clear.

Post-Crisis

Just because a crisis is declared "over," it doesn't mean communication stops. Stakeholders want to be reassured everything is okay. So, messaging must be repositioned and possibly even re-directed to rebuild credibility and trust and to re-establish or reinforce the nonprofit's positive reputation.

What does this messaging look like? First, people need closure. Therefore, it is necessary to inform them when the crisis is over. Remarks must be honest and realistic but positively framed. If corrective action measures were taken or structural changes are underway, these updates should be shared.

If it is determined now that the crisis could have been prevented by or was caused by the nonprofit, responsibility must be accepted. The public is forgiving when accountability for a "human error" is acknowledged, an apology issued, and corrective action taken. A commitment that the same mistake will not occur again helps to restore trust and belief that the organization will do the right thing in the future. However, when denial or blame are used to avoid accountability, there is the likelihood the organization will experience a greater erosion of trust.

If a lawsuit is pending or an investigation isn't concluded, there still will be requests for updates, which post-crisis messaging must address. Stakeholders should receive details and updates in a timely manner to assure them the nonprofit is acting in a transparent and responsible manner.

For consistent communication, the key messages, which were foundational to crisis messaging, should be leveraged in the development of post-crisis communication. Crisis recovery commentary must have a clear linkage to these messages as they embody the very essence of the organization and emphasize the nonprofit's prime directive.

Crises can create an opportunity for organizational value clarification. If the nonprofit remained true to its ethics and values throughout the crisis, these values can be stressed in post-crisis communication by offering examples and emphasizing the organization's commitment to doing the right thing.

If the nonprofit strayed off course and the crisis was caused by or poorly managed because of ethical issues, a subsequent evaluation can identify the root cause of this occurrence. Standards or processes must then be implemented to help prevent this from happening in the future. In these instances, the communications department must do damage control by explaining what happened and issuing a guarantee the nonprofit is committed to ethical behavior and high standards, and as such, will do everything possible to avoid a similar situation in the future.

Stakeholder Contact

Following the crisis, it is critical to initiate contact with all audiences. Basic communication content must be consistent. However, message customization may be required because of the nonprofit's diverse stakeholder base. This means some messages may need to be framed slightly differently than others, emphasizing the key elements that are most important or of greatest interest to the group. And, some informational exchanges may need to contain more detail than others or even offer guidance.

Employees, board of directors, volunteers, donors, members or recipients of services, vendors, government representatives, the media, and even the public-at-large ... all have a vested interest in knowing the nonprofit's future plans. Notice the word "plans." Obviously, the future cannot be predicted, but it is important the nonprofit state what the "new normalcy" will look like to help establish the crisis recovery process is underway.

If not already developed, a two-way communication design should be created to encourage stakeholders to ask questions, voice concerns, and make suggestions. This model can lead to better audience engagement and emphasize organizational transparency. While there is no prescribed formula as to how this two-way interaction should be accomplished or what represents sufficient communication, the department must seek opportunities to initiate dialogue with employees, within the community, with other key stakeholders, rather than merely pushing out all communication. Not only will such an interactive process provide important input that can influence subsequent messaging, but this feedback will reveal related issues that are percolating and have the potential of developing into a crisis.

Debriefing

Debriefing should occur on two levels. First, the communications team should have "a seat at the table" during the organizational debriefing process. As this department has held a leadership role prior to and throughout the crisis, it is crucial this continues. It is essential communication professionals share their insights and recommendations with the cross-functional team.

As a member of the debriefing task force, the communication officer is exposed to a more complete picture of what happened. In turn, these findings should be relayed to the communication team during the department debriefing, as these critical details could shape future messaging, enhance the internal communication process, or improve the crisis communication plan.

Communications is integral to the crisis management process. Open, honest, and efficient internal communication is required, if critical material is to be conveyed to leadership, situation-specific particulars shared in a timely manner, and issues addressed or problems solved as quickly as possible. That's why debriefing must include a thorough examination of how internal communication practices contribute to the flow and quality of communication before, during, and after a crisis.

If a crisis is averted, the nonprofit must do more than simply celebrate for "having dodged the bullet." Instead, introspection is recommended to detect the reason for successfully avoiding a public catastrophe.

Every crisis or near crisis presents a learning opportunity; and, the art of discovering what that lesson is occurs by conducting a thorough debriefing. A few questions that should be posed during this process are:

- Had the communication prior to the crisis instilled sufficient trust in the nonprofit, so credibility was established prior to the crisis or was the not-for-profit already dealing with a negative image?
- Was there sufficient communication with appropriate stakeholders throughout the course of the event?
- Was communication prioritized and appropriately timed to reach all audiences on schedule and with pertinent facts and/or necessary guidance?
- Did messaging include organizational values, ethics, and key messages?
- Was outreach sufficient and audience-appropriate?
- Was the spokesperson credible, measured, and purposeful in interviews?

Finally, the communications debriefing examines the context surrounding what occurred as well as the influencing people or factors, which impacted the outcome or escalated the sensitivity of the situation. This can be accomplished through an environmental scan, which will reveal the signs and conditions triggering this event and which could cause similar ones. By knowing what these triggers are, warning protocols can be established to alert the nonprofit of future crises.

During debriefing, hindsight will serve as a valuable tool. However, this reflection can be a hindrance. By knowing the outcome of the crisis, it may be difficult for participants to imagine any other outcome. This can encumber the group's ability to recognize and prepare for other consequences or solutions to similar situations. Therefore, it is necessary to keep an open mind as to how a crisis could manifest differently than in the past.[11]

The results of these post-crisis reflections should be shared with the crisis management team and used to improve the crisis communication plan. Depending upon the significance of the enhancements, the board, executive management, or attorneys may have to review and approve the changes.

Always Acknowledge

At some point following the crisis, employees must be recognized. Depending upon what the crisis was and the stakeholders involved, others may need to be commended as well. Volunteerism is exemplified when people stack sandbags to protect property from flood waters; community service groups collaborate with a nonprofit to buy and deliver fans to the elderly during an unprecedented heat wave; and animal shelters throughout the country assist with the placement of pets following a hurricane, fire, or flood. In each of these cases, the nonprofit serving as the focal point should articulate its appreciation of the other groups, teams, or individuals.

Acknowledging the time and effort of others is proper etiquette and helps volunteers to feel valued and their work appreciated. The "thank you" could be delivered by email, a hand written note, a plaque, a billboard, a national television advertisement, or a party. In many ways, the action of acknowledgement is more important than the selected form.

Demonstrating gratitude to others for their assistance during the crisis can produce other benefits. Having been recognized for contributions, these same groups and individuals will be more likely to volunteer in the future. This "thank you," then, contributes to the relationship-building process, potentially leading to a long-term, personal commitment.

What If There's Litigation?

It is conceivable litigation could result from the crisis. This means the organization's reputation is still in jeopardy. Dealing with the media as well as communicating with key stakeholders and even the public at-large during this stressful time poses a challenge. To avoid creating additional damage, it is important to limit communication. Over-communicating when a trial is underway could create the perception of attempting to sway a jury, which would be considered unethical. There is also the possibility significant publicity could undermine the legal strategy. Consequently, communication only should occur when it is in the best interest of the organization and attorneys are alerted to the interview or statement prior to release.

Reputation Restoration

A primary goal of post-crisis efforts is to restore trust. Having dealt with the crisis and all related issues, the nonprofit must concentrate on rebuilding confidence through reputational repair. This can be achieved by:

- Conveying organizational emotion and/or humanizing the nonprofit;
- Demonstrating a commitment to transparency;
- Repeating an apology if appropriate and/or necessary; and
- Returning focus to the nonprofit's primary mission and goals.

Measuring Recovery

It is important to be aware of the progress an organization is making in its reputational recovery. This insight will be helpful in developing subsequent communication as well as determining the ideal timing for instituting new operational procedures, holding events, and conducting campaigns. But for measurement to occur, it is necessary to clearly define what is to be measured and then select the best methodology to do so.

Staff morale and attitudes can be an indicator of reputational recovery. Knowing how these brand ambassadors feel is critical as they represent the organization to all stakeholders. This outlook, reflected through both verbal and nonverbal communication, reveals their perception of the organization and conveys these thoughts to others. Are employees optimistic about planned changes and trusting of leadership? Or, are they anxious the crisis hasn't truly passed and the worst is yet to come?

Their issues, concerns, and attitudes during the post-crisis phase can be monitored through informal pulse surveys, conference calls, and face-to-face meetings. The size of the organization, scope of the crisis, and communication budget will impact the vehicles used for this task.

If data from previous morale and engagement surveys is available, this new research can be compared against the benchmark findings. This will produce a snapshot comparison of employee sentiment. Depending upon the severity of the crisis and its impact on employees, morale may need to be very closely tracked over an extended time period.

Another way to measure the reputational recovery process is to examine the group's social legitimacy. To determine if the nonprofit has regained its status, chat rooms, blogs, and media can be monitored for content and tone. A town meeting, forum, or teleconference opens an avenue for dialogue with members, employees, or the community, permitting first-hand data collection. Questionnaires, telephone polls, and Internet surveys can be used as well. Principles to keep in mind when measuring the reputation quotient are to:

- carefully select the best methodology to secure a solid sampling,
- vigilantly monitor and carefully listen, and
- meticulously analyze stakeholder sentiment.

More Important than Ever for Communicators

It is a primary duty of the communication team to protect and enhance the nonprofit's reputation. This duty must be taken very seriously because it is the nonprofit's image that helps to:

- instill trust;
- establish credibility
- raise money;
- promote membership, encourage involvement, and/or inspire volunteerism;

- achieve the organizational mission; and
- position the nonprofit as a leader in its sector.

This does not, however, mean the professional communicator should take unethical, illegal, or immoral measures to ensure the organization's character remains untarnished. Instead, this individual must act as a leader in the effort of helping the not-for-profit fulfill its prime directive and embody its values and ethics.

This professional is expected to think beyond boundaries and to recognize the full implications of the crises, challenging with "what if," and even presenting worst case scenarios. Although such actions may not be popular with the crisis team, executives, or board members, the organization must prepare for the worst possible outcome and hope for the best. As Marion Pinsdorf succinctly summarized: "Crisis managers need wise, trusted devil's advocates, not neophytes and naïve do-gooders."[12] The communications officer should be this trusted advisor ... to the crisis management team, the executive leadership, and the board of directors.

Plus, a high degree of ethical and professional conduct exhibited by the entire communication team will safeguard the department's credibility with the nonprofit's board, executive management, crisis team, the media, and community leadership. Exemplary behavior before, during, and after the crisis will build and reinforce credibility at every level and with every audience. Actions representing such conduct are: providing accurate information to all stakeholders; returning calls and providing responses promptly; and offering an honest and direct assessment of the situation. If credibility, integrity, or moral standards appear to be questionable or are lost during any of these stages, it can be a career-altering experience for the communicator.

Thoughts on the Subject

Dick Meisterling
Vice President for Advancement
Coe College, Cedar Rapids, IA

Q: Cedar Rapids, Iowa, faced a catastrophic flood in 2008. It caused many companies and nonprofit organizations to rethink their crisis communication planning efforts. How has the college changed its approach to strategic crisis communication planning as a result of this event? As a result, do you have any guidance you would like to offer others in regards to crisis communication planning?

A: The disastrous Cedar Rapids flood of 2008 caused horrific damage throughout the community, displacing thousands of families and businesses and costing billions of dollars. Coe College, although sited beyond the 150-year flood mark, was nonetheless affected. A solitary building was inundated despite heroic sandbagging efforts by many of its employees. Unfortunately, that one building housed—in its lower levels—much of the campus' switching equipment and its electronic distribution system. Most importantly, the city's century old power plant was destroyed and more than 200 businesses, including Coe College, lost hot water and the heat it provided. This presented the college with several challenges and easily qualified as an emergency.

Because it was summer, Coe had only 100 students in residence; but for them and employees, communication was critical. With no telephone, Internet or email, senior staff gathered to build a plan. Scores of details had to be managed, from locating housing for our students to finding temporary power generation. Most every decision had to be disseminated among faculty, staff, and students. Text messages were sent to as many as possible, and, at a gathering of all students, they were told we would evacuate campus within 90 minutes. Arrangements were quickly made with nearby Cornell College that had graciously agreed to house them.

Coe had refined its plan for such emergencies on the heels of the Virginia Tech tragedy in 2007. The plan was considered reliable and efficient. At its core is an emergency alert system that sends texts and emails to the entire campus community. The system is tested on a monthly basis. To educate the community, a leaflet is given to employees and students each year. It is also provided on Coe's web site (http://www.coe.edu/uploads/pdfs/aboutcoe) and outlines the levels of emergencies as well as lists the directions associated with each.

Following the flood, we learned that text messaging was a vital component of our communication system. With other systems unavailable, we exploited that medium immediately. We also built an off-campus web site, expanded our Facebook presence, and created a special telephone number with a recording that was regularly updated. Though we did not have cell phone numbers for all constituents (despite robust efforts), we expanded various social networks, so we were able to disseminate information quite effectively.

Every organization should consider such a plan, the foundation of which should focus on communication with all individuals who might be affected. This preplanning step is imperative and includes the foundational element of determining how best to share information in a timely manner. It is impossible to anticipate the many specific decisions that have to be made in an emergency, but knowing in advance that senior management decisions will be efficiently shared, will save time and lead to a better outcome.

Kate Meier
Regional Communications Director
American Red Cross, Carolina Piedmont Region

Q: How has the Red Cross leveraged social media during crises?

A: The Red Cross utilizes social media during disasters in several ways. First, when disaster strikes, the Red Cross social media machine is in action immediately, disseminating information on what has occurred, how people can help and what the Red Cross is doing to help the people affected.

There are countless success stories about how the Red Cross has been able to leverage social media into donations of time and money:

1. The millions and millions of dollars from text donations after the Haiti earthquake, stemming from Twitter lighting up with instructions on how to give.
2. During the North Carolina spring tornadoes in 2011, we utilized Facebook to recruit volunteers for a call center.

The Red Cross also uses social media to spread awareness of what the Red Cross is doing on the ground, which assures our donors of where and how their money is being used; informs the public about what we're doing; and communicates to people affected of where they can turn to for help. Examples include:

1. Media outlets have actually sourced Red Cross tweets without calling for verification (on the national level and even here in Charlotte).
2. We post blogs that feature Red Cross-generated YouTube videos, pictures and stories of our volunteers in action after a disaster and share those blogs via RSS, Facebook, Twitter, and our national and local web sites.
3. We use social media to disseminate messaging about our Safe and Well site, where people can register themselves as being okay after a disaster and their families can find them there.

Social media is also a good way for the Red Cross to communicate preparedness messages. If a storm is expected, we disseminate preparedness tips and messages via Facebook and Twitter.

Something to Think About

1. What considerations should be taken into account when selecting a site for a crisis news conference?

2. When would it be advisable to have the nonprofit's logo seen or not seen in a media interview, YouTube video, video news release, photograph, or other visual?
3. What types of crisis issues could materialize, if a nonprofit has its computer files hacked? What types of confidentiality breaches could occur?
4. An element in the image repair process can be an apology. What can be the challenges to issuing one?
5. What are the potential barriers to conducting an accurate risk and issues assessment?

5   Cause-Related Marketing

Be careful of the environment you choose for it will shape you; be careful the friends you choose for you will become like them.

(W. Clement Stone, Businessman & Philanthropist)

There are many facets to the building of a nonprofit's reputation. Its ability to serve its primary mission, transparency, sustainable citizenship performance, and fiscal responsibility are a few of the attributes that help to build a positive identity. Another influencer relates to the old adage: "It's the company you keep."

While it would be nice to simply accept money from any donor or to proudly display the name of any sponsoring organization and not worry about the implications of the association, it is not that simple. Unfortunately, perceptions are formed and judgments are made based on where the nonprofit's support originates.

Example: An environmental group that accepts large sums of money from a business, known to be an air polluter, can find its image negatively impacted. However, if the agreement between the two is to fund a test on equipment to reduce emissions, accepting money could be perceived differently because the purpose would be to solve an issue consistent with the nonprofit's mission.

Similarly, initiating a cause-related marketing campaign with a business or reviewing a request from a company for this type of collaboration must be scrutinized carefully and thought given as to how this affiliation would help the nonprofit achieve its mission and affect its reputation.

A Business Primer on Cause Marketing

For business, there are seven primary benefits from marketing in this manner:

- It drives sales and builds a positive reputation for a company.
- It can attract and retain employees, building loyalty.

- It can target key customers in a company's overall market and enhance loyalty within specific niches.
- It creates product/service differentiation in the marketplace.
- It contributes to the social responsibility platform of a business.
- It can drive shareholder value.
- It creates opportunities for business to engage with employees, customers, and other key stakeholders.

While not philanthropy in its purest form, this approach is "steeped" in the philanthropic world, as one goal is to raise money for the nonprofit. So a donation is involved, but there is also the profit-making focus.

If sales are so slow as to create a negative balance sheet or if a business is simply breaking even, the funding typically given to charity becomes out of the question. So when a company faces incredible economic challenges or needs to increase market share, cause-related marketing may be an appropriate avenue to both drive sales and support the firm's community-based goals.

There is yet another return on this business investment. Companies have been able to increase both customer and employee engagement as a direct result of such a campaign. In fact, today's savvy consumers are driving the growth of this marketing technique. If there was no response, corporations would not engage in it, and nonprofits wouldn't waste time on this fundraising effort. But, "purpose" influences purchasing behaviors.

On a global level, social purpose has intensified. According to Edelman's "Goodpurpose 2012 Executive Summary," 72 percent of consumers will recommend a business that supports a good cause. This reflects a 39 percent increase over 2008 survey results. Similarly, 71 percent of consumers indicated they would promote the products or services of a brand, if a good cause was associated with it. This represents a 34 percent increase. Even more compelling is that 73 percent of consumers say they would shift to a different brand, if it was affiliated with a good cause. This is a 9 percent increase over 2009 figures.

In fact, just over half of the respondents believe companies should donate a portion of their products or services to a good cause, and 80 percent of the global respondents believed business should educate them about these socially responsible efforts.[1]

Socially responsible consumers want to participate in a company's cause-related activities. According to a 2008 Cone Communications/Duke University Behavior Cause Study, 83 percent of the respondents said personal relevance was key in these shopping decisions, and 65 percent found emotional incentives, such as feeling good or alleviating shopping guilt, as important in this purchasing process. In addition to this emotional key, an appeal to logic is necessary. Seventy-seven percent said saving money or time for their participation in such a campaign was important to them.[2] So, emotion and logic work together in the buying equation.

In 2010, Cone's Trend Tracker reported 78 percent of Americans believed a partnership between a "trusted" business and a nonprofit, helped the cause cut through clutter to bring positive attention to it. This increased awareness to both organizations produces mutually beneficial results, generating sales and nonprofit funding while also increasing the likelihood of additional donations and volunteers for the nonprofit.[3]

Millennials, with their growing purchasing power in the marketplace, support cause marketing. According to a 2011 study, conducted by Barkley, Boston Consulting Group, and Service Management Group, Millennials are more likely to develop a positive image of a business due to its cause marketing efforts than those in other age groups. The research also said Millennials would attempt to purchase products supporting a cause about which they care (52 percent) over non-Millennials (45 percent).[4]

Because of the different models and the flexible approaches, large and small businesses can utilize cause-related marketing. Effective programs leverage the power of a company's brand to generate sales; fulfill the firm's commitment to society; create shareholder value; engage the workforce; and enhance reputation by publicly communicating the corporation's good works.

But to make such a program viable, the opportunity must be mutually beneficial for both the business and the not-for-profit. The time, effort, and money invested by each organization must surpass expenses, including labor costs. This is especially true if the two intend to enter into a successful, long-term relationship.

Companies also are sensitive to research showing some consumers view cause-related marketing as exploitative.[5] This fact carries a potential reputational risk for business because the perception would cast a negative light on the company and such an action would be in direct conflict with its corporate social responsibility platform. Consequently, a business would want to avoid any such appearance. This would contribute a firm's receptivity to making a very equitable agreement with a nonprofit.

Successful cause-related marketing, then, is a partnership, which must be interconnected and interdependent in a manner that addresses societal needs and corporate goals. When these come together, a successful campaign results. As Jocelyne Daw explains: "Above all, cause marketing is where purpose, passion, and profits meet in a productive, strategically-aligned partnership."[6]

For business, there is a thin line between opportunism and altruism. Being a realist, Daw recognizes to make this a successful collaboration, nonprofits must "think like businesses and understand their needs and objectives."[7] This statement should not be misconstrued to indicate the nonprofit's point of view is irrelevant. Understanding what drives the corporate world will aid the nonprofit in approaching a business, negotiating an agreement, and developing a long-term cause marketing arrangement.

The Approaches

In 1996, Professor Allan Andreasen placed some structural parameters around this large and rather nebulous marketing activity by creating three categories: transaction-based promotions, joint issue promotions, and licensing.[8] Daw prefers to use other marketing terminology for this same discussion: products, promotions, and programs.[9] However one views cause marketing, it is clear this approach to the marketplace is continuing to evolve. As it does so, there likely will be exceptions, which may fall outside the parameters of the current descriptors.

One emerging trend in cause marketing is the shift to long-term associations between nonprofits and businesses. The effort will advance to become what Carol Cone calls "cause branding." This describes a scenario where a long-term partnership is established, developing into a "corporate identify, culture, and corporate social responsibility palette"[10] for the business and long-term connectivity with an established nonprofit brand generating benefits. Consumers and employees will help drive this lengthier and more complex business relationship between the business and tax-exempt worlds.

Regardless of how one wants to examine the cause marketing world, there are a plethora of opportunities and many ways to finesse an agreement's structure. Descriptions of a few of the models follow, along with a brief explanation as to the benefits they bring to both organizations.

Sponsorship: When a nonprofit event or activity is sponsored by a business to help raise funds for a good cause, it is called a sponsorship. There is some disagreement as to if a sponsorship truly qualifies as a cause marketing campaign. Given fundraising occurs as a result of a joint collaboration between a not-for-profit and a business, this marketing tactic is being cited as one of the models.

Benefits: Size doesn't matter. A multi-national company can sponsor a major event, such as the Olympics, or a local restaurant can sponsor a community walk to raise funds for juvenile diabetes. Both can exemplify the qualities of a sponsorship.

In addition to raising funds, there is an increased awareness for both the nonprofit and the for-profit company through marketing and PR efforts. The two "brands" benefit from the halo effect of each other's positive reputation through this affiliation, resulting in an enhanced image with donors, volunteers, and customers.

Licensing: In this case, the company pays the nonprofit for the privilege of licensing the use of its logo on the company's products and promotional materials. There is an implied benefit in that the business expects a halo effect from using the charity's logo.[11]

Benefits: As this is a straightforward commercial relationship, it can stand on its own. However, many times it is linked to additional opportunities, such as a special event. Contractual in nature, both entities are aware of the parameters of the agreement, including formal permission in regards to how, when, and where the logo can be used. The nonprofit must take care to ensure is receives full value for this usage of its logo.

The nonprofit has no upfront capital invested. There will be projections as to the revenue generated by the agreement. In some cases, the organization will know exactly how much money it will receive and can access this funding immediately. Depending upon the length the contract, ongoing royalty payments may be received. Plus, if the nonprofit wants to use the t-shirts, mugs, or other promotional materials to promote its own brand apart from the company-specified retail uses, these materials will be available to the organization at a lower cost because of the benefit produced by large manufacturing runs.

Whether a supplier markets directly or in a retail store, the nonprofit gains additional exposure opportunities than it wouldn't normally have.

Licensing agreements also include affinity card programs. In this case a donation is made to the charity or cause, whenever someone signs up for the credit card. Subsequent contributions are made to the charity, based on card usage. Consequently, revenue continues to be generated rather than being solely dependent upon additional credit card applications being approved. For obvious reasons, the charitable organization's database of donors and volunteers is leveraged.

The corporation benefits from the consumer goodwill derived through association with the nonprofit, the publicity for the funding support, and the increase in number of credit card holders.

Product or Service Sales: This is a common cause-related marketing initiative. Donations are made to the not-for-profit in conjunction with a transactional sale. This approach can be used with everything from candy bars to haircuts. The purpose is to drive product or service sales with a percentage of the purchase being donated to the cause.

Benefits: The organization benefits from the fund-raising efforts while at the same time increases its brand awareness. This visibility can lead to further donations and an increased number of volunteers. If the business is well known and respected, the nonprofit may have its reputation enhanced through the association.

The company may attract a new customer group. Also, its association with the not-for-profit can provide product differentiation that drives sales. The collaboration can be promoted through marketing materials, communicating the value of the company's investment in its corporate responsibility platform, thereby leading to better brand positioning.

Purchase-Plus Sales: A perfect illustration of this cause marketing technique is the "ask" by the cashier at a retail outlet. The customer is requested to purchase a candy bar, a school supply, or other item, which goes to a local charity rather than going home with the customer. In this case the retailer facilitates and collects the donations.

Example: The retailer works with the nonprofit to identify the needs of the typical school child, provides employee labor to package the products into a school bag, has sales associates "make the ask," and dedicates collection space. A shopper is encouraged to buy the pre-packaged bag of school supplies and then physically places the bag in the drop-box at the front of the store. The nonprofit is responsible for picking up the product donated by shoppers and delivering it to the qualified needy recipient.

Benefits: Overall, this is easy to implement and doesn't require extensive capital outlay. It can be executed in a single store or nationwide. Retail employees feel engaged in the process and good about helping a charity. By pre-packaging the materials, it makes it easy for a customer to donate and to know indispensible items go directly to the neediest.

The result? The nonprofit meets an important organizational goal without capital outlay. The company and the nonprofit benefit from positive media coverage. And, the business is positioned as a strong community partner while also making a profit.

Socially Responsible Branding: This collaborative arrangement brings attention to a social issue through the nonprofit and corporate collaboration. The joint promotion requires public relations and marketing materials but is not involved with a product or service purchase. Instead the company, with its direct access to a large consumer base, makes a public call to action about a key issue faced by society or a specific community, which is also aligned with the nonprofit's concerns.

Benefits: The business may contribute financially to the nonprofit helping to deal with the social issue; but this is not required. The real benefit for the nonprofit comes from the additional personnel needed to conduct a major awareness campaign and the group's "placement" in front of the company's customers. The business may experience reputational enhancement and increased customer loyalty because of its stand and public support of an important societal issue. This stance can generate pride and a loyalty in the work force. It's possible this call to action could lead to increased enthusiasm and engagement in the workplace, based on employee pride, while generating additional volunteers for the not-for-profit.

Co-Branded Events, Competitions, Etc.: A popular cause marketing technique is a co-branded event. Examples of these are runs, bike-a-thons, dinners, dance competitions, and performances. With this approach, a firm provides most of the resources necessary for the marketing and operation of the event. Promotional communication, event materials, and even trophies or awards may be donated by the business.

Benefits: Of course, the proceeds go to the nonprofit. In addition, the joint branding increases the likelihood of producing more revenue than if the event was conducted solely by the nonprofit.[12] Plus, the nonprofit has access to many more promotional opportunities than it would without the assistance of the business.

The synergy creates a perfect opportunity to involve key stakeholders from both groups, including employees, volunteers, donors, and board of directors. This event can be linked to other cause marketing initiatives, such as product purchases like t-shirts, posters, or jewelry. And as always, the business can use this event to publicly demonstrate its commitment to being socially responsible.

If the event directly correlates with the goals of both institutions, even more educational and reputational benefits result. For example, a five-mile walk hosted by the American Heart Association and a drug company known for manufacturing medications for heart disease patients complements the missions of both organizations.

The Trade-In: Another common retail cause marketing program, this involves a customer bringing in a gently-used item, such as a business suit or a lady's handbag, to donate to a particular cause, such as a shelter for abused women. The item is given to the nonprofit for distribution. In exchange for the contribution, the customer receives a discount on the same type of merchandise from the store. Thus, the shopper may receive $50 off of a purse or be able to purchase a new suit at 50 percent off.

Benefits: This type of exchange offers several benefits. The shopper has the satisfaction of knowing an in-kind donation is going to someone who needs the item. Also, the customer receives greater value for the in-kind contribution than the tax write-off would have provided. So, the customer is rewarded with great value for "doing good."

As a result of the donation, the nonprofit receives tangible goods that can help its constituents. Plus, the advertising to promote the program is covered by the business partner. The company benefits from the transaction, providing a discount that may be exactly the same as if the item would have run on sale, with the bonus of being positively recognized for socially responsible actions.

Voucher Collection: The objective of a voucher collection program is to gain active customer participation. The product contains a special label or voucher the customer removes after purchasing the item. The label or voucher is then given to the nonprofit. The charity collects these and submits them to the company in exchange for a donation or product.

This cause-related fundraiser is very popular with schools. One example is the Betty Crocker Box Tops for Education program. Ten cents is paid by the company for each box top submitted by the nonprofit. Since it was launched in 1996, the program has paid out over $400 million.

Campbell Soup Company, with its Labels for Education program, is similar in structure but the collected points earned through the box top collection process are combined and then redeemed for free arts, athletic, or academic merchandise. With over 400 items in the catalogue, a school can get anything from laminating machines to basketballs to microscopes.

Benefits: Obviously, the company sells the product. But with this approach, shoppers are engaged more deeply in the process. The customer selects the recipient. The nonprofit acts as a collection point. It also can launch a campaign to raise awareness for this fundraiser to capture a greater percentage of the donations.

The corporation makes a contribution, which would have been part of its philanthropic program anyway. No additional expense is incurred. The company gains positive visibility for its social or environmental platform, profits from the product purchase, and experiences reputational enhancement and goodwill because of its donation. Plus, this approach ensures the organizations of greatest importance to customers benefit. Shoppers participate by purchasing products, collecting labels, vouchers, or container lids, and passing them along to the nonprofit, thereby increasing shopper involvement.

It's All About Timing: They say "timing is everything." Particular events or holidays can help promote a cause-related initiative. In the United States, the July 4 holiday may be the perfect time for an annual veteran's fundraiser. A food bank or soup kitchen may find it beneficial to partner with a grocery chain on a food drive at Thanksgiving.

Even if timing seems to be a critical element in the program, it's necessary to survey the market to see if other programs are already successfully leveraging the same time frame. Becoming a "me too" addition, when donors are already weary of the number of "asks," will not produce the desired results. If the nonprofit intends to launch the initiative when the market is already saturated by similar requests, the lack of program uniqueness could undermine the success.

Benefits: Understanding both the motivation and donation pattern of target audiences are important for this cause marketing model.

Examples:

- Hoping to receive a tax write-off, a specific demographic group may be more inclined to participate in an end-of-year program rather than in January.
- Employees may be more willing to promote the program because they are "in the spirit of the time," thus increasing the degree of positive work place engagement.

While both the nonprofit and the company want to avoid launching a "me too" campaign, visibility during a particular time frame may be essential. For example, a Christian-based religious group often is expected to be seen "doing good works" at Christmas. The absence of such an activity could be noticed and negatively perceived. Likewise, if a significant portion of the company's business is generated at a particular holiday, a lack of community involvement during this time frame could be conspicuous and viewed as symbolic of withdrawing from a cause or even misinterpreted that the business is no longer supportive of the fundamentals represented by the particular day or event. Hence, the benefit of being highly visible with cause-related marketing and public relations efforts during a particular time frame can protect as well as enhance reputations.

Despite the many benefits, cause marketing is not without flaws. These must be taken into consideration before launching a campaign based on one of these models (see Box 5.1: Potential Barriers to Cause Marketing Relationships).

Whatever model is selected, it's important to apply the K.I.S.S. theory to program specifics. "Keep It Simple, Stupid" is good advice because an overly complicated cause marketing program alienates shoppers, donors, volunteers, and employees. A company employee needs to be able to explain the program to a friend, neighbor, vendor, or customer. This brief speech also should be articulated by the nonprofit's staff and volunteers. After all, if these brand ambassadors don't understand the program and can't describe or explain it, how would anyone else?

Finding the Right Partner

Choosing the right partner is a requirement for a successful cause marketing collaboration. The nonprofit must think about the competitive advantage it has by combining its strengths and assets with those of a potential business partner. What does the not-for-profit hope the relationship will ultimately do for it?

Given the nature of this relationship, it is essential the values of the two entities match. This means internal perceptions and conduct must be consistent with public statements and actions and understood by each. Both cultures must respect and appreciate the other's professional behavior and

---

Box 5.1   Potential Barriers to Cause Marketing Relationships

There are numerous benefits to cause-related marketing programs, but this tactic isn't for all organizations. The drawbacks as well as the benefits must be weighed. For that reason, a benefit/risk analysis should be conducted. To begin this process, consider the following barriers, which could derail a cause-related marketing effort:

- It takes time to successfully launch a cause marketing campaign that generates significant funds.

- When it comes to some cause marketing models, such as licensing, it is necessary to receive a guaranteed minimum level of funding or royalties.

- It can be challenging to find a business that fits the culture and has a corporate responsibility platform sufficiently similar to the nonprofit's mission.

- If the program is being driven at the national level, individual chapters may experience difficulty executing at the local level or engaging the business partner within a specific community.

- Agreeing on terms that make the cause-related marketing effort mutually beneficial and that satisfy both the nonprofit's board of directors and the company's executive leadership can be difficult.

- A social marketing campaign may not be an effective match for the culture or the way in which the not-for-profit operates.

- It could be challenging to identify a business that is financially stable or able to underwrite the costs associated with or supply the necessary employee resources to implement and execute the cause marketing campaign desired by the nonprofit.

- A corporation's publicity and promotional efforts may overshadow the nonprofit's brand visibility or cause.

- Developing and instituting an effective cause-related marketing program requires an extensive investment of time. The nonprofit may not have sufficient personnel with available hours to dedicate to launching and supporting an additional fundraising tactic.

- The nonprofit's board of directors may not be fully supportive of this type of fundraising technique and would be unwilling to publicly endorse the initiative.

- The company's public image may not align with or reflect values consistent with those of the nonprofit brand.

---

culture. Without this value match, neither synergy nor a long-term relationship is likely.

A clear and appropriate affinity is important, says Sue Adkins in her book, *Cause Related Marketing: Who Cares Wins.* She explains some affinities are "too close for comfort" and emphasizes it isn't about the size nor the "fit" between the two organizations; rather, it is about the appropriateness, the objectivity and independence of each, and the clarity of communications between the two.[13]

The nonprofit must determine if partnering with a local, regional, national, or global company offers the greatest benefit. Perhaps, the company's footprint matches the nonprofit's target audience perfectly for the goals of raising funds and expanding its volunteer base. Or, a small nonprofit may be approached by an international corporation because the company's reputation in the particular region is less than stellar. In this situation, the corporation may be very willing to negotiate a cause marketing agreement highly favorable to the not-for-profit's bottom line, hoping an alliance will improve its community image.

This concept is further supported by research conducted by Cone Communications. According to the report, *Past. Present. Future. The 25th Anniversary of Cause Marketing*, "Global corporate leaders will empower their brands and business units to invest in localized solutions to meet societal needs in the areas in which they operate."[14]

Particularly during a recessionary period, the nonprofit must be careful to select a partner capable of providing the necessary support, tactical execution, and financial backing to conduct a cause-related marketing initiative. Partnering with a financially floundering company can make it difficult to collect the funds generated from the cause marketing program in a timely manner. The last thing needed is to embark on a collaborative campaign, invest time and energy on this type of fundraiser, and then learn it is one of many organizations trying to collect from a corporation in bankruptcy. Finally, the corporate partner must be financially able to compensate fully the nonprofit for any and all uses of its name and logo.

It is advantageous if the partnership brings additional value to the equation. For example, a media outlet could guarantee a strong advertising campaign and promise news coverage. A business could engage its celebrity spokesperson to promote the cause or organization, free of charge to the nonprofit.

Board of directors commitment is critical. Members must be supportive of this undertaking and have a comfort level with the potential corporate partner. Possible conflicts of interest must be considered during this selection process. Would a member of the board benefit personally or professionally to a disproportionate degree by a cause marketing initiative with a particular business? If this is the case, the nonprofit should not tempt fate. A careful examination of what type of accusations or reputational damage can be expected should be discussed before pursuing the collaboration.

To broaden and deepen internal support for this type of fund-generating activity, the nonprofit can solicit recommendations and input from staff, the board, and possibly even key donors or volunteers. This approach makes the selection process inclusive, helping these brand ambassadors feel more vested in the process and creating strong advocates for the program when it's launched.

An important question for the nonprofit to ask itself is, "Does this company have a corporate social responsibility platform and business that is a good fit with our mission, values, and culture?" If the corporation manufacturers food and has a CSR mantra focused on child obesity, it may be an excellent organization but it would not be a "natural fit" with a nonprofit focused on educating or training displaced workers.

Introspection at this stage is critical as well. The nonprofit must reflect upon what it can bring to the collaboration. Business personnel, trained in negotiating techniques, will want to be sure this agreement has merit for the company. Examples of unique advantages a nonprofit could bring to the cause marketing equation are:

- A traditional event already exists and is well received. It simply requires a new sponsor.
- The nonprofit has a strong volunteer program and donor base, which can be leveraged in conjunction with executing this particular cause market program and which represents a potential customer base for the for-profit.
- The organization has strong community roots that may be helpful to a business just entering the particular geographic market.
- The nonprofit has prepared cause marketing and collaborative materials ready, which can be customized for easy use by the business.
- Touching stories and other emotional community connections are part of the nonprofit's history, which could be leveraged by the firm for the selected cause marketing model.
- A camp, historical property, or educational institution is owned by the group and can be made available to a corporate partner for training events or meetings.

Working through the selection process is not a quick or easy task. Much research is required to develop an initial list of "good" companies, not aligned with other causes, and to which the nonprofit has a natural connection. Further analysis of these candidates will be required before the nonprofit can identify the best and most strategic cause-related marketing partner with the greatest likelihood of producing the desired program outcomes from the nonprofit's perspective.

Making Sense of It All

As Adkins explains: "The opportunity that cause-related marketing potentially provides the charity sector is fantastic, but it must be considered thoroughly. The risks are as significant as the potential rewards. The strategy therefore must be clearly relevant, well thought through, and clearly targeted."[15]

Armed with a better understanding as to the types of cause marketing models available and the attributes of a good business partner, the nonprofit should re-check the value this reputationally influential fundraising activity will bring to the organization (see Box 5.2: Cause Marketing Program Query).

Box 5.2   Cause Marketing Program Query

Before entering a cause marketing relationship, logic must prevail. Questions to consider are:

- Does the nonprofit have the capacity to undertake this fundraising effort?

- What risks are involved with initiating this particular cause marketing model? Do these overpower the potential positive outcomes?

- Does the company's corporate responsibility platform align with the nonprofit's organizational values?

- Are the cultures of both organizations compatible?

- Does the selected business have the capacity necessary to launch and support this type of collaborative effort with a nonprofit?

- Are there any reputational drawbacks to collaborating with this particular business?

- Is the company's market a good geographic fit for the goals of the not-for-profit?

- Will the firm's customer base strengthen or expand the nonprofit's donor or volunteer base?

- Will embarking upon this type of fundraising initiative build donors, volunteers, or members?

- What type of increased visibility can the nonprofit expect?

- Will the nonprofit experience a "reputational boost" by its association with the business?

- Would any controversy be generated by affiliating with the selected business partner?

- Will this association create a conflict of interest with other major nonprofit donors?

- Does the revenue or fund-raising ability of this program sufficiently offset the cost of the resources the nonprofit will invest to launch and execute this initiative?

- How much does this compete with and how similar is this initiative to existing cause-related marketing programs?

- How will this effort complement the nonprofit's existing fundraising efforts? Or, will it cannibalize established programs?

- Will this cause-related marketing activity resonate with the nonprofit's staff, donor base, and volunteers?

- Can the essence of the program be easily communicated and understood?

- Does the initiative lend itself to transparency and does its structure validate the integrity of both organizations?

Working Together

It's important to remember that, at its very foundation, cause marketing is a business relationship. Consequently, an infrastructure must be in place to manage this program successfully. Formal assignments must be given to the staff of both the nonprofit and the company. All responsibilities should be accounted for and assigned in advance to ensure program execution is flawless and nothing is overlooked. By delegating duties at the onset, it makes it unnecessary to negotiate particulars about a job in the midst of a campaign. Plus, this ensures accountability is linked to every aspect of the plan.

When setting ground rules, it is essential to realistically assess the resources and talent both organizations have to offer. Can volunteers be of service in this endeavor? If so, what type of controls or accountability is required? If the nonprofit has a two- or three-member communication team and the corporation has five people dedicated to social media, is it logical to expect the charity to handle the entire social media promotion? Or, if a sole proprietor is sponsoring the fundraising opportunity at his or her restaurant, is it fair to expect the business to provide the facility and all of the labor?

Time parameters should be established. Is this a single event? Or, is an event to repeat annually? If so, for how many years? Whether a pancake breakfast, a trade-in-your suit, or a collect the lids from your yogurt labels, establishing a program end-date is recommended. Including this target date should not be viewed as "the absolute death" of the program. Instead, it should be seen as assurance that both organizations value the affiliation and respect the possibility of differences and changing organizational needs over time. Of course, there is always the opportunity to renew the contract.

If a long-term arrangement is developed, periodic reviews should be formally built into the contract. This will ensure both organizations are continuing to benefit, and their respective and mutual goals are realized. Depending upon the outcome of these discussions, a re-negotiation may be necessary before the contract expiration.

Of course, a question haunting every nonprofit executive in such a business relationship is, "What if we are in the middle of a cause marketing program and realize we selected the wrong partner?"

Having invested significant time and resources into the decision-making process and cause marketing launch, this question can make even the bravest leader shudder. But, failing to select the correct company with which to collaborate is always possible. For this reason, planning must include an exit strategy.

It's important not to take any disagreements or program issues personally. Assuming both partners have performed exemplary, there are times when collaborations simply don't appear to be working. Here, open communication is essential. It may be possible to "save" the partnership if each entity states its issues, acknowledges the relevance of each other's concerns, demonstrates mutual respect, and keeps the interaction positive. But if this behavior doesn't occur, then it may become necessary to discontinue the arrangement.

Earlier, the advantages of a program end-date were discussed. Depending upon when the decision is made to "part ways," the natural ending date may provide the perfect opportunity to discontinue the relationship without having to explain to donors, staff, volunteers, or customers as to why the program is ending.

If the cause-related tactic is based around an event, it is hopeful the two entities can make it through this affair before severing the collaboration. The nonprofit must balance the risk of discontinuing involvement with the particular business versus continuing in the collaboration. However, if the business is found to be financially unstable, has major brand image issues, or demonstrated egregious behavior, the nonprofit may be forced to discontinue the relationship earlier. If this occurs, the nonprofit must prepare for investigative press inquiries, negative feedback from key stakeholders, and possibly even law suits.

The nonprofit also must recognize the tenuousness of the situation. Other businesses will watch how gracefully this relationship has existed. If the collaboration was particularly unhappy and the nonprofit feels abused, it may be tempting to state candidly how the nonprofit was used by the big company. But, one must remember there is tactful way to communicate this, and it is always best to yield to professional conduct and a polished demeanor. After all, the nonprofit still has its reputation to maintain.

A final reminder: Cause collaborations are like any other relationship. They have a life cycle. The need to discontinue the relationship could be linked directly to some program element or it could be triggered by an unrelated event, such as the company being bought by another business or a plant or store closing. For this reason, it is always wise to watch for new partnership opportunities and to retain independence from the business partner (see Box 5.3: Before You Sign).

Communication Tips

The importance of strategic communication planning and critical plan elements were covered in Chapter 2. Working closely with the development department to design a comprehensive, cause-related communication and marketing plan, which is integrated into the nonprofit's annual communication and marketing plans, is essential. This strategy work should focus on generating funds and enhancing the group's reputation. Clear and transparent informational and persuasive messaging technique should be utilized by the nonprofit's senior staff during these eight stages:

1. Gain board of director backing for the cause marketing initiative.
2. Pitch to target company.
3. Secure support of key internal and external stakeholders for program.
4. Pre-launch marketing and public relations.
5. Publicity and promotion during the life of the campaign.

Box 5.3   Before You Sign

Recognizing the importance of a cause marketing relationship, it is critical to study the document and reflect upon key elements prior to signing the contract. Use this checklist to assist with your final review of the agreement:

- Are the responsibilities of both organizations clearly defined?

- Have all potential liabilities and risks been considered?

- Will an appropriate sum of funds be generated to make it worth the nonprofit's investment of time and resources?

- Is a program end-date and/or "check-ins" scheduled or the timing for this/these outlined?

- Is there sufficient differentiation of this particular program from others within the nonprofit's sector or geographic area of operation?

- If the participation of other vendors or organizations is required, are these other groups addressed in the document?

- Is the budget clearly defined, including which organization will be responsible for which program expenses?

- Are program goals clearly stated and/or success criteria specified?

- Is a timeline included in the appendix or in the document itself?

- If appropriate, has a confidentiality clause been included?

- Is there an exit strategy?

---

6. Post-campaign/program announcements, including results.
7. Feedback loop from key stakeholders regarding communication effectiveness.
8. Communication debriefing and measurement.

To ensure program effectiveness and that both partners realize success, the following communication factors are worth emphasizing:

- Strategic communication is essential to promote the cause marketing initiative and to benefit from the reputations of both the nonprofit and the corporation. All communication must be authentic, regardless of the size of the marketing and public relations budgets or the tactics used. It's critical the unique mission and values of each are accurately represented and key organizational messages are consistent and clear. Honesty is essential in sharing the work to which both organizations are committed. A description of the joint action being taken to accomplish the societal or environmental goal should be made and publicly shared through multiple venues. This helps reach participants to ensure they understand the necessity of the cause marketing effort, the related objectives, and their role in successful program execution.

- Compelling stories enhance the communication process. The corporation and nonprofit's work forces must understand the difference their employers are making within the community or in helping a specific cause. Stories help to make a personal connection and can lead to improved workplace engagement as well as invest employees more deeply in the nonprofit and its mission.

  Stories can complement the marketing efforts by adding "the human touch," thereby creating ethos and pathos "differentiators" in the cause marketing program. This will help separate this particular initiative from others in the endless sea of advertisements.

  Donors and volunteers want to know the difference their participation makes in helping the not-for-profit reach its service goals. Already dedicated to the organization, these key stakeholders want proof of what their purchase or action accomplished or how the raised funds were allocated. Persuasive, individualized stories reinforce the emotional connection to motivate continued support for the effort and to create further goodwill for the NGO.

- The web, social media, and location-based services will be critical in the growth and development of cause marketing.[16] In fact, "social marketing is where commercial benefit and social benefit combine to achieve social change."[17] For these reasons, its applicability to cause marketing must not be overlooked or understated.

  Designing promotions specifically for web-based and mobile interaction can produce additional benefits such as: eliminating direct mailing costs; eliminating printing and possibly reducing marketing expenses; supporting the company's eco-friendly or sustainability platform; and emphasizing the not-for-profit commitment to sustainable citizenship.

  If the product purchase is made online of if the event is "virtual," it is possible to realize even more benefits: fewer resources are required for event execution; less demand is placed on volunteers, nonprofit staff, and the company's employee base; additional funds are generated because of the program's cost-effectiveness; and time-crunched, program participants are not required to attend a physical event to participate.

Measurement

What does "success" look like for a cause marketing program? How should it be evaluated? These questions should be agreed upon prior to both parties signing an agreement. The expectations and outcomes of each entity should be clarified and documented. A cost-benefit analysis can be conducted at the end of a campaign or at agreed-upon intervals to ensure the effort is financially justified and the less tangible goals of both parties are met.

Obviously, making sales and raising money are at the heart of this collaboration, but what are other ways success can be measured? According to Cone Communications, "Companies will be forced to redefine measurement metrics no longer based on outputs, but on the outcomes for society and their business. Stakeholders will hold companies more accountable to align their business practices with cause-related initiatives."[18]

Businesses need for additional measurement mechanisms, which focus on intangibles and societal or environmental results, are applicable to nonprofits as well. Examples of other measurement criteria, which could be used to determine the success of a cause marketing program by both nonprofits and companies, follow:

Creating New Connections

The nonprofit and business may be seeking new markets or want to strengthen their relationship with established target audiences. Does the business have an expectation in regards to sales leads, expanding its customer base, or gaining a competitive edge in a new market? Or, is it hoping to realign its brand so as to be viewed differently in particular target markets? Is the nonprofit hoping to introduce itself to new donors or recruit a specific number of volunteers? Knowing current donor, volunteer, and customer statistics and having specific target goals makes a comparative analysis easier, when it comes evaluation time.

Increasing Visibility and Building Reputation

Each may want to increase visibility and enhance reputation. Whatever the desired results, it's important to know these goals and the planned form of measurement. Visibility may be determined by the number of appearances in newspapers, blogs, television news reports, and tweets; or, it could mean appearing in a business publication much coveted by the corporation or the nonprofit capturing headlines on a national newscast. While this discussion may sound ego-centric, both organizations must be frank about what they hope to achieve in terms of positive media exposure, increased awareness, and reputation building.

If the nonprofit wants to increase its visibility as a leader or become better known in the community, aligning itself with an extremely well-known business with excellent brand recognition may be helpful. The relatively unknown or small nonprofit then could be catapulted into the spotlight, directly benefiting from the visibility of its sponsor. Interestingly, Cone Communications examined this concept in a 2010 survey. Results showed 56 percent of respondents said they were more likely to donate to a charity aligned with a for-profit partner, and 41 percent were more likely to volunteer.[19]

From a business perspective, the positive affiliation with a nonprofit may provide much-needed local exposure and credibility enhancement with a critical target audience. And, a positive reputation earned by the company for "donating one of its most valuable resources to a project, namely employee time."[20]

Benchmarking

Many nonprofits and businesses have already participated in cause marketing campaigns, so if it is the first time an organization is considering undertaking such an initiative, goal-setting and measurement can be gauged against best-of-class standards and adapted according to desired outcomes, organizational type, and the cause marketing model used.

If the entity has participated in a similar marketing initiative in the past, it has its own benchmark against which it can be compared or the measurement features adjusted to accommodate changes in goals and circumstances. Measuring against the campaign's previous performance, such as with a re-occurring annual event, can be beneficial in determining if program performance is improving or its effectiveness is decreasing.

It is, however, still wise to benchmark against other cause-related campaigns in the market to determine the true effectiveness of the effort.

Employees and Volunteers Engagement, Job Satisfaction, and Pride

Studies have shown a company's social responsibility platform is helpful in employee recruitment and retention. These actions are believed to build loyalty and elicit positive feelings toward an employer. Demonstrating the degree to which a cause marketing initiative, in particular, impacts day-to-day engagement is challenging. But despite the ability to identify direct and concrete results, its influence on morale can be determined through focus groups, surveys, or similar techniques. Anecdotal evidence could possibly be produced, which could demonstrate the link to between the cause marketing program and the outlook of some employees.

If a business is new to a community or if lay-offs occurred, the grass roots activity involved with a location-specific cause marketing campaign could help elicit employee goodwill and positively position the business in the community. Particularly in the case of a national or multi-national corporation, a cause-related marketing campaign at the local level could create an experiential opportunity for the work force, engaging employees in a manner that positively connects them to the company and instills pride in their ability to make a difference in the community. This, in turn, can heighten the degree of connectivity employees have with the company. But again, it may be difficult to assign a dollar figure to the degree of engagement and job satisfaction produced by this specific program. Consequently, its impact likely will need to be viewed in terms of its relation to the overarching CSR goals.

Even if only empirical evidence is feasible in regards to the contribution a cause marketing program can have on an individual's work place morale or job satisfaction, it does not mean this initiative should be discounted. The company should simply be aware of the challenge in possibly capturing statistical proof.

The nonprofit can incorporate questions about the cause-related marketing program into its regular employee survey to learn how this initiative is perceived. If previous survey data is available regarding employee loyalty, job satisfaction and organizational pride, new questions can be crafted to help determine how this particular initiative impacted employee outlook.

Focus groups can be conducted with both staff and volunteers following an event or campaign to discover how well the initiative was received; to determine if the opinion about the effort was positive, negative, or neutral; and to ascertain feedback regarding how the event could be more effective. Thus, multiple goals could be achieved with this form of feedback.

Finally, the nonprofit could measure the number of new volunteers and donors originating from the company's work force. Such results would be interesting to the business as well.

A Look into the Future

Cause marketing—in concept and form—will continue to morph, becoming increasingly sophisticated and influential in the corporate philanthropic arena. Here are a few of the trends that should be monitored during this evolutionary process:

1. Waters and MacDonald predict even more growth in the cause marketing arena and a decrease in traditional philanthropy. They suggest several reasons for this. First, Wall Street's emphasis on earnings and return on investment are so strong many businesses can no longer fund generous philanthropy programs. Then, there are the consumers, who understand the necessity of business making a profit but also view commerce as capable of generating social change, possibly even more effectively than government. Finally, nonprofits cannot overlook any funding source, including small and mid-sized businesses, which may not be able to endow large contributions but could participate in a cause marketing initiative. Consequently, cause marketing creates a win-win solution permitting companies of all sizes to be philanthropic in some manner.[21]
2. Harnish Pringle and Majorie Thompson see the emergence of what they call "brand spirit. Considered the third way of branding, a "promise" is created due to the ethical or spiritual dimension of the

brand, exemplifying personality traits and potentially even creating a persona with which people can interact. Consumers need to understand what the brand "believes in."[22] Cause marketing is a concrete way to demonstrate an otherwise esoteric explanation, which is less visible or too complicated to easily comprehend.

3. With social media demonstrating more and more power in its ability to connect people and causes, location-based cause marketing will increase in importance. The premise on which this type of cause-related marketing model is based deals with potential customers or donors "checking in" their location with a nearby business. The company rewards the check-in activity with a donation to the cause, which is an action-triggered donation emanating from the smart phone. With GPS-enabled smart phones, the development of additional mobile apps for web-based businesses, and the emergence of location-based social networking services, it is only a matter of time before considerable growth of this application occurs in the cause marketing arena occurs.

4. With corporate America experiencing a "trust crisis," companies are looking for more ways to gain and retain consumer and employee trust. Recognizing both reputation and sales may be at risk because of waning trust, one solution to which business is turning is its corporate responsibility platform. Cause marketing is one tactic in an organization's multi-prong approach to achieve its CSR goals. If properly designed, a cause-related marketing program—once operational—can demonstrate the social conscience and transparency of a business, thereby building credibility and trust. Communication is critical for consumers to witness the system integrity of both organizations and to provide assurance program recipients truly benefit.

5. In tough economic times, consumers will look for value on two levels: (a) the emotional reassurance their "investment" supports a worthy cause, and (b) they receive excellent value for their monetary investment.

Thoughts on the Subject

Dave Stangis
Vice President, Public Affairs and Social Responsibility
Campbell Soup Company, Camden, NJ

Q: What criteria does Campbell Soup Company consider when selecting a nonprofit partner for a cause-related marketing initiative? How is this similar to what other companies seek in this type of nonprofit partnership?

A: Cause-related marketing efforts at Campbell Soup Company begin with two questions:

1. Does the mission and do the objectives of the proposed program align with the mission of the company's corporate social responsibility efforts?
2. Will participating in this initiative permit us to make an impact?

When we examine what Campbell Soup Company does and where it can make the greatest social contribution, we have determined we can make the biggest difference by tackling issues related to food, such as childhood obesity and reducing hunger.

Our next step is to determine how we can differentiate our efforts from those of other food companies. We do this by looking at both the social value that can be generated through the initiative as well as the value it brings to our brand.

Using these criteria in reviewing requests, we have found some programs are perfect for achieving these goals. In these initiatives, we have acted as a catalyst and provided marketing materials, educational information, administrative assistance, or other necessary support. We may have partnered with both nonprofit and for-profit entities to ensure every aspect of the process is addressed. Plus, we have discovered that by involving others, you have the chance to make a significant impact rather than one that is simply ordinary.

We also like to see our customers engaged in any philanthropic process we undertake. For that reason, we ask our customers—who have participated in programs ranging from our Labels for Education program to Help Stamp Out Hunger food donations—to post their thoughts and reactions.

The reality is that Campbell Soup Company isn't interested in simply writing out a check. We are strategic in our efforts and want to develop robust programs that deliver socially responsible results and support our brand image. We believe it is important to educate, engage, and interact with our customers. We also look to involve our business partners, such as the retail outlets where our product is found.

While there might have been a time when companies opted to become involved in a cause-related marketing program because it was an executive's pet project, those days are gone. Today, companies, such as Campbell, are focused, impactful, and brand conscious. With this approach, a true difference can be made with a cause-related marketing program."

Jane Meseck
Director of Citizenship & Public Affairs
Microsoft, Seattle, WA

Q: What guidance can you provide to a nonprofit that plans to approach a company for a cause-related marketing partnership? When looking for a nonprofit partner in a cause-related marketing initiative, what type of criteria do you have?

A: Prior to approaching a company for a cause-related marketing venture, it is essential the nonprofit learns as much as possible about the business.

One of the first steps is to discover how the organization manages its cause-related marketing program. Is the cause-related work centralized or decentralized? And, is the corporation only likely to respond to major requests that have national or international implications? Or, does the corporate office consider large cause-related initiatives and manage smaller program requests at the local level?

An example of the latter is apparent in some national retail chains. There, a store might be funded for community or regional requests, while large or nationwide cause-related programs are administered from corporate headquarters.

On the other hand, a corporation such as Microsoft, which has very few retail outlets currently, is more likely to centralize its campaign.

In addition to understanding the company's infrastructure, it is critical to understand how the nonprofit and company's missions align. Microsoft, for example, examines the similarity in purpose of mission as well as analyzes the purpose of the proposed cause-related marketing campaign to ensure it is compatible with the business. So, be sure to research what social or environmental concerns are important to the corporation.

Microsoft also considers the similarity in target audiences. It is essential a strong connection exists between Microsoft's market focus and the nonprofit's primary stakeholders and interested donors. This helps ensure the philanthropic messages and efforts will be communicated to the company's customer base.

Disasters can be a game changer. It is not uncommon for a business to respond to a natural disaster, such as a hurricane, earthquake, or tsunami. Here, a corporation may not follow its typical course of action or implementation process. Instead, the company may be very receptive to partnering with a nonprofit on a joint venture that will engage customers quickly in a cause-related fundraising campaign.

Creative thinking is an attribute that Microsoft seeks in a nonprofit partner. Many times a nonprofit's creative approach contributes to the development of a unique, cause-related campaign that is effective and memorable as well as emphasizes donor engagement. This thinking can set the campaign apart from other, more traditional philanthropic approaches. We really want the donors to be able to participate to ensure we engage our customers in this activity.

The reputation of the nonprofit's brand and strength of leadership are two other components we carefully examine. Because we are concerned about our reputation, we want to be associated with a nonprofit that also has a very good reputation. In turn, the nonprofit should consider the reputation of the company with which it is seeking affiliation. Similarly, we look at the leadership demonstrated by the nonprofit's executive director and its board.

Before an agreement is reached between the nonprofit and a business in regards to any cause-related marketing program, it is necessary that both parties mutually agree to the goals of the initiative, the strategic approach, and the anticipated outcome."

Something to Think About

1. In what instances would it not be appropriate for a nonprofit to engage in a cause marketing campaign?
2. How could a cause marketing campaign be created that would bring in multiple business partners in order to increase the fund-generation capabilities for the nonprofit?
3. What role could a nonprofit's board of directors play in a cause marketing program?
4. In the future, how is social media likely to influence the promotional efforts of a cause marketing campaign?
5. When approaching a business for a cause-related marketing partnership, what materials or information should a not-for-profit present?

6   Social Connectivity

Before beginning a Hunt, it is wise to ask someone what you are looking for before you begin looking for it.

(Pooh's Little Instruction Book, Inspired by A.A. Milne)

Setting Communication Context for New Technology

Well-performed business negotiations make both parties happy and a deal is closed. Feuding nations identify root causes of problems and arrive at mutually acceptable terms sufficiently adequate to sign a peace accord. Students listen to an inspiring classroom lecture and follow the instructor's advice to dedicate time and resources to nonprofits in order to advance social causes. One could just as well cite examples where effective communication resulted in conspiracy, started a war, or created apathy among members of an audience.

Eliminating both the motivational and ethical components from the previous examples, one must acknowledge the relationship building capacity of this communication and the results produced. Relational communication theory addresses the behavioral changes, human interactions, and social processes that evolve through the emotional and values-based tensions, playing a significant role in human discourse.

Recognizing the complexity of motivational, ethical, and relational communication concepts in the communication process, this chapter will limit significantly the examination of these subjects but reference them in conjunction with web-based communication and their use by the nonprofit sector. However, time will be dedicated to addressing how basic communication characteristics, including listening, mutual respect, transparency, two-way informational exchange, risk taking, messenger credibility, and nonverbal communication, are linked to this relatively new and continually evolving technology.

Taking a Step Back

When mass communication entered the scene, studies reported its influence as ranging from having no effect to being a powerful force. Regardless of the degree to which you believe mass media influences people, it is generally agreed upon that it impacts our perception of the world. We are exposed to sites, words, and actions we otherwise may never encounter in our homes or communities. And even if we opt to limit our personal exposure to mass media, we experience its effects through others who are exposed to and/or participate in it and find ourselves responding in some manner to their behavior.

Many people rely on mass media to create a trustworthy picture of what is happening outside of their functional areas. This is true, despite an acknowledgement of the possible bias on the part of a news outlet or material presented.[1]

Because of its ability to push content out, using a one-to-many broadcast approach, mass media can send information quickly to multiple audiences. But, its ability to engage in two-way dialogue is controlled. In response to a news report, one can write an editorial, pay to place an op-ed piece in a magazine, interview with a television news reporter, or go on a radio talk show.

In setting additional context, it is worthwhile to reflect briefly on key technological advancements impacting media. One can look at publishing, for example, where hand-written manuscripts were replaced by printed books and are now available online.

With the debut of the web, news is available real time. Journalists constantly post new content and story updates. No longer must one wait for the daily paper or an evening television newscast to learn what is happening in the world.

Consequently, the web has transformed public relations. Online communication makes it easier for professionals to share information directly with target audiences. Communications teams can act as news producers, tweeting about an issue or posting content on a web site or blog. Thus, the role of the gatekeeper, found in a traditional news outlet, is diminished.

While there are many benefits to web-based communication, such as the speed with which messages can be sent and more options to communicate directly to key audiences, the pros and cons of this communication methodology must be studied before adding specific tactics to the strategic communication plan. Considerations include:

- advantages and disadvantages over existing tactics;
- the complementary possibilities in combination with other forms of communication such as mass media and face-to-face interaction; and
- value-add components, such as efficiency, cost-effectiveness, transparency enhancements, and message quality.

For example, making an emotional connection is integral to nonprofit communication effectiveness. Therefore, online and mobile technology must be examined for the ability to inspire, motivate, and engage multiple audiences. If not sufficiently present, techniques must be incorporated into this web-based format that will emotionally move people from a state of passivity to that of engagement with a dedication to support and even actively promote the not-for-profit.

During this overview, Walter Lippmann's concept of the silent majority is worth mentioning. Lippmann, an American journalist, philosopher, and political commentator, observed that individuals may not see their point of view being communicated. Believing this opinion is not that of the majority, these individuals may become silent. Yet, it is possible for those who believe themselves to be in the minority to actually represent the majority. The majority's silence and lack of activity to express a viewpoint permits the vocal minority to appear to hold the popular opinion.

Using the silent majority phenomenon as a foundation, it is feasible to extrapolate a similar web-based scenario. Today's social lurker monitors web conversations of others yet is reluctant to voice an opinion or become engaged, even though this individual could easily share thoughts and opinions through blogs, online chats, and tweets. Ironically, these same venues makes it possible for the vocal minority to intensify its voice in web-based conversations. Thus, web-based communication faces some of the same challenges as mass media.

Today's communication professional should draw from these communication concepts, applying them to online and mobile tools. After all, these are an outgrowth of earlier forms of messaging and steeped in the evolution of human communication.

Web 1.0, 2.0, and Beyond

By the time this book is published and distributed, new web-based and mobile tools will have emerged and more will be on the horizon. Consequently, this discussion will address some of the existing tools with the intention of providing "lessons learned" that can be applied to current and emerging communication technologies.

Web-based technology can be broken into three categories:

- *Web 1.0* refers to the static web. Similar to traditional mass media, 1.0 uses the "push technique." Most users simply consume the content. E-newsletters, web sites, and email blasts, are representative of this era of web development. These now are considered basics in most nonprofit communication plans.
- *Web 2.0* describes the next phase in the web evolution, which includes social networking. This movement takes the nonprofit from merely broadcasting information to creating a platform for

engagement. Interaction and collaboration are emphasized. It's important to remember the various communication tactics and techniques do not operate in isolation. They interrelate. Consequently, it is possible to build community through online interaction while other tools, such as e-newsletters or e-advocacy campaigns, are promoted.

- ***Web 3.0*** represents the mobile era, according to Heather Mansfield. Texting, texting-to-give, and smartphone apps characterize this phase. But given the rapid rate of development, additional advances in mobile web technology are expected.[2]

Strategy

This separate discussion of online and mobile communication should not be misconstrued as a recommendation to treat these tactics separately from the overarching communication strategy. Instead, this is a breakout discussion of the "new possibilities" available to today's communication teams. Because additional personnel may be required to successfully establish a more social culture, it's important the nonprofit begin by asking if creating channels that promote web-based interactivity are important to the organization and in line with budget constraints. The nonprofit also should examine its reputational goals in relation to social media positioning possibilities. For example, will use of these channels build the nonprofit brand, enhance its relationship-building capacity, improve transparency, or establish greater credibility? If the answer is "yes," then individual web-based tactics should be reviewed for effectiveness.

Some of the evaluation criteria for online and mobile tactics are:

- capacity to fit into and across the nonprofit organization;
- ability to reach the intended audience(s);
- audience preference and responsiveness;
- ability to influence audience perceptions and behaviors;
- resources (effort, budget, number of personnel required, etc.) required to implement, monitor, and maintain the selected tactics;
- connectivity with new stakeholders or expanded public bases;
- complimentary and complementary uses in conjunction with other communication tactics;
- vehicle effect on the message; and
- ROI (return on investment) of the tactic.

The online and mobile communication journey is unique for every nonprofit because different groups are at various stages of adoption and experimentation. One organization many only have a web site and use email. Another may be more sophisticated, even accepting donations through mobile apps. Regardless as to how aggressive an organization is in applying web-based technology, it should rely on a four-step process to ensure successful communication results, when integrating this new technology into the arsenal of communication tools.

The initial step is *research*, which involves listening and observing. What social media tools are other nonprofits employing? How successful are their web sites in fundraising? Have their tweets or texts inspired volunteers or donations? What types of communication vehicles work the best in a particular sector? Much can be learned by studying the web-based communication approach of others. So as new technologies emerge, closely monitor the successes and failures of others.

To develop long-term relationships and build loyalty with critical stakeholders, a nonprofit must learn the interests, concerns, and communication preferences of its targeted audiences. This comes from closely listening and carefully monitoring key audiences and their habits on all web and mobile technologies used by the organization. Examples include:

- How long do visitors stay on the web site and does it get a "thumbs up" on Facebook?
- Which pages are visited the most frequently?
- Are blogs receiving comments?
- What is the response to email blasts?
- Which tweets get retweeted?
- Are there bloggers who reference the nonprofit's work?
- Is there information that draws stakeholder criticism?
- Which tactics best engage or produce the desired behavioral results?

The list could continue, but it is clear much information can be mined through this data analysis. Then, thoughtful decisions can be made as to how which online and mobile communication should augment the strategic communication plan.

Testing is the second stage. Rather than automatically implementing a particular tactic, it is advisable to test it. This will help determine how well a new form of communication will be received, the type of training or awareness campaign required to launch the new vehicle, and the resources necessary for implementation and ongoing maintenance.

For example, adding board of director members to the nonprofit's Facebook page and expecting these individuals to become social weavers is possible, but training is likely required to fully leverage the opportunity.

Blogs or Twitter may be under consideration for the communication portfolio. However, before fully implementing either, it is advisable to test such tactics—even on a personal level—to ensure the nonprofit has the bench strength to support this vehicle on a long-term basis. Uncovering implementation issues or identifying problems during a test scenario enables one to avoid failure and the added effort of a re-launch. If issues and problems can't be resolved, it is less embarrassing and easier to delay the launch and circumvent the additional effort required for a re-launch.

Testing also presents an opportunity to see how key stakeholders will respond to the communication. In fact, an organization may want to test both its internal capacity to become a more social organization and the communication vehicle by first representing the nonprofit through online forum participation. Whether posting comments onto the blogs of others, participating in chat rooms, or retweeting, a nonprofit can glean critical information, learn the amount of time required for such an activity, and determine the level of interest in the posted content.

Next, is *adoption*. How can new communication tools be integrated effectively into the organization and its overarching communication strategy? What will entice staff to be supportive of the process and stakeholders to use it? If employees don't retweet or participate in relevant on-line discussions, how can others be expected to do so? Both awareness-building and educational campaigns may be required to transform a web-based technology from simply languish to a robust, two-way communication platform.

Finally, there is *strategy integration*. To fully integrate and support any web-based communication tool, it is advisable to formally enter the tactic into the communication strategic plan. This includes determining its role in relation to existing tactics and strategies; stipulating goals and/ objectives; clarifying target audience(s); assigning responsibility for execution; ensuring budget accommodations are made to support the added communication channel; and identify measurement techniques to track performance.

For web-based communication to perform to its maximum potential, staff must be involved. In his book, *Social Media ROI*, Oliver Blanchard addresses the importance of starting every day with a short team meeting. He emphasizes the necessity of reviewing overall objectives and keeping everyone up-to-date on progress.[3]

Because of the speed with which social media moves, it represents a medium that cannot simply be discussed on a quarterly, monthly, or even weekly basis. While a daily meeting may not be feasible, given staff size and individual responsibilities, some type of briefing should be provided. Example discussion topics are: suggesting employees check out an update to the Facebook page; alerting staff to concerns being voiced on Twitter; notifying personnel and volunteers where fundraising campaign updates are posted; and requesting assistance in promoting an in-kind donations appeal.

Governance

To ensure strategic and proper use of current and emerging web-based technology, an organization must develop guidelines and establish policies that protect its reputation while effectively leveraging these communication opportunities. These standards should:

- Create a framework that clarifies responsible employee social media usage in both internal and external settings;
- Offer behavioral guidance in regards to representing the nonprofit on personal sites;
- Serve as a reference point for training, organizational procedures and policies, and other critical materials, which have interactive potential;[4]
- Establish best practice protocols for web-based communication use; and
- Introduce directions for effective two-way communication that enhance and strengthen the nonprofit's internal and external relationship-building, problem-solving, and networked governance options.

When developing these guidelines, it is important to remember the organization is not in a position to "grant" employees the ability to use social media or other web-based technology. Employees have a right to personal communication and self-expression. A paid employee or an intern may opt to share his or her thoughts about the nonprofit very publicly through social media, when sitting in front of a laptop at a coffee shop or in front of a desktop at home. Employees, carrying smart phones loaded with mobile apps, can share opinions easily during lunch time. If workers posts videos, tweet, or text on their own time and using their own equipment, what right—if any—does the nonprofit have over this communication, if its name is used or organizational visuals posted?

While the legal system is still exploring answers to some of these issues, it is advisable to give employees rules apprising them of the nonprofit's expectations of social media usage. These policies should address subjects such as: security procedures; crisis communication guidelines; directions regarding the treatment of confidential information and privacy issues; the loading of social media-related software onto equipment owned by the nonprofit; personal use of social media during working hours; web site access limitations; content discussion parameters; file sharing protocols; and directions for posting on the nonprofit's blogs, Facebook page, or web site. Depending on how the volunteer base is utilized, the same regulations may need to be shared with this group.

For nonprofits that rely on staff, volunteers, and board members to use personal social media outlets to solicit volunteers, share updates, or post pictures and video of organizational events, the line between nonprofit and personal social media use becomes even more blurred. Thus, questions are raised such as, "Should employee use of social media be controlled?" and "If so, how should it be controlled?"[5]

Regardless of the depth or the breadth of a nonprofit's social media policy, the following are foundational elements:

- internal and external usage guidelines;
- definitions of accepted practices and behavioral expectations;
- disclosure policies regulating the discussion of employment; privacy issues regarding employees, members, or other key stakeholders; and confidential information controlled by nondisclosure agreements;
- file sharing and Internet safety (The integrity of an organization's IT system can be compromised. The need for accessing and sharing information must be balanced against technical requirements to guard against hackers and spammers.);
- rules addressing areas of character defamation, slander, libel, and cyber bullying; and
- nonprofit site content loading and password security protocols.

Beth Kanter and Allison H. Fine explore a secondary dimension to social media nonprofit governance: How can board governance leverage this? The pair believes governing boards can better connect with broader communities of people for input and guidance by leveraging social media tools. They suggest social media can close the gap that may exist between boards and the organization itself, thus making the nonprofit more representative of the communities being served and better designing the communication process for productive dialogue. They acknowledge the concept of combining board governance with social networks can be disconcerting. However, they advocate doing just that because of the effectiveness in guiding nonprofit organizational practices through peer-to-peer governance principles.

Without requiring a change to the board of directors' charter, a social media governance structure can be practically applied to help boards act more like social networks. The goals would be to: achieve greater operational transparency; improved engagement with the people within the nonprofit's ecosystem; enhanced accountability; and more timely and enriched communication.

How can this approach be tested? A few of their suggestions follow,[6] along with strategic communication considerations.

- *Post board meeting agendas online and include open space*: With the open space, a degree of calculated risk taking is necessary. However, this creates an opportunity for others to provide input and enhances the organization's transparent image.
- *Issue a public invitation to board meetings*: By inviting everyone to attend (even providing a conference call-in number or broadcasting online), a reputation for transparency is developed. Unless sensitive matters, such as personnel issues, are being discussed, there is little reason why a board of directions meeting should require a "closed door" approach. While a loss of control may be felt through the extension of such an offer, diverse viewpoints are gained and

potential issues can be identified earlier and solved prior to escalating into a crisis.

- ***Share information through social networks***: A private social network can be established for online information sharing. If some board members are withdrawn or shy, this forum may encourage them to participate in a conversation they may otherwise not join.
- ***Develop online profiles for board of directors***: Add profiles of board members to the nonprofit's Facebook page. This serves a two-fold purpose: establishing a venue for more informal conversations with board members and positioning these individuals as organizational ambassadors, establishing a "more human connection" with this visual.
- ***Encourage board network weaving***: Board members should be trained to use social media, so they can engage in online discussions about the nonprofit. If all board members participate, they can facilitate conversations across multiple channels. This can strengthen relationship while increasing organizational visibility.

If the nonprofit pursues this more public approach to organizational governance, specific parameters incorporated into the social network governance document are critical.

Committing to a more open environment is not without challenges. Increased interaction means more public discussion, some of which could be negative. Questions such as these will likely arise:

- What if a decision or organizational work is criticized?
- Can we be sued more easily because of the increased exposure?
- What happens if confidential information makes its way online?
- If someone posts false information or makes derogatory comments about us, how can we defend ourselves?

All of the aforementioned are logical questions. Even with stringent guidelines and policies, it is feasible confidential information could be inadvertently posted by the nonprofit. This situation validates the reason for social media protocols and procedures. Rigorous scrutiny and control must be applied to confidential material handling to help avoid security breaches with employee records, donor credit card data, or other secure content and information.

Law suits over social media issues are possible, just as in any area of the nonprofit's operation. Clearly articulated protocols should stipulate expected employee behavior and use. With employee awareness, training, and careful monitoring, the likelihood of misuse is reduced and even avoided.

Because it is never possible to please everyone, it's likely the organization will be criticized; and individuals may make negative remarks, possibly even lie. But this could occur whether or not the nonprofit has a robust social media plan or a web site. And should rumors, crisis, or inaccuracies occur, possessing online and mobile channels is actually a benefit because the nonprofit is better positioned to respond quickly.

The Tools

Apps: This three-letter word refers to computer software applications. An "app" makes it easier for a mobile device user to perform a task. Facebook, LinkedIn, Foursquare, Twitter, and others utilize this technology, so it is easy for mobile users to stay connected with their favorite sites. Apple offers over 500,000 apps, and in March 2012, the company hit the 25th billion app download mark. As David Meerman Scott said in his book, *The New Rules of Marketing and PR*, "There really is an application for anything."[7]

Many nonprofits have successfully used apps to make personal philanthropy more convenient. And as mobile technology continues to evolve, it is likely there will be more and more reasons for nonprofit communication and development teams to leverage this technology.

Blogs: It's a good idea to participate in the world of social media before initiating this tactics. Commenting on the blogs of others provides social media experience with minimal risk. This also provides the opportunity to monitor content, track trends, and learn who the influencers are.

Why should the nonprofit consider having a blog? Blogs can lend a human face to an organization, create a personal connection, promote the nonprofit's reputation and brand, and serve as an information source for volunteers, donors, and other key audiences.

It goes without saying that significant consideration must be given to selecting a name for the blog. Because search engines will index the name, it's best to spend time on this process upfront rather than attempting to change later. The tag line and avatar are important for branding purposes, too.

The blog can be added to the nonprofit's web site or located separately. The advantage to hosting it inside the web site is that, when a blog is published and promoted, traffic is driven to the site and search engines will give content priority to that web page over static pages.[8]

On the other hand, a separate site, which uses a complimentary color palate, font, type face, and logo from the organizational web site without being identical, establishes connectivity between the two yet asserts an independent voice. This can make others feel more confident about posting comments, ideas, questions, and contrary points of view.[9]

Whatever the approach, time should be taken to test the name, tag line, and design elements with key stakeholders. While not everyone will agree on these, the differing viewpoints will pave the way for improvements and likely create a broader-based appeal.

Blogging software offers a comment control feature. Comments can be turned off. While this ensures no one can post a derogatory or negative remark about the organization, this approach undermines the benefit of conversation. By opening up to comments, user-generated content can spark discussions, reveal shifts in opinions, capture trends, and identify issues or concerns. Plus, the more compelling and interactive the blog, the greater the likelihood of improving search engine results and growing the number of fans and followers on the nonprofit's social networking sites.

Permitting comments can help to "keep the organization honest." Authenticity is critical to well written blogging. In *Blogging Rules*, Nancy Flynn notes: "Blogging culture demands absolute honesty. The blogosphere hates a phony!"[10]

Permitting guest blogs has several advantages, too. Naturally, this means the communication department doesn't have to create all of the content. So, from a time-labor perspective, it's practical. If relying on guest bloggers, strategically incorporate them into the editorial calendar. Consideration should be given as to who should contribute content and how frequently a guest blog should appear. Advantages are: enhancing the nonprofit's image through affiliation with respected community or nonprofit sector leaders; an apparent openness to welcome commentary by others; and a broader range of subject matter.

To ensure subject matter is timed with the release of other organizational communication, stays focused on key messages, is supportive of critical issues being faced by the nonprofit, and is not redundant, an editorial calendar must be developed. Topics can be strategically mapped in terms of content and timing, and appropriate personnel can be assigned to the task of updating blog content and engaging in conversation when comments are posted.

Content must be fresh, relevant, and authentic to encourage and build a subscriber base. But, thinking about what to say on an ongoing basis can be challenging. Blog content ideas for nonprofits are:

Give readers something to do. Encourage others to post a comment by asking a question or suggesting an opinion be voiced. Perhaps, an e-newsletter article is being referenced. Include a link that will permit the reader to subscribe. Or, link to the results of an opinion poll or white paper.[11]

Share resources and tips. Useful information—applicable to everyday life—attracts readers. Analyze the purpose of the organization and how the nonprofit is in the position to provide guidance or helpful hints on related topics. For example, if the nonprofit focus is helping abused and abandoned pets, blogs could include links to coupons for pet food, remind pet owners of the importance of having pets spayed, or offer tips for pet care during summer or winter months.

Recognize. Most people like to be thanked, whether it is for a monetary contribution, consecutive years or service, or chairing a major fundraising event. Have a summer intern? Consider featuring this individual who is donating time in exchange for experience. These examples underscore the gratitude recognized by a handwritten thank you note and publicly announce how much the agency appreciates the support. The recipient may encourage others to read the complimentary copy. So by simply extending the courtesy of a public thank you, it's possible to gain blog subscribers and increase the exposure for this tactic.

Break news and announcements. Want to get the word out quickly? Blogs can aid with the announcement of new service offerings, fundraising campaigns, research results, collaborations and partnerships, and organizational response to crises.

Make a call to action. A request for volunteers to help with an event or to donate to a specific cause can be posted quickly and then follow-up communication distributed to keep the campaign visible. Consider addressing the topic of in-kind donations in a blog. In such instances, you can ask readers to make suggestions for companies that could donate the products, if readers are unable to do so.

Interview experts, conduct research. Affiliation with experts and producing reputable research are two means by which an organization can help to build its leadership reputation. Consequently, interviews with subject matter authorities, reports on white paper findings, and thoughtful analyses on reports produced by others can be very interesting to readers. Content-rich discussions are likely to follow and even appear in tweets and other blog posts.

Create Lists. While developing lists can be trite, they also can serve as informative and interesting blog content. Plus, lists keep writing concise.

Reference other bloggers (and post on their sites). Referencing other blogs has advantages. It can create an ongoing exchange of ideas, as the blogger who initiated the subject may post a comment on the nonprofit's blog or write subsequent blogs referring back to the nonprofit. An ongoing discussion of this nature can elevate the importance of the subject matter while keeping content fresh, relevant, and reflective of diverse viewpoints. Of course, there is added exposure for the nonprofit's blog, the potential of at least one new subscriber (and possibly others who follow the initial blogger), and the likelihood of other social media picking up the conversation.

Share stories, photos, and videos. Stories, photos, and videos add to a blog's effectiveness. They create a personal connection, enhancing the relational link. Photos and videos leverage nonverbal communication to help convey – and even emphasize –salient message points.

Emails: Emails have become a staple in the communication arsenal. And while social media reduces some of the reliance on email, this format should not be discounted entirely. Emails can be sent or received via desktop or a mobile device, making this an incredibly accessible technology. Ideal for sending documents, images, and presentations, including Word, Excel, and PowerPoint files, its flexibility permits distributing to a single individual or to a large group. Targeted distribution lists can be developed to avoid spamming, while making sure critical audiences receive the message. Inexpensive to use, it offers budget relief over other forms of communication that require mailing or advertising expenditures. Plus, emails can be written when convenient, sent according to a schedule, and opened when desired by the recipient.

Despite its advantages, there are drawbacks. There is a proliferation of emails. Companies routinely request email addresses to send special offers and promote products or services. Organizations consider email a critical tool to conduct business. And, personal emails, which replace a considerable amount of postal communication, add to the size of the content of an individual's inbox.

So, how does a nonprofit make its emails appropriately relevant to be opened and sufficiently compelling to connect with its intended recipients? How can an organization make this form of communication seem more personal? How could a not-for-profit better brand itself to raise organizational awareness with existing and potential stakeholders? What if the audience is comprised of multi-lingual individuals? All of these questions must be examined to ensure the decision to use this form of communication is strategically beneficial and well designed.

Tips for using this communication for nonprofit promotion are:

- Create strategic and interesting subject lines to grab attention.
- Leverage the signature by including a tagline or simple organizational description. Include a link to the nonprofit's web site in addition to personal contact information.
- Write in a tone which reflects the content and is appropriate for the audience.
- Be concise.
- Limit the size of attachments, so there aren't complications in opening files.
- Strategize on how to best personalize and make emails interesting.

Remember: There are times when a face-to-face meeting, phone call, or online chats are more appropriate for the message and the group.

The Dragonfly Effect offers the following guidance to inspire action and spur change through email campaigns: Make it personal, informative, and direct.[12]

When trying to make email communication informational, relevant, and well branded, carefully crafted *e-newsletters* are one solution. For starters, the low cost to create and send is advantageous over its print predecessors. E-newsletter solutions, offered by companies such as Constant Contact, VerticalResponse, iContact, and MailChimp, provide templates to brand a nonprofit's newsletter; automatically add an individual's name to personalize each mailing; incorporates features such as opinion polls to entice interaction; and possesses easy-to-insert link capabilities to set up "click-throughs" to web sites, Facebook pages, or "donate now" pages.

Photos and other graphics can be added to entice readers to linger at least a few minutes longer and take in more of the content. Links to videos can be inserted, enhancing the information-sharing capacity of the e-publication and incorporating "the human face" of the organization. And, the outcome of those previously referenced opinion polls can be reported.

Because of the ability to easily customize content and target audiences, multiple e-newsletters can be produced. However, there are two cautions. First, content must be relevant and interesting. Repetition and old news will drive readers away as opposed to toward the e-newsletter. Also, it is critical to remember readers are time-crunched. If distributed weekly, it shouldn't be assumed readers will welcome them. A well-done monthly e-publication may be better received than a more frequent one.

E-newsletters should be promoted on the web site and in other outlets to encourage subscribers. Regardless if the e-newsletter is developed in-house or with the help of an outside service, each e-newsletter must include an "opt out" function. The last thing the nonprofit should want is for the e-publication to become an annoyance. It is better to have the recipient opt out of the e-newsletter but continue to receive other email communication rather than blocking all emails.

E-cards or SendOutCards create a unique opportunity for personal interaction with donors, volunteers, and other key audiences in a convenient and cost-efficient manner. Hallmark, 123Greetings, and Blue Mountain greeting card sites offer e-cards free of charge.

With SendOutCards, an online greeting card system, the communication team can select from a large database of templates, which can be used for an invitation, congratulation, thank you, birthday, years of service, reminder, or other appropriate communication. The inside message can be personalized and an electronic signature added to the paper card. A file containing U.S. postal service addresses can be set up and stored online. Mailings can be made to an individual or an entire group. Although there is a cost associated with this arrangement, there are advantages to surprising people with this form of personalized communication.

Whether an e-card or an actual greeting card is sent, both offer more of a "personal touch" than an e-mail blast or e-newsletter. This vehicle should not be overlooked as it helps to emphasize the value the nonprofit places on relationship building.

Facebook

With more than 901 million active users by March 31, 2012, and more than 500 million mobile monthly active users by April 20, 2012, the influence of Facebook is significant. These numbers clearly demonstrate the power of this social site and make a compelling case as to why nonprofits cannot overlook this particular social media platform.

With Facebook, a nonprofit can raise its visibility by creating organizational, cause, and group pages. It must be emphasized that these pages have distinctive purposes. If the nonprofit only has personnel to support one of these options, the nonprofit profile page is the logical choice (see Box 6.1: Facebook Set Up).

TechSoup, a nonprofit that offers technology products and information geared to nonprofits and libraries, provides tips online for nonprofit Facebook administrators. One of its recommendations includes leveraging existing video content, podcasts, interviews, and documents to begin creating a presence quickly. Even if the nonprofit already has a Facebook page but hasn't taken advantage of broadening the exposure of its already prepared marketing and communication materials, it is advisable to

---

Box 6.1   Facebook Set Up

Nonprofit Page: To create a nonprofit page, log into Facebook. At the bottom of any page, the words "create a page" can be found. Click on this link. This leads to a page where labeled boxes can be found. Click on the one that says "Company, Organizations, and Institutions." A menu will appear. There are several options from which to choose, including: "Nonprofit Organization," "Non-Governmental Organization (NGO)," "School," "University," and "Political Organization." Select the correct description and then add the name of the nonprofit. Because the name cannot be changed later, take care when entering this information. Directions, including prompts, follow.

Group: To create this community, go into "Groups," located on the left-side of the page. Next, select "Create a Group" and a screen will appear. Enter the name of the group, member names, and degree of privacy desired (open, closed, secret). Once finished, click on "Create Group."

Group details can be edited at any time by simply going to the "Group Info" tab. The Group can be promoted though its built-in invitation feature.

It's fairly easy to set up a nonprofit page, group, or cause on Facebook because of the prompts and directions. However, if extra help is needed, there are several Internet sites, such as www.ehow.com, that provide more detail.

pursue TechSoup's recommendations. Plus, sensory experiences are created through videos, photos, audio files, and slide presentations, possibly strengthening all three Aristotelian appeals and heightening the degree of donor or volunteer engagement.

A Facebook Group serves as an excellent venue for keeping people informed about particular aspects of the nonprofit in which are interested. For example, individuals passionate about the organization's advocacy efforts may want in-depth communication on the subject. If set up properly, only registered members can see this private space; so, this targeted audience could be polled or invited to chat on a confidential basis. If transparency is desired, the group site can be public, showing the names of its members and the postings.

Other Facebook page tips are:

- Encourage board members, staff, and volunteers to be active on the nonprofit's Facebook page. To give greater exposure to status updates, encourage these loyal supporters to "like" the content or, even better, to post a comment.
- Have more than one administrator who knows the account password (even though this should be protected). This will help guard against the nonprofit being locked out, if an employee quits or is ill. This advice is true for all social sites, such as the nonprofit's Linked In account.
- Use "Favorites" functionality to build a relationship, demonstrate appreciation, or even initiate partnerships. For example, to recognize a company that is a major donor, simply go to its Facebook page and click on the "thumbs up" button to indicate that the nonprofit "likes" that business.
- Take advantage of the tagging functionality by posting status updates or photos on other Facebook walls. By tagging the page of another nonprofit, foundation, or cause-related partner, there is the ability to promote both the nonprofit and the other organization.
- Leverage the free event-posting capabilities to advertise upcoming events.
- Send updates twice a month to keep content fresh and interesting while not appearing too aggressive or burdensome.

It also should not be assumed board members and staff are savvy on Facebook use. Training may be required to familiarize key audiences on this site's functionality. Or, as this site become increasingly sophisticated in its offerings, employees and volunteers may need to receive training updates in order to help the nonprofit fully leverage the capabilities of this social site.

LinkedIn

LinkedIn, a social networking site for professionals, was launched in 2003. In March 2012, the site reported being the world's largest professional network on the Internet. It has more than 161 million users in more than 200 countries and territories.[13]

The nonprofit's executive and communication team should have LinkedIn profiles. The profile summarizes personal work experience, educational background, awards, affiliations, skills, and other professional information. While the focus is on an individual's personal career, this social site can raise visibility for the agency or charity as well. For example, "causes" and "volunteer" information can be added to one's profile. This acts as an endorsement of the nonprofit, linking the credibility of the account holder to the charity while helping to drive name recognition and brand awareness of both.

The degree of professionalism projected by the content of one's profile and photograph reflect on the nonprofit, too, as the lines between personal and professional brands are blurred.

Connections are an integral element of this social networking site. Time should be spent inviting contacts to be LinkedIn connections. People leave jobs, change careers, move to different parts of the country, and work abroad. It isn't always easy to follow an individual. LinkedIn stays connected to these people, as long as they continue to participate in this social networking platform. Thus, it is possible to remain connected with individuals through the course of their careers.

The "people search" function can help one locate colleagues from previous employers or past professional and business relationships. Assuming these individuals have progressed in their careers, it may be very beneficial to reconnect. By entering the person's name and possibly a few other identifying features, one can locate the individual, if they use this social networking site.

Finally, it is possible to make a new contact, extending beyond the confines of the typical networking options, by conducting a search and going through a virtual introduction process sponsored by an existing contact.

All three approaches present opportunities to broaden and strengthen an individual's professional network, which can be personally rewarding and extremely beneficial to the not-for-profit. This extensive network can serve as an excellent base from which to recruit donors or volunteers or hire employees.

Each profile has a "home" view, which includes a place for postings. Post something each week, so the content is picked up on the LinkedIn Updates sent to contacts. These postings can promote upcoming nonprofit events, request a professional opinion on an issue, solicit help for a project, advocate a cause, and recognize an individual, company, or foundation.

There are two important guidelines for posting updates: be professional and be authentic.

LinkedIn provides the opportunity to recommend others. Some volunteers, such as an intern, may be looking to gain experience or learn skills. By providing a professional recommendation about this individual's quality of work on this social media site, the nonprofit publicly recognizes the volunteer. And, the individual gains a professional career reference.

An organizational page can be created for the nonprofit, too. The American Red Cross and The Nature Conservancy have LinkedIn pages worth checking out. Each provides an overview of the organization, shares job opportunities, describes services, is set up to receive endorsements through the recommendation process, and has a significant number of followers.

A nonprofit can create a "group" to manage the online community affiliated with it. The LinkedIn Learning Center has easy-to-follow directions for creating and managing a group. It's a good idea to require approval to join. This permits the group manager to better monitor growth and reduce the possibility of spammers. If the not-for-profit intends to use this tool to grow online community support, existing tools—such as the web site, e-newsletter, and email blasts—will need to promote its existence.

As with other social media, relevant content is critical, so it is important to keep individual profiles up to date and groups and nonprofit pages interesting and engaging. It should be cautioned that establishing a successful LinkedIn nonprofit page or group takes time.

Texting

A real-time collaboration tool, texting offers several benefits. But one of its biggest assets is its ability to reach a group instantly. Content should be timely as text messaging conveys a sense of urgency. This communication tool is particularly helpful during a crisis when a call to action is required for notifying and updating members or staff about a situation; mobilizing key volunteers; and permitting employees and volunteers to connect quickly with each other.

Of course, texting is an important tool in addition to its crisis communication uses. Periodic texts can be sent to remind people to donate or to issue a reminder for upcoming events and registration deadlines. It also is a very effective means for polling a group to schedule a meeting or to receiving feedback quickly on multiple options or ideas requiring small group vetting.

Twitter

Twitter is a free social messaging utility, providing yet another avenue for the nonprofit to reach critical audiences quickly and directly while avoiding the traditional gatekeeper.

This microblog communicates real-time through a 140-word count tweet. People who subscribe to a Twitter feed are called "followers." A Twitter feed can drive traffic to the nonprofit's web site where more detailed information and links are shared.

Because of the brevity of this form of communication, Twitter is considered to be more informational—both seeking and providing—than it is conversational. This form of communication also tends to be very much "in the moment." What do people want to know now? What is trending currently? This can help guide the nonprofit's tweet content.

But, a nonprofit should leverage this social media platform for more reasons than simply addressing subjects of immediate interest to followers.

Because of the time-sensitive nature of a crisis, Twitter is in incredibly helpful tool. Safety advisories can be transmitted and followed by subsequent alerts or security updates. Volunteers can be rallied. Donations requests can be issued to help crisis victims. Status updates can be sent to staff.

Twitter can be a particularly effective communication tool in other instances, too (see Box 6.2: Potential Uses for Twitter).

Celebrities have proven Twitter's ability to gain attention and initiate relationships. Much can be learned from these high profile people in terms of what is effective and what has created issues for their brands. With this in mind, nonprofits must be cognizant of how their brands appear. A

Box 6.2   Potential Uses for Twitter

Twitter is excellent for reaching people quickly during a crisis. However, this tool can be leveraged strategically in other ways:

- Requesting followers to sign online petitions or to contact government representatives and officials about emerging legislative issues;
- Apprising key constituents of advocacy campaign progress;
- Alerting members about an upcoming event or a registration deadline;
- Sharing breaking news;
- Notifying donor and volunteers upon reaching an organizational goal;
- Expressing thanks for an overwhelming and immediate response to an appeal;
- Updating a progress report on a critical project;
- Reminding followers of a fundraising campaign;
- Encouraging members or donors to go to the nonprofit's web site to participate in an opinion poll;
- Posing an intriguing question to obtain diverse viewpoints;
- Conducting a quick survey to prioritize key organizational causes; and
- Gaining feedback on a blog or marketing materials.

140-character message can severely tarnish an organization's reputation. In fact, negative or inaccurate information can go viral in an extremely short period of time. Consequently, an organization's Twitter feed must be monitored regularly.

Finally, the nonprofit should take great care when developing its Twitter page. Although there are obvious differences among the various social media, message consistency and visual appearance among all social media sites are important for branding purposes.

A nonprofit's tweets should have personality, too. They should be friendly, genuine, and professional. Followers need to feel there is a "real person" tweeting. Developing this reputation takes time.

Web Sites

According to Patterson and Radtke, "A well-organized, well-written, well-maintained, and graphically compelling Web presence is one of the best ways to educate and influence key constituencies."[14] Consequently, effective web site development is critically important.

The effective web site can draw people in, engage volunteers, inspire donors, inform members or service users, and encourage visitors to return. A well-designed site makes it easier for search engines to find the nonprofit's online presence, too.

If a nonprofit doesn't have an online presence, a web site is the first step. If the organization already has one, it is wise to analyze its use by visitors, study the search engine optimization (SEO) data, and scrutinize the site with a critical eye to ensure it is highly effective in its ability to help the nonprofit achieve strategic communication goals and objectives.

It's important to remember two rules when developing or critiquing the web site. First, the site must complement other tactics, so that—together—they will help the nonprofit achieve its strategic communication goals, further its organizational mission, and enhance and protect its reputation. Second, it must be about the visitor. Visitors must find the web site's content interesting, relevant, and beneficial (see Box. 6.3: Recommended Web Site Content).

Nitish Singh and Arun Pereira emphasize culture is the "new imperative in web design."[15] They address the need to develop a site that permits instant global reach and the ability to interact on a worldwide basis. Although their emphasis is on business use, the premise is a sound one for nonprofits. Some not-for-profits already are global in nature, but even those that aren't must be forward thinking. If their primary mission resonates across the globe, it is possible it will draw interest from geographic regions beyond its current scope of operation. Or, a similar nonprofit located in another country or region may see benefits to collaborating on causes or even fundraising efforts. In this world of web and mobile tactics, there really is no limit as to when, where, or how a nonprofit's brand

---

Box 6.3   Recommended Web Site Content

What are people likely to search for on your site?

- Mission statement and overarching goals
- Staff list, with bios and contact information
- Organizational history
- Services, programs, issues, and causes
- Message from the executive director and/or board president
- The nonprofit's general contact information
- The nonprofit's official tax status
- Frequently asked questions
- Annual report, including financial data, number of members or persons served, highlights from the year, annual goals, etc.
- White papers, speeches, reports, polls, videos, webcasts, or podcasts
- Press releases
- Awards, testimonials, endorsements
- Board of directors listing
- Upcoming events or activities
- In-kind donation requests
- Sponsorship opportunities
- Online monetary contribution functionality
- Links, including social networking sites such as the organization's pages on Facebook, Twitter, and LinkedIn
- Sign-ups for e-newsletters or other materials
- Privacy and security policies
- Netiquette rules, if the site is interactive

---

may be seen, its communication and image evaluated, or its reputation regarded.

Basic web site development principles are:

- Register the web site with popular search engines and monitor its "findability;"[16] and create page titles that increase search engine optimization.
- Limit the number of columns used. Heather Mansfield suggests using only two columns, one of which takes up two-thirds of the page and other which would comprise the remaining one-third.[17]
- Ensure site navigation is simple and intuitive.
- Ensure consistent design throughout all secondary navigation and content pages.

- Include all pertinent contact information for the nonprofit, including key staff members.
- Limit the number of links that will take visitors to other sites.
- Establish a professional and memorable reputation. The site should represent a personality that is unique to the nonprofit and distinctively represents the organization in a manner consistent with its mission and brand.
- Offer relevant and up-to-date content.

Include social media icons (such as Facebook and Twitter).

With the growing popularity of mobile technology, it is critical the nonprofit's web site be mobile friendly. Scott emphasizes the need for designing a site that can be displayed quickly and is optimized for viewing on smaller screens. Thus, the necessity of using mobile-friendly architecture is of increasing importance.[18]

Additional Features

Photographs, videos, audio files, and slide presentations can enhance the sensory appeal of the nonprofit's messaging, thereby strengthening the communication connection with audiences. While these tools and tactics cannot fully replace face-to-face interaction, they can enhance communication by sharing compelling nonverbal features, such as facial expressions, and vocal characteristics, such as inflection and tone of voice. Not only do these dimensions help to emphasize the written word, but they can create a stronger connection and emotional link in the online storytelling process and help those, who learn more effectively through other sensory appeals, better understand and retain the data and messaging.

Currently, there are several sites available to assist the nonprofit with this effort. A brief discussion of each follows.

Founded in 2005, *YouTube* has demonstrated no indication of declining in popularity. This social site reports, "We have hundreds of millions of users from around the world." Its global profile includes 24 countries and 30 languages.[19]

YouTube offers a nonprofit program. In addition to the video hosting capabilities it provides, YouTube has a strong, online community. So when a video is posted, the nonprofit should consider permitting comments. If a mean-spirited or extremely negative comment is posted, it is always possible to remove it and block the sender.

To present an identifiable and consistent visual image, the nonprofit should use the same avatar for its profile picture that it does with other social media. Remembering the importance of the single boiler plate paragraph used in a news release, a similar description should be added to the YouTube site. However, as with all online communication, particularly in this case where visitors are on the site to watch videos rather than read content, it's best to be brief.

Of course, YouTube relies on apps to reach mobile devices users. With this technology, a nonprofit's audience is not tied to a desktop to view a quality video.

As a photo and video sharing and management application with over 5 billion photos and over 1.5 million active users, *Flickr* stores, sorts, searches, and shares these visuals online.[20] There is a free version, but the upgrade offers more features.

TechSoup partnered with Flickr to create Flickr for Good, which offers a discount, making the upgrade a cost-effective addition to a nonprofit's budget. In fact at the time of this writing, Flickr was committed to the donation of 10,000, one-year, Flickr pro accounts for good causes as a result of this partnership.

If a nonprofit has photos or videos it wants to share with volunteers, staff, board members, donors, or event attendees, this platform makes it easy to do so. Photos should be named and the best ones tagged. When adding photos or videos, it is important to remember any guidelines that protect the privacy or personal rights of those pictured. For example, a photograph of a disabled toddler, a recent accident victim, or a senior citizen suffering from a debilitating disease may convey an important message but using this picture could land the organization in a court of law. Although the intentions for posting such visuals may be admirable, it is essential to obtain permission from the individuals or their guardians.

Similarly, visuals must support the conveyance of the nonprofit's mission. And, do the photos and videos support the written text regarding the benefits, programming, or work of the nonprofit?

Slide presentations can be developed to strengthen written copy. For example, pictures can be taken to document the progress in building a new hospital, camp, or school. An emotional and compelling story can be told through an online photograph scrapbook, creating a greater emotional hook than mere words, such as photographs capturing the tragedy of September 11 in New York. These visual are more likely to tug at the heart strings and convince people to open their wallets to support the cause.

A thank you presentation to acknowledge volunteers for their work throughout the year shows appreciation while also demonstrating the many avenues for volunteerism. Thus, two benefits are derived from a single tactic.

The site permits comments, notes, and "favorites," encouraging dialogue and creating a potential avenue for engagement. And as with any form of social media, contacts can be added to build key audiences. As with YouTube, Flickr has an app.

Calling itself an Internet-based, social expression and personal publishing service, *Shutterfly* offers free, online photo storage capability. In 2008, it launched Shutterfly Share sites to combine photo sites, blogs, and social networking to make it easy to collaborate in a secure environment. Its Gallery is a community platform for sharing and connecting with others.

In 2009, Shutterfly "went mobile" with free photo sharing through an iPhone app. The following year, it announced the integration of the Simple Path photo book with Facebook, allowing users of that social medium to access their photos and those of their friends. Other services, such as the ability to print customized greeting cards and to make photo gifts (like thank you t-shirts or mugs for volunteers) from online photos, can generate additional branding opportunities that also lead to the development of a stronger personal connection.[21]

SlideShare supports slide presentations, webinars, videos, PDFs, and documents. Content is shared through blogs and social networks, including LinkedIn, Twitter, and Facebook. Although these files can be uploaded and privately shared, the focus is on collaboration.

Since its launch in 2006, companies have used this site for a wide variety of business purposes. But, nonprofits have found SlideShare's platform to be helpful as well. UNICEF, Pew Internet, the Bill and Melinda Gates Foundation, and the University of Illinois are examples of not-for-profits that rely on this social medium.

Organizations may find it beneficial to leverage the site's technology for webinars, slide presentations, and other forms of web-based communication that are effective in conveying details and explaining complex elements about critical issues, a cause vital to the group's mission, or an important problem. Thus, SlideShare is yet another venue for nonprofits to share important material and to tell their story in a highly visual, very compelling, and public manner.

Even though there is a fee associated with SlideShare, nonprofit invoices are discounted by 50 percent, if proof of tax-exempt status is provided.

Pinterest is a social photo-sharing web site that allows users to create and manage theme-based images in a style indicative of a bulletin or pin board. In this case, a "pin" is simply an image that can be uploaded to the Pinterest site from a computer and placed on a virtual "board."

According to its site, Pinterest's mission is to connect "people all over the world based on shared tastes and interests."[22] Growing in popularity, this social site is even monitored by journalists who are looking for trends and other potential news story ideas.

There are a plethora of social media channels available to nonprofits. The ones addressed in this chapter represent only a few of; even more importantly, by the time this book is published, it's possible the particular ones identified will no longer be trendy and will be replaced by others. What is an accepted fact is social media has changed forever the communication landscape. Consequently, staying abreast of trends, watching for technological enhancements in existing tools, monitoring the evolution of new technologies, and being cognizant of the collaboration possibilities among social media sites are necessary to strategically leverage all communication opportunities.

Final Thoughts on Web-Based and Mobile Technologies

It's clear the role of web-based and mobile technologies in a nonprofit's communication toolkit will continue to grow. Web 1.0, 2.0, and 3.0 have demonstrated influence; the ability to evolve to meet audiences' ever-changing communication needs, preferences, and demands; and adaptability to complement more traditional communication tactics. Although a number of points have been made in this chapter, there are a few other aspects that must be touched upon to provide a more complete picture of web and mobile technology influence.

The Most Critical Audience.   While it is easy to think of social media as an excellent tool for external audiences, it can deliver impressive benefits to the internal communication process. Social media permits secure communication in real-time, which keeps employees abreast of critical information in a timely manner. Use of web-based and mobile technology helps staff be more productive and effective with communication and other job-related tasks. Just think about how much time can be spent on emails and phone calls to schedule a meeting. Group texting can expedite this process.

Stacy Wilson, president of Eloquor Consulting, Inc., shares several other examples where social networking contributes to employee performance:

- *Microblogging* can connect project teams, create awareness for and update staff on a project, expedite problem resolution, and leverage skills and expertise cross-functionally.
- *Blogging* can promote dialogue, which can lead to innovation; keep team members informed; and enable sharing, capturing, and archiving intellectual capital.
- *Discussion Forums* can expedite the answer-finding process, enable in-community support, and capture and share subject matter expert knowledge.
- *Social Networking for virtual teams* can help employees find each other, particularly in a large, national, or international nonprofit; identify group expertise and skills more quickly, connect and educate specific teams, and permit individuals to see the contributions of others.
- *Podcasting and Video* can provide an alternative learning method, enable the sharing of intellectual capital, and serve as a very good visual reference for task instructions.

Wilson adds there is great opportunity to connect employees working in similar disciplines but at different locations. Consequently, social media can be an extremely powerful, internal communication tool for nonprofits with large staffs, a work force where a significant number of people work remotely, or in the case of a national or international organization, which represents a geographically large area.

Push vs. Pull.   One must remember today's message recipients expect dialogue. So although the nonprofit must push out key organizational messages, informational briefs, and basic data, people must be pulled into the conversation. Consequently, the nonprofit must offer social dialogue opportunities to increase the likelihood of building community and producing the desired behavioral results from key audiences.

Conversion Rate.   Just as a business needs to "close the sale" to achieve its goal of staying in business and making a profit, a nonprofit must motivate people to take action, whether that means transforming individuals into donors, volunteers, event attendees, or members. So while a nonprofit's web-based and mobile technologies may inform, entertain, share, and acknowledge, its ultimate goal should be to fully engage advocates, supporters, volunteers, donors, and other critical stakeholders.

Measure Relationships.   While the importance of goal-setting and identifying social media objectives have been emphasized, it is equally important to measure against these to ensure the time spent developing, maintaining, and monitoring specific social media tactics has been worth the investment. There will be some fluctuations in online mentions and metrics, so it is important to take this into account. But due to the speed with which social media moves, it is necessary to examine this data on a granular level as well as to analyze trends.

K.D. Paine warned not to simply look at the number of visits, click-throughs, and retweets but emphasized the need to audit at the relationship level. She comments, "While relationships impact the bottom line in any organization, in the not-for-profit world relationships take on even greater importance … Relationship are the foundation of the reputation and awareness that your PR and other marketing efforts have built. And without those relationships, chances are no one would be donating or volunteering or anything."[23]

Manage Reputation.   While it's necessary to observe and monitor social media for measurement purposes, it's equally important to do so from a reputation management standpoint. Online crisis communication and reputation monitoring and management serve in an early warning capacity by detecting emerging problems and reputational issues. But manually culling through the overwhelming volume of online data to identify such situations requires considerable time and personnel. That's why RSS feeds are recommended. Since RSS feeds consolidate and deliver syndicated versions of online content to end-users, without spam and viruses, this technology permits the communication team to select what it needs to monitor in an efficient manner. Blogs, chats, web sites, and other online and mobile technology are included in this scan.[24]

Finally, it should be noted that for all of the advantages of promoting a nonprofit's image and engaging critical audiences, social media produces risks. Inherent to social media is the inability to completely control online reputation. An inadvertent posting or inappropriate tweet by a staff member can draw unwanted attention to the nonprofit. And, a web site hijacking can produce undesirable effects requiring significant energy on damage control.

Instituting social media policies and employee and volunteer protocols and guidelines can minimize this risk. By clearly articulating procedures and online behaviors, an unintended fiasco possibly can be averted. And with diligent monitoring and strategic social media planning, a positive online reputation can be achieved by determining how, when, and where to employ these tools in an effective and robust program.

Thoughts on the Subject

Catherine (Kitty) Keller
Director of Communications & Outreach
Business Civic Leadership Center, U.S. Chamber of Commerce,
Washington, DC

Q: How has social media helped you in your strategic communication efforts? How do you plan to further leverage this communication tool?

A: My job got way more exciting four years ago. This was about the time that I, along with many other communication practitioners on behalf of their organizations, started to explore social media as a tool to communicate. It began as somewhat of a tiptoe into this new, ultra-connected world of digital technology—a few peeks behind the curtains to see what we could see.

We liked what we found, and we've never turned back. Why? To put it simply and briefly, we now have more options and more connections to help us get our job done.

The Death of Old-Fashioned Communication?
Is the press release dead? has become a common query in recent years. Of course, this question reflects the changing nature of how news and information are pitched and consumed due to the changes that digital technology has brought us.

The press release isn't dead; it's more important than ever to communicate with precision, focus, and brevity. The traditional press release format pushes us to be disciplined.

The Next Generation Is Very Much Alive

What's different is that the options available today to communicate the press release's content are so exciting. In just the last year, we've taken traditional press release content for various campaigns and projects and used it to create YouTube videos, Twitter launches (breaking our news first via Twitter), tweet chats, LinkedIn conversations, people's choice polls, and multimedia news releases, among others.

One of our aims this year is to better leverage Facebook as a key medium. The impending switch to Facebook Timeline for brand pages is something we're planning for and are actively managing, as this change creates new opportunities as well as questions. We're also planning to launch a mobile app in the Android Marketplace this year, and Google+ still remains uncharted territory for us.

It will be interesting to read this article in a year—heck, in six months!—from now and see how far we made it. That's how fast and creative social media allows us to be.

The Importance of Style and Professionalism Hasn't Changed

To be clear, social media won't take the place of the "age-old" communication and outreach practices. Basic communication skills—writing clearly, speaking persuasively, listening to your constituency, for example—are the cornerstones of what we do on social media, as well as what we did as communicators before the social media advent.

The more casual, conversational nature isn't cause for lax technique and poor habits. While our profession's ability to get the job done might require less face-to-face time, the need to know and practice "netiquette" (Internet etiquette) has increased—and strong communication skills remain central to professional behavior and a respected reputation.

The Future of the Digital Network

I read last week that chief marketing officers will soon spend more on technology than chief technology officers. Our experience might be a supporting point to this; our technology costs have dramatically risen. Like many communication teams, we're diverting sums of money from other tactics to our digital assets. After all, in these times the pot doesn't get much bigger much faster, but the key ingredients have to mix differently.

We do this because we've built a digital network that is one of our most valuable assets for fulfilling our mission. The virtual connections we've been able to make enrich the live relationships we have; the digital network has introduced us to new people and organizations and has made us a better, more valuable partner to other organizations.

This stuff matters. It's not always easy to measure or to evaluate the return on investment. But being an influencer, a conversation-starter, and an active participant in other organizations' conversations will make a difference to your brand. At no time has there been a better way easier to accomplish this than social media.

Final Note

I'd be remiss if I didn't mention my boss's significant role in this social media exploration. In 2008, neither of us quite knew what to expect with social media. We thought it might lead us somewhere, but we didn't know where. He allowed the freedom to explore and experiment. That helped us get to where we are today, which is not a bad place. We've hit a nice stride but we still have a lot of terrain to cover.

Not all organizational leaders are open to exploration and experimentation with the unknown. My advice? Spend some time building your case. Research success stories in organizations similar to yours. Attend Meet Ups or conferences about social media—there are many! Ask role model organizations to help you think through the risks and rewards. Put some questions out on discussion boards. Monitor the accounts of organizations you respect and see what you can learn. Engage openly—just like you will on social media.

Cheryl Carpenter
Managing Editor
The Charlotte Observer, Charlotte, NC

Q: With the increased popularity of social media, how are journalists leveraging this tool to learn about story ideas, access news releases, etc. from nonprofits? In other words, how is the social media landscape impacting how journalists receive information from nonprofit entities?

A: Social media gives us an alert that an idea is catching fire within a community. We watch what is trending on Twitter daily. We all see what is being shared and forwarded on Facebook. Pinterest has also emerged as a place to watch ideas bubble. All of these sites are where journalists overhear conversations. They are valuable as listening posts. They are also valuable as sites where we share our news and enterprise. If we write an exclusive story, it often is not exclusive for long. We share it on those sites to add volume to our share of voice.

If a nonprofit has an extraordinary idea for raising money, it is likely to be seen and heard on social media sites. If fans of the nonprofit are using those sites in unusual or fresh ways to share news or fundraise, that could emerge as a story worth covering.

Best advice for nonprofits still is to know which writers are more likely to write about your organization or the issues that affect your nonprofit.

Follow them on Twitter; friend them on Facebook. If, for example, you work for a nonprofit concerned with children's issues and a wounded or abused child case is in the news, watch for how media are covering it and use it as an opportunity to remind journalists that your organization serves that need in a community.

While social media are amplifiers for what journalists are working on, the best practice for nonprofits is still to understand what is news. If you've broken a fundraising record or have a great story to tell about someone who has been helped by your organization, then share that and offer access to those who can speak to your effectiveness. Often we hear from nonprofits that are running campaigns and ask for coverage. Journalists always need stories to tell; that is what we do. Ensure that you have told your best story with your impact on your community.

Something to Think About

1. What are likely challenges a nonprofit will face as it begins using more social media tools?
2. How could donors, who are social media influencers, be identified?
3. How do the social media and crisis components of the strategic communication plan interrelate?
4. How can social media be used to strengthen a nonprofit's sustainable citizenship efforts?
5. How can communication and development personnel leverage each other's work in the social media world?

7 Creating Nonprofit Engagement

> There are three kinds of people: those who make things happen, those who watch things happen, and those who ask, "What happened?"
>
> (Casey Stengel, Baseball Hall of Fame)

Setting Context

When I have the opportunity to informally chat with nonprofit leaders, I ask, "What are the biggest challenges you face?" Of course, fundraising is mentioned. There are always more resources needed than available. But another subject is referenced consistently: engagement.

Dedicated volunteers and donors are critical to a nonprofit's existence. Without them, a not-for-profit could not accomplish many of its goals. It also is impossible to talk about these target publics without discussing the nonprofit's staff, due to the highly interactive relationship between employees and each of these other two stakeholder groups.

The quality of the staff's work determines how efficiently and effectively the operation runs. Their passion and actions serve as role models for those making contributions or giving their time to the cause. Yet, these individuals typically work for less money than those in the private sector.

So, although the nonprofit has many key audiences, this chapter's engagement discussion will focus on involvement with the three highly relevant groups of staff, volunteers, and donors.

What Does Engagement Look Like?

"Engagement" has become a hot topic in many circles. Marketers want to engage customers to instill loyalty and increase sales. Human resource professionals want engaged employees to improve retention, lower absenteeism, and maintain positive morale in the work place. Business executives want an engaged work force to deliver quality customer service and to create an organization adept in adapting to change, focused on efficiency and productivity, and capable of generating innovative solutions.

Consequently, when asked to define what "engagement" means, it can be a challenging task as it is dependent upon one's perspective. Using a dictionary may not be of significant help in this particular application. For example, *Webster's Encyclopedic Unabridged Dictionary* defines "engagement" as "employment," "an encounter," "a battle," "a pledge," "betrothal," and simply "the state of being engaged." But if the definition of the root word is examined, the meaning for the aforementioned context becomes clearer. "Engage: choosing to involve oneself in or commit oneself to something."[1]

Thus, a necessary element in the engagement process is free will. Engagement is not a program. It cannot be forced or bought. It must come from within the individual. Understanding this, it becomes clear "engagement" is personal and is exhibited in different forms, depending upon the audience or the group demonstrating the behavior. So what does engagement look like for each of a nonprofit's key target publics?

- Employees passionate about their jobs, who believe in the cause, who feel they are helping to create a better world, who find meaning in going to work every day, and who deliver their best effort—day in and day out.
- Volunteers who are enthusiastic about the organization's mission and demonstrate their excitement by willingly devoting time and energy toward helping the nonprofit reach its goals, who want to be known for their affiliation with the group, and who are strong advocates who speak highly of the ethics and work performed by the institution.
- Donors who believe in what the not-for-profit represents, who want to be known as supporters, and who feel this entity is worthy of their hard earned money on an ongoing basis.

If one could capture the energy represented by such behavior, a powerful image comes to mind. It indicates a type of "absorption" into the cause. The resulting psychic energy[2] becomes an incredible force, rallying strength from these organizational ambassadors who possess a laser-like focus on successfully achieving the group's prime directive.

This highly visible energy sends a positive public message. People are drawn to this momentum, since there is a natural desire to be "where the action is" or to belong to a group of "winners." So, in addition to the high degree of productivity and fundraising originating from engaged employees, volunteers, and donors, these critical audiences become a recruiting tool through their very actions.

Why Worry About Engagement?

Engaging these three powerful groups delivers highly desirable results:

- They make two-way communication a reality. Acting as a conduit, these ambassadors introduce or carry the nonprofit's key messages to others. They observe and take information back to the organization. These stakeholders are knowledgeable about issues and community concerns. They are aware of how the nonprofit is perceived and provide feedback, which permits the not-for-profit to refine its message, offer additional materials or programs, or correct misinformation.
- They adapt to change because they embrace new opportunities. Rather than negatively responding, these individuals may actually suggest change. Willing to bring in fresh ideas, they seek ways to improve what they—and others—are doing to help the nonprofit achieve its goals. Consequently, as community needs change or budget restrictions impact how the organization must operate, these engaged stakeholders are poised to assist with the required adjustments to ensure the not-for-profit can continue its good work.
- They desire to remain involved and to perform to the best of their ability on a consistent basis. This means the donor, who loses his or her job, may only have a dollar to spare and is willing to contribute it to the cause; the individual, who may not have money but has time, volunteers; and, the employee, who is off duty for the weekend, attends a new fundraiser. In all three examples, the committed individual is focused on consistently bringing what he or she can to support the good work being performed. Their caring intents are reflected in the quality of their work.
- They understand team work and encourage others to join. The field of sports is often given credit for instilling team work. However, these three groups, when fully engaged, are a powerful team as well. This group rallies to raise funds and to execute the organization's strategic plan. A synergistic advantage is produced as engaged stakeholders become fully committed on an emotional level to the organization's work or cause and are interested in success rather than personal reward.
- They are resourceful, permitting the nonprofit to overcome obstacles. Intensity, purpose, urgency, and conviction are evident in their actions. Need more volunteers? They will find them. Need more funding? They will dig deeper into their pockets or find others willing to contribute through a fundraiser. The "can do" attitude of these stakeholders helps the nonprofit reach seemingly impossible goals.
- They are confident in and feel connected to the organization. Their aspirations are aligned with the nonprofit's prime directive. These people are interested in areas beyond the immediate scope of their involvement and ask questions. Ultimately, this broader interest leads to further engagement in other aspects of the organization. For example, a donor may decide to volunteer time as well as give money. An existing volunteer may want to take on the added responsibility of a committee chair or board seat.

Why Disengagement Hurts

By understanding what engagement can do, it's obvious why disengagement hurts. Having a donor, employee, or volunteer "in name only" results in a copious number of missed opportunities. The disgruntled employee or volunteer who speaks poorly of the organization tarnishes the nonprofit's good name. Donors who pledge but "forget" to provide the promised monetary support means loss of funding. The list of examples could continue; all lack positive outcomes.

Unfortunately, disengagement is common. According to global findings released by Blessing White in January 2011, fewer than 1 in 3 (31 percent) of employees are engaged in their workplaces. On average, 17 percent are disengaged.[3]

Although the Blessing White statistics vary some by geographic location, one can view the workplace disengagement figures as an opportunity for the not-for-profit. Why? Because if individuals feel stifled in their jobs, they may seek to use their talents elsewhere.

Sometimes, an individual will change jobs in the hopes of finding a "more meaningful career" where it's possible to "make a difference." Thus, the nonprofit may be able to recruit a highly talented individual who is willing to take a pay cut in order to feel valued or to support a cause. But, this is not always possible. Perhaps, the healthcare benefits at the current employer exceed what the person can access at the not-for-profit. Or, they may want to leave but are too near retirement. In these situations, people may remain with present employers but seek outside opportunities offering a positive feeling, mental stimulations, and training. If a nonprofit can provide this, it can attract and turn disengaged employees into engaged volunteers.

Therefore, disengagement elsewhere can create a positive recruiting environment for the nonprofit. However, the nonprofit itself can suffer from employee disengagement.

As an employer, the not-for-profit should look closely at its staff. Are employees challenged? Are the attributes of an engaged workforce apparent in performance? Do those on the payroll proactively present themselves as brand ambassadors? Or, do they simply appear to be coming to work to pick up their pay checks? Productivity and brand image are influenced by an employee's engagement level, so closely monitoring the culture is important.

There's also an old adage that one bad apple can spoil the bunch. Nothing could be truer when it comes to engagement. Those who are engaged can become irritated—and even frustrated—with those who are disengaged. This impacts the ecosystem in which both employees and volunteers work. For example, the dedicated employee sees others not doing their jobs. Yet, these unengaged individuals receive paychecks and appear to face no repercussions.

Similarly, a dedicated volunteer may witness employees not applying themselves. Meanwhile, the volunteer is picking up some of the staff work. The upset volunteer becomes distressed. A negative opinion is formed about the employee, the organization's ability to manage personnel, and the effectiveness with which the organization operates.

Or, the dedicated helper may see other volunteers who receive the same degree of recognition but who do very little to help the organization reach its goal or even undermine progress. This volunteer may wonder why the other person is receiving significant rewards or accolades.

In these scenarios, it's possible the devoted and enthusiastic employee or volunteer will experience a change in attitude, possibly becoming disengaged. Of course, the individual could sustain his or her high level of engagement. However, the person also could withdraw, leading to a performance equal to the disengaged employee or volunteer or quitting and moving to an organization where he or she finds an environment reflecting the type of passion and work ethic with which there is a comfort level. When this occurs, the high performer is lost.

A similar parallel can be found in donor activity. When a person signs a pledge card, commits to a donation over the phone, or promises a contribution to a capital campaign, the nonprofit counts on this funding. However, the money may never materialize, if the donor isn't committed.

For example, a fundraising auction may be used at an annual black tie dinner. Attendees bid up prices. At the end of the event, everyone pays. What happens when the person, craving public attention, outbids others during an auction, leaves early, and then never "buys" the item—or takes the item but pays for it with a check from an account with insufficient funds? It happens. And, how the nonprofit manages the collection of these funds is important to the outcome of the fundraiser and the nonprofit's reputation.

The root cause of this behavior may not be easy to diagnose. It's feasible the person's financial situation could have changed suddenly. But more likely, disengagement is present. This status occurred and could have done so for any number of reasons. The lack of desire to take a promised action could result from the individual not feeling that his or her needs are met. Maybe, the nonprofit's decisions affected the employee, volunteer, or donor's opinion and created a desire to disconnect from the organization. Or, news, damaging to the not-for-profit's reputation, emerged.

The charity or agency may—or may not—be able to solve the enigma surrounding the disengagement, much less re-engage the person. But, the result is the same. The disengaged behavior harms the nonprofit financially and causes extra work for staff and volunteers.

Burnout is sometimes mistaken for disengagement. The conditions of burnout are similar to those of disengagement:

- A lack of vigor or energy; exhaustion on an interpersonal, cognitive, or physical or combination of these elements;
- A sense of detachment; of distancing oneself from the work or the cause; and
- A loss of positive self-worth, self-efficacy; profoundly affecting how one feels about oneself.[4]

It's easy to understand how an employee might experience burnout, but what about volunteers or donors? Can burnout occur there, leading to the loss of engagement and the many benefits it provides for the nonprofit? Absolutely.

Just because a volunteer or donor can be counted upon to "never say no," it does not mean the person should always be asked. When the same individual is asked repeatedly to chair a major fundraiser or to be the lead donor, there is incredible pressure. If requested to "do even better this year," the stakes may rise beyond what a committee chair can imaginatively and effectively create or a donor is capable of giving. Always fulfilling the same role may not provide the necessary change of pace or interesting challenge that leads to continued inspiration, motivation, and engagement. It's conceivable a repetitive role also could become nothing more than an exhausting chore. The result is less verve, excitement, and passion for participation, much less a successful outcome.

In pushing a volunteer or donor to the point of burnout, there is another extremely negative byproduct: reputational damage. The nonprofit can gain a reputation for "working people to death." People become afraid of or timid about taking on a committee chair, lead donor, or board president role because they have witnessed what they perceive to be an abusive situation in which the organization takes advantage of individuals.

Or, the nonprofit's actions could be perceived as demonstrating favoritism or bias. By repeatedly relying on the same individuals for what may be seen as key leadership or select roles, those who consider themselves to be "outside of the clique" decide they will never be selected. Consequently, they never volunteer. They withdraw. Once again, the organization's image is impacted because of its lack of diversity and perceived closed environment.

Retention Implications

Many benefits of engagement have already been mentioned. However, it is worthwhile to pursue an in-depth discussion on how engagement impacts retention on multiple-levels and effectively permeates an organization's culture and operation. Perhaps, this concept can be seen most easily by examining a case in point.

When staff members become long-time employees, the nonprofit saves money because it doesn't need to invest in expensive recruiting and training costs. So, retention has a very real—and potentially significant—impact on a nonprofit's budget.

When employees leave, others must pick up the work load. If there is a budget shortfall, the nonprofit may opt to delay hiring to save on the salary expense line. Or if the job market is tight, it may be very difficult to locate an individual who has both the skill set and the personal attributes beneficial to the organization. Either of these scenarios can cause a lengthy replacement process.

During this time, existing staff can grow weary—especially if the economy or other factors have created a highly stressful environment. In turn, this can create a spiral effect in which morale issues materialize.

If the remaining employees are not fully engaged in their work, a further downward trend can occur because disengagement could surface through negative behaviors appearing in the existing employee base. These individuals could demonstrate their displeasure for the requirement of assuming additional tasks. At this point, the negative or uncaring attitude becomes public through a worker's interactions with key stakeholders, family members, friends, and professional contacts.

Of course, there is the possibility the existing staff can't keep up with the work, so the nonprofit loses funding opportunities or experiences a reduction in contributions or volunteers.

One must not forget the original disengaged or displeased employee who has left and continues to speak negatively about the organization. This can potentially damage the organization's reputation in a broader sense.

If you map the relational possibilities that could be linked to one disengaged employee, the endless possibilities can be visualized (see Figure 7.1).

Highly engaged volunteers, who donate time and talent to accomplish tasks for which the nonprofit would otherwise pay, are an incredible asset. These individuals do administrative work or event planning, provide strategic planning guidance or network contacts, or help with fundraising or policy writing. Retaining this talent and dedication is critical to keeping the nonprofit operating at a high degree of effectiveness with minimal budget.

The volunteer looking for "name only" involvement will not sufficiently engage to his or her full potential. Remembering "full" engagement must occur "of free will," the effectiveness of guilt, fear, or other negative motivational techniques is reduced or possibly even not effective at all. In this situation, the nonprofit must determine if more information, greater opportunity for visibility, or other positive possibilities could inspire this individual to become more involved. If not—or if the time isn't right for the nonprofit to invest heavily in the person—then the organization must determine to what degree it does want to invest in the volunteer.

Because of an individual's talent, contacts, or resources (leading to potential monetary contributions or in-kind donations), a nonprofit may

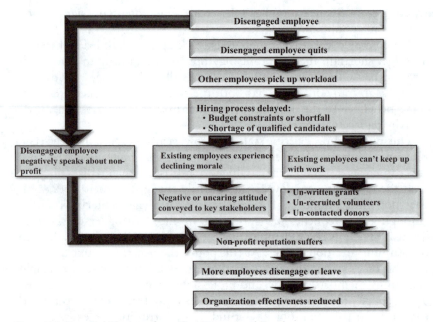

Figure 7.1 Potential Damage from One Disengaged Employee.

determine someone would be perfect to move into a board position, to assume a committee chair role, or to enter into the succession planning line for an officer position.

Remembering engagement cannot be forced and the high level of productivity produced by a fully engaged volunteer, the nonprofit's recruitment and orientation methodology must be skillfully managed to maximize this engagement (see Table 7.1).

In Chapter 2, the importance of leveraging demographic and psychographic insights in the communication process was explained. The application can be seen in the engagement-creation process.

What could motivate this potentially high-performing volunteer? Turning to Maslow's Hierarchy of Needs, it's likely this candidate has his or her basic needs met on the physiological, safety, and love levels (see Figure 7.2). But, there must be a compelling reason to motivate this individual to move from slacktivist status to full engagement.

Using the aforementioned example, is the nonprofit's brand sufficiently impressive to motivate the person to become a leader in the organization? Is the organization's reputation untarnished, so the person is proud to be affiliated with the group? Could the role of president appeal to the individual's ego or serve as a resume builder? Would the position—despite the required time—enhance the individual's visibility in the community? Does the mission of the nonprofit align with the individual's passion or concern, such as mirroring a personal or family healthcare issue, to produce an emotional link with the organization?

Table 7.1 Volunteer Management Readiness Questionnaire

Volunteers are critical to a nonprofit's success. Their passion and dedication combined with their skills, knowledge, and resources make them an invaluable asset. But to maximize the effective use of this talent pool, a nonprofit must be prepared to strategically utilize these individuals. The following list represents some of the necessary considerations for effective use of a volunteer base.

- Has the nonprofit developed an effective means to identify and recruit volunteers?
- Is volunteer orientation in place?
- Has the organization developed practices that will help to motivate volunteers on an ongoing basis?
- Does the nonprofit have a recognition protocol in place that ensures volunteers are thanked for their efforts?
- Has the organization assessed which volunteer functions are needed and the job description prepared?
- Although all staff members are "responsible" for volunteers, is there a coordinator in the organization? Are the duties assigned to this role clear?
- If there is not a volunteer coordinator on staff, is there a separate volunteer organization affiliated with the nonprofit to ensure proper coordination and management of volunteer work?
- Is there duty-specific volunteer training or instruction provided?
- Does the nonprofit have clearly established procedures and documentation for volunteers, which will serve both as instruction for the participant and help to minimize any risk for the nonprofit?
- Are guidelines in place for managing inappropriate or problematic volunteer behavior?
- Are volunteers aware of their brand ambassador role in addition to any duties or expectations affiliated with the specific volunteer duty?

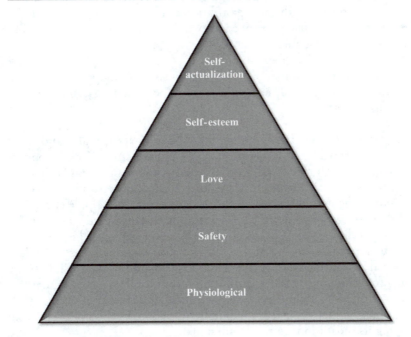

Figure 7.2 Maslow's Hierarchy of Needs.

Remember, one or all of the three appeals (ethos, logos, pathos) may need to be infused into the communication process. The nonprofit must be strategic in creating an environment that feels personal and engenders a feeling of "belonging with benefits" to motivate individuals. If this can be achieved, the organization increases the likelihood of engaging volunteers over a long period of time, maximizing the individual's degree of involvement, and producing long-lasting benefits for the nonprofit.

While it is essential to add to the donor base, it is equally important to retain long-time, faithful donors. These individuals can be counted upon to continue to support the organization during tough times. Because their degree of loyalty has continued to build through the years, they have gained both an affinity for the nonprofit as well as a better understanding as to the good work performed. This goodwill is demonstrated when the donor continues contributions, even during a reputational crisis or severely depressed economic times.

When discussing the benefits of employee, volunteer, and donor retention, it is necessary to acknowledge there may be a time when the nonprofit must discontinue a relationship. Any number of reasons could necessitate the severance of the association:

- A donor is shown to be unethically leveraging its relationship with the nonprofit to make money from services or goods sold to the nonprofit.
- A major donor is conducting business that either undermines or is in direct conflict with the organization's mission.
- A volunteer is using connections with the nonprofit to make money in an unethical manner.
- An employee is embezzling money.
- A volunteer or employee is sexually harassing or inappropriately taking advantage of other employees or the beneficiaries of the nonprofit's services.

In such instances, the nonprofit must investigate the allegation and then move swiftly and professionally to pursue the most appropriate course of action. It should be noted—whether the nonprofit is "firing" an employee, board of director member, or volunteer or refusing to accept a donation—the manner in which this is done produces a ripple effect.

The person with whom the relationship is being severed was an advocate. Regardless of what has occurred, the nonprofit must be concerned about its reputation and what this individual says about the organization. Others are watching the management of this relational break. Is it being done professionally? Is the organization refraining from making derogatory comments? Is the break following organizational procedures? If sexual misconduct occurred, potentially what caused the nonprofit from delaying its separation from the individual?

"Letting go" of an engaged individual is a delicate matter with potential repercussions on the organization's reputation. And, since many are watching—including the media—the discontinuation of the relationship must be conducted timely, appropriately, and respectfully, with the utmost civility.

But, what if this fully engaged individual wasn't simply a leader, but an icon within the ranks of the nonprofit? Whether the executive director, the board president, the clinic's doctor, or primary sponsor, the "removal" of such a figure head impacts those employees, volunteers, and donors still associated with the nonprofit. In addition to observing how the break is handled, there is a risk of losing these engaged stakeholders or, at the very least, disenchanting them. Proactive measures and authentic communication must be employed in a retention strategy to try to avoid this occurrence (see Figure 7.3).

Audience Segmentation

Thus far, the concept of engagement has been applied across three critical stakeholder bases because of their importance to the nonprofit. Although the principles of engagement can be applied generally, it is equally as

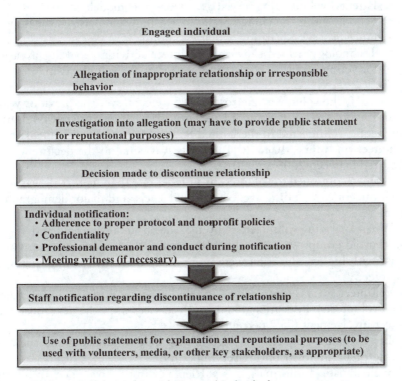

Figure 7.3 Severing Relationship with Engaged Individual.

important to segment these audiences to better understand the nuances of engagement in relation to each particular group. In addition, it's critical to account for the segmentation within categories.

The importance of employee engagement is mentioned frequently throughout this chapter. Therefore, a brief break-out discussion follows on volunteers and donors. Examples of further segmentation, including board of directors, generational considerations, and gender differences, will be included to illustrate salient points.

Volunteers

In 2010, Americans devoted 8.1 billion hours to volunteering. Generation X, also referred to as Gen X, volunteered more time to service than this age group ever did before. Over the previous year, these individuals donated 2.3 billion hours of time. This is not surprising as parents, who have children under 18, volunteer at a higher level than the rate for persons without children.

Teen volunteerism between 2002 and 2010 was higher than in earlier years. It is likely an increase in this rate was seen because:

- Parental volunteering served as a strong role model;
- Schools across the United States increasingly emphasized the importance of service-learning activities; and/or
- Technology helped showcase volunteer activities, making it easier for young people to access information about volunteerism.[5]

In 2011, the volunteer rate rose by 0.5 percent over the previous year, according to the U.S. Bureau of Labor Statistics. Approximately 64.3 million people volunteered in the United States. Interestingly, the increase in volunteerism from 2010 to 2011 actually was equal to the decline which occurred between 2009 and 2010.

Women continued to volunteer at a higher rate than men. This was true in all categories including age, educational levels, and major demographic characteristics.

When analyzing volunteerism by age, the 35- to 44-year old and 45- to 54-year-old groups were most likely to engage. And, married persons and those with higher education were more likely than their counterparts to volunteer.

Volunteerism was most evident in religious organizations (33.2 percent of all volunteers). Educational and youth services drew the next most volunteer involvement (25.7 percent).

The two most frequent volunteer duties were fundraising and the collecting/preparing/distributing/serving of food.[6]

Such statistical information is particularly impressive when an hourly wage is attached to the work performed by these individuals. While this dollar amount varies from state to state, the hourly rate for volunteer time ranges from $33.61 in Washington, D.C., to $11.41 in Puerto Rico.[7]

Understanding the monetary worth of volunteerism, which groups are most likely to become involved, and the demographic and psychographic profile of key volunteer categories influences a nonprofit's recruiting and retention efforts. And for visionary nonprofits, which understand the necessity of keeping the pipeline of volunteers flowing, the information is helpful in long-term strategic planning. These organizations realize Millennials represent an important volunteer base, which must be cultivated to ensure future support.

Establishing relationships with Millennials is becoming an increasingly vital task. This age group wants to connect online with nonprofit through web sites, emails, social media, and smart phones. And, they feel underutilized by nonprofits. They want options when it comes to volunteering time.[8] They are very interested in sharing their experience and skills with a cause. They also want more opportunities to lead on boards and committees.[9]

Understanding both the psychographics and demographics of Millennials and developing a plan to recruit and retain volunteers from this emerging and highly connected generation will be critical to the long-term success of the nonprofit.

But the Internet's influence on volunteerism goes beyond providing a strong connection with Millennials. Virtual volunteerism is a growing trend. For those eager to volunteer but unwilling or unable to work on site, this form of volunteerism can be harnessed to design and update web sites, write e-newsletters or ezines; conduct Internet-based research; prepare reports or white papers; develop advocacy materials; create surveys; or even teach online classes.

And, it's not just Millennials who find this form of volunteering to be ideal. An elderly person, a stay-at-home caretaker, or someone immobile due to a disability might be restricted from volunteer opportunities otherwise. This non-traditional approach also can be perfect for the busy person who cannot commit to a specific location or time for a volunteer activity.[10]

When it comes to Baby Boomer volunteerism, the more flexible the opportunity, the greater the chance the nonprofit will be able to locate and engage a qualified volunteer in this age group.[11] Given their age and experience, volunteers in this category want support, not supervision. Because these individuals view their volunteer efforts in a more collegial manner, they typically like to partner with the not-for-profit, reaching an agreement on accountability, communication, project or initiative outcomes, and even timelines. Consequently, customizing a volunteer plan can be an extremely effective tool to cultivate a deeper and more sustainable degree of volunteer engagement with this age category.[12]

Donors

When it comes to wealthy households, women play a major role in determining which charitable organization will be supported. According to the 2011 *Study of High Net Worth Women's Philanthropy*,[13] women create and control a growing share of wealth in the United States, and they are using their influence in philanthropy.

Results showed women spend more time on due diligence when making charitable decisions than their male counterparts. Consequently, they place greater importance on effectiveness and efficiency and look for opportunities where their donations can make an impact. They also seek a deeper level of engagement and prefer more communication.[14] In fact, wealthy women (82 percent) said a nonprofit's ability to communicate plays an integral role in the gift-giving process.[15]

When it comes to Millennials, a multi-channel approach, particularly relying on the technology of email, mobile, and social media, should be used. Because these individuals want to know the impact of their gift, sending solicitations too frequently without any other communication is not well received. Since this age group has grown up in a world of instant communication, consistently reposting the same messages on Facebook and Twitter are unwelcomed forms of messaging.

Due to their reliance on the Internet, long letters sent via mail, with a request for checks and the need for stamps to return donations, are not preferred. Mail actually ranks third in terms of gift-giving solicitation preference (34 percent). Seventy percent of the *Millennial Impact Report* survey respondents preferred to donate online.[16]

The board of directors represents another important subset of the donor group. It is critical all board members participate in annual gift giving as they must serve as role models for other donors.

In striving for board diversity, varying degrees of financial status may be present in this particular donor base. But regardless of the dollar amount a board member is able to contribute, it is essential to achieve 100 percent board participation. After all, if those who accepted the role of a board member don't feel compelled to provide financial support for the cause, others notice. And right or wrong, the perception can be that the board member accepted the duty for its prestige or other self-serving purpose but is not invested fully in the nonprofit's work; equally as bad, would be the public perception that an organizational leader does not fully support the nonprofit's mission.

Capitalizing on the existing donor base as well as initiating the relationship building process to engage new donors will keep funds coming into the nonprofit. Stories as to why people continue to give, reporting statistics about the number of people who are long-time supporters, or featuring an individual who has included the nonprofit in his or her will can create interest, demonstrate the organization is considered "worthy" of ongoing financial support and can motivate others to give or to increase their monetary support. Thus, engaged individuals are valuable to the fundraising effort because of their financial support, ability to role model, and ethos.

Sustaining Engagement

Engagement occurs on an individual level, and some people are more inclined to engage with a nonprofit than others. But if the nonprofit intends to chart the degree of engagement it wants from employees, volunteers, and donors, it is essential a culture is created for engagement to thrive. By executing a proactive engagement strategy, it is feasible to instill a desire for involvement and a yearning to maintain participation that far exceeds a temporary condition. Thus, by developing and maintaining an environment in which individuals "crave membership," it is possible to sustain a high degree of engagement with employees, volunteers, and donors.

Paul Marciano introduced what he calls the Principles of RESPECT to the discussion of employee engagement. He cites seven critical drivers: Recognition, Empowerment, Supportive Feedback, Partnering, Expectations, Consideration, and Trust.[17] But, this approach is applicable to and can help maximize engagement in volunteers and donors as well as employees.

Volunteers and donors will feel more engaged if they believe they are relevant partners in achieving the nonprofit's mission and appreciate the courtesy and consideration of being recognized for their contributions. They want to be aligned with an organization they trust to "do the right thing." They want feedback in regards to how the organization is progressing through the assistance they and others are providing.

What strategic communication elements help to inspire a desire to become engaged?

Transparency and Trust

Being open and honest is essential to establishing a trusting relationship, which is foundational in the engagement process. People want to know, even if difficult to materially confirm, the organization will protect them and work in their favor.[18] In the case of a nonprofit, transparent communication conveys a sense of honesty and integrity. It represents professional conduct and ethical behavior. It creates an atmosphere, which inspires employees, donors, and volunteers to give freely of their time, talent, and resources because they know the not-for-profit will "do the right thing." Whereas, hidden information or exemplifying covert behavior instills a feeling of mistrust.

Establish and Emphasize High Standards

This doesn't mean goals or standards are set so high as to be unattainable. Goals should be developed to accentuate quality and to give the individual something for which to strive. From an employee to volunteer's perspective, the opportunity to gain a new skill, to try something different, or to learn something can be motivating.

If people believe they are assigned tasks consistently beneath their capabilities and there appears to be no way to improve or grow, personal pride suffers and ultimately is reflected in the work output. Productivity wanes and performance becomes inferior on even small or simple chores. Thus, offering opportunities keep the job or the assignment exciting and interesting for the employee or the volunteer.

Unfortunately, it may not be possible to always offer such a position. Tasks can become mundane or boring. Sometimes, unpleasant duties are involved. Fortunately, most people understand every job or volunteer opportunity will not be "glorious" in nature. Nevertheless, a quality performance must be emphasized, no matter how small the task. If the volunteer or employee is engaged, he or she trusts the organization, believes proper consideration will be given when better opportunities materialize, and understands the link between the simple task and strategic organizational goals.

Respect and Recognize

The value an organization places on employees, volunteers, and donors, as evident through respect and recognition, produces two highly visible results.

First, when people feel respected and acknowledged for their contributions, a strong emotional link is developed with the nonprofit. Whenever possible, a personal thank you should be issued. This customized communication heightens the emotional connection and may be prized by the recipient. Whether there's a "thank you" penned at the bottom of a computer-generated letter, an acknowledgement in a newsletter, personal praise delivered during a meeting, or a phone call from a committee chair, this recognition goes a long way. After all, it is a human tendency to desire to be appreciated.

But recognition need not only occur on an individual level to resonate. Recognition of a group effort generates pride as well. It is important, as mentioned earlier, to be part of a winning team, and therefore it is wise to celebrate success on this level, too. For example, reaching a major fundraising goal is important for the organization. But, donors need recognition for their contributions; volunteers must be acknowledged for their part in the fundraising activity; and staff should be thanked for the hard work to conduct the event.

In Marciano's model, he talks about "consideration," explaining how it goes beyond a thank you. Clearly, consideration is linked to respect. For example, in today's time-crunched society, employees and volunteers appreciate their time being respected. Consequently, he cites tactics, such as conducting on-time and efficient meetings,[19] as representative of thoughtful behavior. Such small acts can lead to an individual's willingness to engage to a greater degree because people do not enjoy being taken for granted.

The second benefit to displaying proper appreciation for services, dedication, and contributions is indirectly related to engagement: reputational enhancement. A nonprofit, which understands the value of each contribution as well as the synergistic achievement of teams, will be inclined to demonstrate consideration and to recognize selfless efforts naturally and genuinely. Such conduct serves as a "commercial" and can draw a diverse group of people who have talent, money, a strong work ethic, and unique skill sets they want to invest because of the appreciative behavior.

Paint the Big Picture

Whether working with employees, volunteers, or donors, it is essential to share the nonprofit's vision. If these key stakeholders don't know where the organization is heading or if they don't know what the goal is, there is no sense of purpose, no urgency, no challenge, and no focus.

In *Louder than Words*, Bob Kelleher explains it is difficult to expect anyone to invest more than a minimal amount of energy toward achieving a goal or executing a strategy, if an organization has neglected to articulate a clear vision or the future.[20]

Chris Gay, owner of Bridge Consulting, often speaks of the necessity of adding context to this description. She believes it's important for stakeholders to understand the reason behind the strategy, as this can lead to a shared understanding of the organization's mission and improve one's knowledge of the overarching strategy. With this better grasp of the nonprofit's work, an engaged employee, volunteer, or donor can fulfill the role of brand ambassador by effectively communicating the not-for-profit's "elevator speech."

Connect the Dots

Creating line of sight for employees, volunteers, and donors is an essential component of engagement. If members of these target groups can see their role clearly and understand how it connects to the overarching strategy, these individuals are more likely to engage and to do so to a greater degree than if this linkage is unclear.

Line of sight produces two beneficial outcomes. First, people who understand their roles in relation to the overarching strategy are more likely to be progressive and initiate actions advantageous to the organization, rather than feeling intimidated or un-empowered. Also, the understanding of the interrelatedness of the work contributes to the knowledge base of these individuals, making them feel more self-assured, willing to ask questions, offering feedback, and openly sharing information.[21] This communicative behavior can contribute to organizational improvements.

When it is understood how individual contributions link to the bigger picture, the individual also comprehends the synergistic effect produced through his or her unique contributions.

But "connecting the dots" should not simply be a PowerPoint presentation or a verbal description during a meeting. This technique will be more effective if these persons are apprised of the desired behavior and offered experiential opportunities to see the manifestation of their involvement.

What's in It for Me?

When discussing not-for-profits, it would be nice to think everyone is motivated to help make this world a better place and to improve the quality of life on this planet. Unfortunately, this is not always the case. For some, there must be personal benefit beyond lofty ideals. And even though personal recognition may be provided, it still may not be enough to engender engagement. Consequently, the nonprofit must identify other strategies, which elicit a desire in the individual to engage.

Chapter 2 emphasized the importance of knowing one's audience to ensure communication customization. And in the introduction, Shelia Brown, FRSM, OBE, discussed the necessity of personalizing nonprofit communication and marketing efforts.

In many ways, addressing needs on a personal level may be the single most important tool the nonprofit can use to engage some individuals. Depending upon the stakeholder, one or all of these communication-linked strategies could act as motivational engagement drivers:

- training or skill-building activities;
- experience working with diverse constituencies;
- committee leadership opportunities;
- intellectual challenges;
- emotional connections because of personal passions;
- involvement in decision-making or other participatory exercises where opinions can be expressed and suggestions offered;
- visibility in the community and/or media;
- a sense of personal power;
- opportunities to work with leaders within the community;
- strategic board experience; and
- networking and/or new contacts.

Communication

The quantity and quality of communication and interaction opportunities an organization provides is shown repeatedly to impact the degree of engagement. Research demonstrates effective and relevant communication positively impacts engagement on multiple levels.

A 2008–2009 employee study analyzed the impact of effective communication on motivation in a business setting. Ouch Point's survey, from Opinion Research Corporation, showed a clear correlation between the positive perception of an organization's internal communication and worker's advocacy of the brand. Messaging particularly appreciated by the work force included:

- thorough explanations of actions taken and the reasons behind the action;
- being updated and the logic behind the decisions;
- early notification of difficult decisions;
- honest and open communication; and
- frequent and routine updates.[22]

A 2011 *Employee Job Satisfaction and Engagement Survey* of U.S. employees conducted by the Society for Human Resource Management (SHRM) pointed to the importance of communication as well. From 2002 to 2011, communication between employees and senior management proved to be an important condition for engagement.[23]

And, an Accountemps poll, which examined the correlation between employee morale and communication, reported senior executives identifying a lack of open and honest communication as having the most negative affect on employee morale and citing better communication as the best remedy for low morale.[24]

Watson Wyatt's employee engagement research showed when individual motivation and an understanding of what is required to achieve organizational goal are combined, engagement occurs.[25]

Traditional Communication & Social Media

With an overwhelming degree of research pointing to the significant role communication plays in the employee engagement process, it is obvious why offering meaningful content in multiple formats that publicize the nonprofit's primary goals, explain the strategic plan, and are transparent and easy-to-understand is essential to engage employees, volunteers, and donors.

According to *Dynamics of Cause Engagement*, Americans continue to rely on traditional communication as their primary information sources in cause-related matters. However, the majority realize the value of social media in facilitating both visibility and support for causes. Nearly six out of every ten Americans agree online social networking permits them to more easily support a cause and 40 percent view social networking sites as important to building awareness.[26]

Because Chapter 2 delves into how to create a strategic communication plan that leverages both social and traditional media formats, further elaboration on tactical selection and methodology will not be addressed. But given the role relationships play in securing and developing engagement, a brief discussion on the use of communication champions in this process follows.

Communication Champions

The communication champion, who also could serve as a mentor, may be a volunteer chair, a long-time board member, or a member of the nonprofit's IT department. The individual's title is not as important to the engagement communication process as the function being served by this champion. In fact, titles may be irrelevant. These individuals are valued for their roles as trusted opinion leaders, rather than the amount of money they give, the role they play, or the job they have.

Some individuals naturally fill this role. Even then, the best outcomes occur when the nonprofit strategically selects key individuals and provides proper training. Instruction should include both an explanation of expectations for this special brand ambassador role as well as a description of the tools available to assist in this endeavor.

Communication champions are specifically recruited with the understanding they will transmit the organization's key messages throughout their network. They should feel empowered to make recommendations to assist the nonprofit in reaching its strategic goals. Acting as allies, these select individuals could assume public leadership positions but are equally committed to working behind the scenes.

For example, rather than the organization initiating a highly visible letter writing campaign to elected officials for funding or legislative purposes, the communication champion may lead a grass roots campaign—both as a supporter of the nonprofit and as a concerned citizen. By changing the lead on this campaign, the communication effort can be positioned very differently.

Communication champions help publicize the nonprofit's needs and successes. These leaders are provided with salient informational points—either formally or informally—and encouraged to cascade the message to others. Whether a manager within the infrastructure, a volunteer committee chair, or a lead donor, these individuals complement the flow of information originating from the not-for-profit.

Because these ambassadors have a natural passion for the organization, it is best to positively direct their desire and energy. If trying to drive traffic to the web site or if nearing the culmination of a fundraising campaign, alerting these individuals to the specific tasks that would help the organization achieve its goals will positively leverage their energy. In fact, the more these communication champions understand the strategy and goals, the better spokespersons they become.

Storytelling

When selecting communication champions, those who benefit from the nonprofit's work should not be overlooked. These individuals can help tell the story by bringing a number or statistical data to life.

While this creates an emotional connection, the storytelling technique will be more successful if ethos and logos are included in the presentation.

Sharing a story about a scholarship recipient who couldn't afford college and now has become a doctor or explaining how a single mother has received training and now is employed full-time may serve as proof the nonprofit's mission is being accomplished. Or, showing an endangered leopard being rescued from a trap, nursed back to health, and re-integrated into the wild may illustrate how the organization is helping to save the species—one animal at a time.

When a highly visible person speaks of disease research or treatment received through a particular charity, that individual describes a personal story, which can increase positive exposure and may be perceived to be of great importance because of the individual's credibility. The desire to be associated in some way with the well-known individual can inspire a person to volunteer or to give money to the charity. Thus, the individual feels an allegiance with not-for-profit similar to what he or she believes the prominent person feels. Plus, if the personality possesses a high degree of trustworthiness, the potential donor or volunteer may assume the person has conducted proper due diligence on the organization and presumes the selection to be worthwhile.

Although celebrity endorsements gain attention for a cause and offer a third-party endorsement, there are pitfalls with depending too heavily on a single public figure or superstar. Caution must be used in this selection process as the nonprofit must weigh the potential risk involved should the individual experience reputational damage, particularly in relation to the cause. For example, a nonprofit focused on women's rights could find itself in a difficult situation if the celebrated spokesperson made media headlines for womanizing or spousal abuse.

Thought-provoking, too, is the *Dynamics for a Cause* research which showed personal relevance overrides testimonials from famous people, when it comes to motivating participation in or engaging in a cause.[27]

Communication champions, such as staff, board, and volunteers, should be able to share these stories in a genuine and compelling manner. Todd Cohen, veteran reporter and editor of *Philanthropy North Carolina*, emphasizes these important stories should be told as clearly, as often, and as broadly as possible[28] because storytelling can generate media coverage, motivate people to contribute time or money, and enhance the public's understanding about the situation.

But despite the incredible value storytelling brings to the nonprofit's communication efforts, it must be remembered this is only one tool out of the many available. Too heavy of a reliance on storytelling, without use of logic or void of other communication strategies and techniques, can lose some of its effectiveness. Too many heart-wrenching stories could cause emotional withdrawal because donors and volunteers feel overwhelmed.

Another form of storytelling, which can aid the understanding of complex concepts, is visualization. This technique can be used by a communication champion to help communicate the strategy, outline goals, or share success. In his book, *The Art of Engagement*, Jim Haudan explains visualizations can capture drama or illustrate risks, threats, or opportunities in a manner that aids the understanding of a complex concept. These mental pictures act as a common language, which minimizes the possibility for misinterpretation. And, visual storytelling can be recalled quickly as mental images can be efficiently retained by most people. In fact, this approach appeals to most learners because it helps them connect the dots, applying a complex concept to a very specific scenario.[29]

Consequently, both styles of storytelling are particularly effective communication techniques in nonprofit communication.

The Value-Add Equation of Engagement

Creating a culture of engagement is not achieved easily or quickly. It takes significant effort and time. So, is it worth the investment? Yes. The nonprofit must think of employees, volunteers, and donors as powerful components within the marketing plan.

A nonprofit does not have a huge promotional budget. It cannot run numerous television commercials during prime time. It can't buy several two-page spreads in magazines or tie up radio waves with countless advertisements. But through the effort of these key stakeholder groups, it can communicate its mission, share news about the good work it does, build its brand, and grow a positive reputation in the huge and highly competitive nonprofit market place. The actions and words of these stakeholders serve as a nonstop, advertising campaign, increasing a not-for-profit's visibility and enhancing its credibility.

In fact, when this positive energy is harnessed and admirable qualities actively displayed through engaged behaviors, a nonprofit has an incredible talent pool and seemingly unlimited resources available. The outcome from leveraging this dynamism goes far beyond the act of merely writing a check or simply showing up to work on time.

Highly engaged employees, volunteers, and donors expand the nonprofit's network. If properly organized and cultivated, these critical stakeholders have the capacity to introduce the organization to a larger but more targeted base of potential volunteers and more qualified donor leads than the nonprofit would ever be likely develop on its own. And, this can be accomplished in an economically advantageous manner, as the stakeholder groups will utilize word-of-mouth and social media to convey information.

Through testimonials, these brand ambassadors can inspire and motivate others to actively support the nonprofit using the three Aristotelian appeals and do so in an authentic and possibly even unassuming manner.

Research has shown when a peer delivers information, there is greater content believability than when an organization communicates,[30] thus establishing a positive and strong introduction to the nonprofit's message on an individual basis. Consequently, these brand spokespersons can rally others and generate results far exceeding what the nonprofit could accomplish through its own message delivery system because of the trust and influence these individuals possess within their independent networks (see Figure 7.4).

Who knew that volunteers might make
the best super information highway?

Figure 7.4 Volunteers at Work.

When it comes to transforming social norms, these engaged stakeholders can demonstrate social activism capable of changing laws, altering opinions, forcing business to change how it operates, creating awareness, and producing a public outcry, without spending significant sums of money on traditional marketing techniques.

Engagement has been shown to trigger behavioral changes in those supporting a cause. Consequently, cause engagement takes the interaction from awareness and participation to impacting personal behavior in a manner that produces even more benefits, thereby furthering the cause. Interestingly, "more than half of Americans (52 percent) affirmed to have changed their behavior as a result of their involvement with a cause."[31]

Finally, if properly cultivated and sustained, these stakeholders will engage for a lifetime as loyal advocates and brand ambassadors. Consequently, the time and effort invested in communication and engagement strategies provide an excellent return.

Thoughts on the Subject

Charlie Becker
Executive Director
Camp Courageous of Iowa, Monticello, IA

Q: Camp Courageous receives no government support and is not affiliated with organizations. Yet, the Camp has successfully raised funds and engaged volunteers at all levels. What are the key elements in your engagement strategy?

A: At Camp Courageous of Iowa, we emphasize that everyone can participate in some way. It's not just about monetary donations.

From the shut-in elderly person who makes quilts for the campers to the person who cleans to the person who saves meals-on-wheels containers to be used in arts & crafts. We recognize these efforts are a labor of love, and they allow everyone to become a part of the camp.

We have found people like the fact that the Camp has no government funding. In fact, people appreciate being able to choose to support the camp rather than having the government choose for them.

The beauty of not aligning with another organization has been twofold. Years ago when the United Way had problems at the national level, Camp Courageous was not pulled into any of the issues, since we have never been one of their agencies. This way, Camp Courageous is in charge of its own destiny because it doesn't have to worry about the possible negative reputational impact which could occur, if there are problems with the other organization.

Second, the Camp would very likely need to employ at least one additional person to manage all of the administrative work involved, when a nonprofit receives aid from the government or another agency. We are a lean operation with the specific purpose of being able to give the most to our campers, so we elect to keep our administrative support to a minimum.

If it succeeds or not, Camp Courageous is responsible for its own destiny.

It also should be noted Camp Courageous believes in setting an example, if it wants to engage everyone. Consequently, we ask everyone to help. If I don't lead by example with my time, my money, and my resources, how can I expect others to do so?

1980 was my first year at camp. A new board member was starting a perpetual fund for us. With the Camp having more liabilities than assets at that point, the board member was searching for 100 people to give $1,000 every year for five years. He told me that I had to be first. So we agreed, as soon as the Camp started paying my $17,000 per year salary, I would pledge the $1,000 per year. He helped me understand that the more I gave, the more it would come back to me, many times over.

During the early years, board members would come to the monthly meeting with money they had collected over the past month. In fact, the Camp Courageous board has always been a hard-working, grassroots board. Our 30-member board represents all walks of life, with the sole purpose of having the Camp succeed. They have been exceptional!

In recent years we have been able to engage more campers as well as their families and friends than ever before. These individuals are involved in walks and other special fund-raising events, thus playing a key role in the success of the activity.

We also give as many as a dozen programs in a week, speaking to civic groups, churches, clubs, those who stop to seep our camp … anyone who will listen. It has caused our organization to grow, now serving more than 6,000 campers with 25,000 supporters. We believe it is this grassroots approach, of sharing our story with regular folks who then fall in love with and commit to our purpose and mission, is the biggest ingredient to our success.

And, we constantly thank volunteers for their help through personal notes, telephone calls and awards. But for many volunteers, they just love what Camp Courageous is all about and are delighted to know a friend or relative who has benefitted from what we do. Or, our supporters feel very rewarded hearing comments from our campers' families who say that coming to Camp Courageous is the highlight of their son or daughter's year.

The moral of the story is: Engagement comes when people witness others demonstrating exceptional dedication and a true love for the mission of an organization. The actions of our volunteers serve as an example to and inspire others.

Michelle Nunn
Chief Executive Officer
Points of Light, Atlanta, GA

Q: The Points of Light Hands On Network is the largest volunteer network in the nation and delivers more than 30 million hours of volunteer service. What do you see as the key to activating volunteers?

A: Points of Light believes that all real change is powered by people. When you look at history, you will find that nearly every great advance was driven by individual people coming together to work for a common cause they believed in. The abolitionist movement, women's suffrage, environmental protection, and the civil rights movement have all been powered by ordinary people working to create change. The enduring heroes of our nation have been citizens who have called upon others to align our reality to our ideals—Frederick Douglas, Clara Barton, Martin Luther King, Jr., Dorothy Day.

Today, people are seeking ways to make a real impact in their communities. They want their time to be used efficiently and productively. They want to bring every dimension of their personal power to the causes they believe in. To activate these 21st century volunteers, Points of Light inspires, equips, and mobilizes people to take action by providing the tools and resources for them to use all their assets—their time, talent, voice, and money—to create change.

To harness volunteers' time, HandsOn Network offers more than 21,000 service opportunities each month through its 250 volunteer action centers that extend to 16 countries around the world. HandsOn Network leads people from impulse to action, turning their ideas for change into impactful projects, like wheelchair ramp construction, watershed protection projects, and tutoring programs. The most powerful projects are those that inspire and activate volunteers to be leaders and problem solvers on their own—creating new opportunities to bring others into service. Similarly, generationOn and AmeriCorps Alums harness the power of youth and national service alumni, respectively, to engage in a lifetime of service.

Things to remember when activating volunteers:

- Identify a real need in the community. Don't manufacture an idea for a project based on what you think a community needs. Get to know the community; talk to people; find out what assets are there and what work is already being done. Then build on that.
- Create meaningful volunteer roles. Volunteers want to know that they're contributing to something that will make a difference. Any service can be meaningful, if you help volunteers make the connection between the work and the greater impact.

- Match volunteers with service opportunities that fit their skills and interests.
- Get to know your volunteers. They will feel more invested in the work and the organization, if they know that you care about them as individuals. It will also help you understand what motivates them to serve so you can keep them energized.
- Say thank you. Recognition is one of the most vital parts of volunteer engagement. Volunteers need to know that you (and the broader community) value and appreciate them.
- Encourage volunteers to reflect on their service. Taking time to think about their service and its impact on a community is powerful and can lead to continued service and deeper civic engagement.

Something to Think About

1. What could be important links or connections that must be made for donors to help them understand why it is important to increase contributions over the previous year?
2. How can volunteer engagement best be measured in a small organization?
3. What do you think most donors want to know about an organization prior to making a contribution?
4. In-kind donations can save money for a nonprofit. What strategy could a not-for-profit employ to improve the number and quality of in-kind donations that it receives?
5. Engaged volunteers can be an invaluable asset when it comes to collecting information, such as learning about emerging critical needs in the community, hearing what the community is saying about the organization's work, and learning if other organizations are using similar fundraising techniques. What would be the best way to collect such insights?

Glossary

Avatar—This visual is used to represent the organization on social media sites. It should be a distinctive design, which can be placed into a square format. The "look and feel" should mirror the organization's brand. In fact, it can be a re-formatted version of the organization's logo.

Boiler Plate—A boiler plate is the standard closing paragraph in a news release issued by an organization. In the case of a nonprofit, the boiler plate could contain the full name of the organization, where it is located or its headquarters, a brief explanation of its cause or the work it does, and who it serves. It also can appear as the "**about us**" paragraph, which is separate from but immediately follows the news story.

Brand Equity—The strength of a brand's value, this is framed by how familiar key publics are with the name, how favorable these audiences perceive the brand, and how distinctive the brand name and image are when committed to memory.

Brand Personality—A brand personality describes a brand as if it is a person. The personality traits are distinguishing features, which help to make it unique in the marketplace.

Crowdsourcing—This approach takes a task, typically performed by one or a very few people, and distributes the work to a crowd. Rather than outsourcing to a specified group of paid employees, the assignment is out-sourced to an unidentified group via social networks in real time. Crowd-sourcing is feasible offline but typically the term is used in the social media setting.

Dark Site—A web page (or pages) developed in advance and not posted until needed. These pages can be developed for Internet or intranet sites. Typically, dark sites are used as part of the crisis preparedness process. For example, content can be prepared and the page designed, but the page may not "go live" until a crisis occurs.

Dashboard—Sometimes referred to as a scorecard, this is a system for gathering and reporting metrics on a particular initiative or project. Its design enables one to track progress through the reporting of accomplishments, statistics, and other data, which can be documented and compared to past performance in the specified areas.

De-construction—In the world of sustainability, de-construction refers to selectively dismantling building components. The purpose is to reuse and recycle as much as possible, providing a second life for items rather than automatically taking them to a landfill. This form of reclaim is very different from demolition, in which the focus is on quickly demolishing a building, treating all materials as waste, and depositing them in a landfill.

Ecosystem—The system or environment involving the interactions between a community of living organisms in a particular area and the nonliving components. Ecosystems are affected by both external and internal forces.

Ezine—This is a magazine, which is online rather than in a printed format. Some print magazine publishers now offer their magazines online. Because a digital format is used, ezines also may be referred to as "digital magazines." Typically, electronic magazines have editors or editorial boards to review submissions, monitor quality control, and ensure deadlines are met. The "ezine" term can be used with small online magazines and even larger e-newsletters.

Global Village—This term frequently is associated with Marshall McLuhan's work. As an author, he has described how the world has "shrunk," becoming more like a village because of technology. He discusses its ability to instantaneously move information globally. Common usage today suggests a new reality, with sociological structures and other cultural contexts emerging due to the enhanced speed of communication and the ability for people to connect and exchange information globally. Because these meanings are strongly linked to the World Wide Web, "Global Village" is sometimes used to describe the Internet.

Goals—Goals are the desired result, the aspirational outcome. They can be operational, reputational, or behavioral in nature.

GPS—GPS, which stands for Global Position System, is an integral part of location-based marketing. By using GPS technology on smart phones in conjunction with mobile social media applications, such as Foursquare or Facebook, a cause, product, or service can be communicated and marketed, based on the physical location of the individual.

GRI—The Global Reporting Initiative focuses on creating a sustainable global economy through sustainable reporting guidance. GRI offers a sustainability framework and guidelines that feature non-financial, integrated reporting methodology linked to corporate social responsibility (CSR) indicators. Global in nature and independent, it is a Collaborating Center of the United Nations Environment Program.

GSE—Global Social Entrepreneur, commonly known as "GSE," is a term used for an entrepreneur who acts as a change agent to improve life globally. This entrepreneur exemplifies the next level of corporate social responsibility by passionately applying a global and holistic perspective to planet stewardship. The comprehensive approach creates an impact in multiple locations and in multiple ways on a simultaneous basis.

Infographic—A visual that succinctly captures a range of information on a complex subject in an easy-to-understand manner. Consequently, a story is told or subject matter is conveyed visually, rather than through words. These graphic representations of data, knowledge, or information also can communicate concepts in a symbolic form.

In-Kind Donations—These are contributions that are made in the form of goods or services, rather than money. Donations can range from real estate and stock to building materials and school supplies. If an individual typically performs a certain task by trade and/or for money, such as plumbing, legal services, or administrative support, and offers these services to a nonprofit for free, the "in-kind" term may be applied.

IPS—This acronym stands for Internet Service Provider.

JPEG—This acronym stands for Joint Photographic Experts Group, which is the name of the committee that created this standard (as well as other standards for still photography). This deals with how an image is compressed into a stream of bytes, so the photograph can be viewed on a computer.

Key Messages—Key messages are the salient points the nonprofit wants its audiences to remember in concise and jargon-free language. Typically, an organization has three to four key messages and no more than five. In order to fully articulate the nonprofit's positioning, these key messages are backed up by supporting points or details.

Landing Page—This is a single web page that appears after clicking on a link. The page is used to prompt a particular action or result. In online marketing vernacular, this also is known as a lead capture page. In this case, the page appears after clicking on an advertisement. Marketing landing pages tend to be transactional in nature. However, landing pages may also be used to provide information relevant to the visitor. Landing page copy can be static or personalized.

Mapping—"Mapping" or the "discovery map" creates a visual depiction of an idea, concept, or complex information in an easy-to-understand format. While not serving as a replacement to text, this graphical representation can complement it. Because many concepts cannot be explained in a linear path, the mind map shows the core elements and how the various components fit together. Visual cues can be added to the map, similar to adding bullets or check marks to copy. Colors can help convey the importance of key elements within the visual, too. By visually presenting the concept, it also may be possible to avoid jargon or complex terminology. Group participants can help develop the discovery map, thereby creating a common vocabulary and reaching a common understanding of the concept or strategy. Mapping can be used as a teaching, problem solving, and strategic planning tool as well.

Microblogging—As the name suggests, this is a form of blogging but the content is smaller, hence sentences are shorter than what is found in a typical blog. Twitter's format offers a perfect example of these small posts.

Netiquette—The rules of etiquette that apply to computer-based communication. This set of social standards applies to communication behavior in everything from blogs to email to chat rooms. Because there is not a universal code of conduct, some online communities stipulate guidelines regarding behavioral etiquette.

Network Weaving—Coined by Valdis Krebs and June Holley, the term is used to describe the skill set required to build or strengthen a social network. Network weaving includes a variety of activities such as introducing and connecting people; inviting individuals with different viewpoints into conversations; working on a multiple-channel level with different publics; sharing links, information, and resources without expecting a direct return from such an action.

NGO—This acronym stands for "nongovernmental organization." These groups possess a nonprofit status and operate independent of government. This not-for-profit or voluntary citizen group can be organized on a local, national, or even international level. Many times, this term is used in conjunction with organizations performing services or serving humanitarian needs in helping the developing world. NGOs may influence the role of government and may be involved with civil regulation, policy monitoring, advocacy, and the encouragement of citizens to participate in the political process. Therefore, this legally constituted institution can have objectives linked to social, environmental, or political aims.

Objectives—Objectives are specific and measurable statements that represent attainable outcomes in support of goals. Usually, communication objectives are informational, motivational, or behavioral in nature.

Primary Research—Information gathered first-hand is considered to be primary research. A person leading a focus group, conducting an interview to gather information, or surveying a population generate the data and statistics. Collected first-hand, these are examples of primary research.

Proxemics—Anthropologist Edward T. Hall pioneered the field and coined the term. This is the study of spatial relationships and requirements of humans and animals, including how these spatial associations impact social interaction, communication, and behavior.

RFP—This acronym stands for "request for proposal." An RFP is an invitation issued to potential suppliers to officially bid on a job. Conducted in the early stages of the bidding process, potential vendors are asked to prepare detailed proposals for providing a service or commodity. Some of these documents are extremely long because of the need to provide all of the information requested by the organization issuing the request. Based on the formal submissions, a selection is made as to which firm to hire.

RSS Feed—"RSS" stands for Really Simple Syndication. An RSS reader is software that scans tweets, blog posts, news headlines, YouTube videos, and web sites. It grabs fresh content and syndicates the material automatically. The results are delivered directly into an individual's computer via the RSS feed.

Scorecard—Also referred to as a dashboard, this is a system for gathering and reporting metrics on a particular initiative or project. This design ultimately enables one to track progress through the reporting of accomplishments, statistics, and other data, which can be documented and compared to past performance in the specified areas. When used in reference to sustainability matters, the term "balanced scorecard" is used and refers to the performance of the Triple Bottom Line's three sustainability pillars.

Secondary Research—Research obtained on a second-hand basis. For example, census data or Internet-based public opinion polls, which are subsequently referenced or reported by other individuals or organizations are shared "second hand." Sometimes, secondary research is referenced as "desk research" because it is a summary or synthesis of research conducted by others in "the field."

SEO—Stands for "search engine optimization." This term relates to the identification and use of key words and phrases in online content so as to draw the attention of search engines. For example, if an individual is conducting a search on nonprofits helping underprivileged children have access to free music education, specific words will be entered, such as "free music education" or "children's music education." If the search engine locates these key words in the nonprofit's online materials, the organization will be listed in the search results.

Slacktivist—The words "slacktivism" and "slacktivist" are created by combining two words. "Slacker" is used in the first half of the word. The remainder of the word comes from the terms "activism" or "activist." A slacktivist is a person who lazily supports a cause. This individual isn't sufficiently engaged to take any action that is inconvenient or difficult. With minimal personal effort, a slacktivist "stands" for a cause, so this individual can "feel good" about his or her actions but doesn't fully engage or commit to the cause. However, this is does not necessarily mean a slacktivist is unengaged in other cause-related activities outside social media.

Social Audit—This term commonly is used to refer to the review or report of a company's contribution to or impact on society. It is often used in the context of corporate social responsibility and can describe legal compliance, such as in regards to diversity, as well as describe a more active social policy.

Spam—Electronic messaging systems can send out unsolicited messages indiscriminately, similar to sending junk mail through the postal service. When this type of bulk messaging is done, it is referred to as "spam."

SRI—Socially Responsible Investing is a broad term used to describe a particular investment strategy. In addition to basing investment decisions on the financial aspect of a stock, mutual fund, or bond, attention is given to how responsible the organization is in its business dealings. These factors are then considered in relation to how they align with an individual's socially responsible values. Factors, such as transparency, stewardship, eco-friendliness, and ethics, are examples of considerations.

S.W.O.C.—The strengths-weaknesses-opportunities-challenges analysis is a variation on the S.W.O.T. (see S.W.O.T.) The analysis is helpful in identifying an organization or department's critical success features. It takes into account a wide range of factors, including influencers such as organizational culture and stakeholder satisfaction. This planning and analysis tool is helpful in the strategic decision-making process.

S.W.O.T.—This stands for strengths-weaknesses-opportunities-threats analysis. The framework typically is applied to a particular issue or element in the marketing arena. During the process, an inventory is conducted in each of the four areas. This outcome then is taken and used to create a shared vision by scrutinizing the results of each of these components through a gap analysis. This gap assessment compares the current status with the desired goal or outcome. An introspective process, the analysis aids in goal achievement by helping an organization strategically plan to make the most of its strengths and circumvent its weaknesses

T.O.W.S.—This refers to the threats-opportunities-weaknesses-strengths analysis. Using the same concept as S.W.O.T. (see S.W.O.T.), the matrix re-frames the four components, conducting the analysis from a different perspective. By changing the order of the quadrants in the review process, this variation shifts the emphasis to an external focus rather than the internal, resulting in a greater focus on opportunities outside of the organization and improved threat management.

Triple Bottom Line—Also known as TBL, this accounting framework uses performance metrics in the environmental, social, and financial dimensions. Many times, these three categories also are referred to as the 3Ps: people, planet, and profits. Although profit can be measured in dollars, the challenge has been to establish a form of globally, agreed-upon standards and to use this form of measurement and indexing for social capital and environmental health.

VNR—These three letters stand for "video news release." This is a video segment made to look like a news report, but is not created by a media outlet. Instead, it is produced by a PR firm, nonprofit, corporation, government agency, or other entity to promote or publicize an issue, product, service, or even the organization itself. Video releases are shared with the media in the hopes a producer will include all or part of the video in a newscast or post the story on line. VNRs carry informational segments about an organization and can project an unbiased appearance because of the news format. Organizations frequently post VNRs on sites such as YouTube, in addition to their own web site.

Notes

Chapter 1

1. Charles J. Kibert, Martha C. Monroe, Anna L. Peterson, Richard R. Plate, and Leslie Paul Thiele, *Working Toward Sustainability: Ethical Decision Making in a Technological World* (Hoboken, NJ: John Wiley & Sons, 2012), 180.
2. "Volunteering in America," Corporation for National Community Service, http://www.nationalservice.gov/about/volunteering/index.asp and http://www.volunteeringinamerica.gov/.
3. "Volunteering in the United States, 2011," U.S. Bureau of Labor Statistics, http://www.bls.gov/news.release/volun.nr0.htm/.
4. Jocelyne S. Daw and Carol Cone, *Breakthrough Nonprofit Branding: Seven Principles to Power Extraordinary Results* (Hoboken, NJ: John Wiley & Sons, 2011), 8.
5. "Executive Summary," The Annual Report on Philanthropy for the Year 2011, Giving USA (Indianapolis, IN: The Indiana University Center on Philanthropy, 2012), 3.
6. Gary M. Grobman, *The Nonprofit Handbook* (6th ed.) (Harrisburg, PA: White Hat Communications, 2011), 24.

Chapter 2

1. Kathy Bonk, Emily Tynes, Henry Griggs, and Phil Sparks, *Strategic Communications for Nonprofits: A Step-by-Step Guide to Working with the Media* (2nd ed.) (San Francisco: John Wiley & Sons, 2008), 4–5.
2. Todd Hunt and James E. Grunig, *Public Relations Techniques* (New York: Harcourt Brace College Publishers, 1994), 10.
3. Erika Andersen, *Being Strategic* (New York: St. Martin's Press, 2009), 99.
4. Todd Cohen, "Nonprofits Face Government Fees, Taxes," *Philanthropy Journal Quarter in Review* (Quarter 2, 2011), 5.
5. David Fitzpatrick and Drew Griffin, "Little of Charity's Money Going to Animals," CNN Special Investigations Unit, June 15, 2012, http://www.cnn.com/2012/06/14/us/animal-charity-investigation/index.html?ref=allsearch.
6. David Fitzpatrick and Drew Griffin, "Tax Records Show Charities Spent Millions on Direct Mail," CNN Special Investigations Unit, May 18, 2012, http://www.cnn.com/2012/05/18/us/veterans-charity-marketing/index.html?iref=allsearch.
7. Tom Watson and Paul Noble, *Evaluating Public Relations: A Best Practice Guide to Public Relations Planning, Research and Evaluation* (2nd ed.) (Philadelphia, PA: Kogan Page, 2007), 237–238.
8. Sally J. Patterson and Janel M. Radtke, *Strategic Communications for Nonprofit Organizations* (2nd ed.) (Hoboken, NJ: John Wiley & Sons, 2009), 157.

9. Glen M. Broom and Bey-Ling Sha, *Cutlip & Center's Effective Public Relations* (11th ed.) (New York: Pearson Education, 2013), 316–320.
10. K.D. Paine, "It's 9 a.m., Do You Know Where Your Membership Is?" (speech presented to the American Society of Association Executives, Minneapolis, MN, Aug. 18, 2004).
11. Institute for Public Relations, "Proposed Interim Standards for Metrics in Traditional Media Analysis, June 7, 2012, www.instituteforpr.org/topics/proposed-interim-standards-for-metrics-in-traditional-media-analysis.
12. Olivier Blanchard, *Social Media ROI* (Boston, MA: Pearson Education,2011), 147.
13. Ted Hart, Steve MacLaughlin, James M. Greenfield, Philip H. Geier, Jr., *Internet Management for Nonprofit: Strategies, Tools, and Trade Secrets* (Hoboken, NJ: John Wiley & Sons, 2010).

Chapter 3

1. William B. Werther, Jr. and David Chandler, *Strategic Corporate Social Responsibility: Stakeholders in a Global Environment* (Thousand Oaks, CA: Sage Publications, 2006), 11.
2. Werther and Chandler, 11.
3. Tom Price, *"Corporate Social Responsibility," Issues for Debate in Corporate Social Responsibly* (Thousand Oaks, CA: Sage Publications, 2010), 12.
4. Stephen Jordan and B. J. Parker. *Two Steps Forward, One Step Back: A Brief History of Corporate Citizenship and Corporate Social Responsibility* (Washington, D.C.: Business Civic Leadership Center, 2010), 16.
5. Price, 10.
6. Ian Wilson, *The New Rules of Corporate Conduct: Rewriting the Social Charter* (Westport, CT: Quorum Books, 2000), 4–8.
7. Wilson, 1415.
8. Price, 10.
9. Charles J. Kibert, Martha, C. Monroe, Anna C. Peterson, Richard R. Plate, and Leslie Paul Thiele, *Working Toward Sustainability: Ethical Decision Making in a Technological World* (Hoboken, NJ: John Wiley & Sons, 2012), 3.
10. "Report of the World Commission on Environment and Development: Our Common Future," United Nations, http://www.un-documents.net/wced-ocf.html.
11. Timothy F. Slaper and Tanya J. Hall. "The Triple Bottom Line: What Is It and How Does It Work?" *Indiana Business Review*, Spring 2011 4–6.
12. Daniel C. Esty and Andrew S. Winston, *Green to Gold* (New Haven, CT: Yale University Press, 2006), 250.
13. Global Reporting Initiative, "About Sustainability Reporting," Global Reporting Initiative, https://www.globalreporting.org/information/sustainabiltiy-reporting/Pages/default.aspx.
14. Landor Associates, "Price Packaging and Perception: Results from the 2011 Image-Power Green Brands Survey," Perspectives 2012 (New York: Landor, 2012), 35–37.
15. Suzanne Benn and Dianne Bolton, *Key Concepts in Corporate Social Responsibility* (Thousand Oaks, CA: Sage Publications, 2011), ix.
16. Benn and Bolton, 41–45.
17. Edelman Trust Barometer: 2012 Annual Global Study, http://trust.edelman.com/about-trust/.
18. Reputation Institute, The 2012 U.S. RepTrack Pulse, http://www.reputationinstitute.com/thought-leadership/category/complimentary-reports-2012.
19. Boston College Center for Corporate Citizenship and Reputation Institute, "Corporate Reputation and Social Responsibility Rankings: 2011 CRS Index," http://www.bcccc.net/pdf/CSRIReport2011.pdf.

20. Landor, Burson Marsteller, Penn Schoen Berland, BAV, *2012 Global Corporate Reputation Index* (Landor: New York, 2012), 1–2.
21. Wayne Visser, *The Age of Responsibility: CSR 2.0 and the New DNA of Business* (West Sussex, U.K.: John Wiley & Sons, 2011), 149–152.
22. Vanita Shastri and Preeta M. Banerjee, "From Corporate Social Responsibility to Global Social Entrepreneurship," *Social Responsibility and Environmental Sustainability in Business* (New Delhi, India: Response Books, Sage Publications), 2010, 2.
23. Shastri and Banerjee, 3.
24. Jim Stengel, *Grow* (New York: CROWN BUSINESS, 2011), 7–8.
25. C.B. Bhattacharya, Daniel Korschun, and Sankar Sen, "What Really Drives Value in Corporate Responsibility," *McKinsey Quarterly* (December 2011), https://www.mckinseyquarterly.com/article_print.aspx
26. Ken Little, *The Complete Idiot's Guide to Socially Responsible Investing* (New York: Alpha Books, 2008), 4–5.
27. Richard Barrett, *Building a Values-Driven Organization* (Boston: Elsevier, 2006), 20.
28. Sarah Kliff, "Susan G. Komen Foundation Revises Policy That Barred Planned Parenthood Funding," The *Washington Post*, February 3, 2012, http://www.washingtonpost.com/business/economy/komen-revises-funding-policy/2012/02/03/gIQAVRa3mQ_story.html.
29. Stuart Watson, "United Way Settles Lawsuit with Former CEO," WCNC, http://www.wcnc.com/video/featured-videos/United-Way-settles-discrimination-lawsuit-with-former-CEO-Gloria-Pace-King-111150384.html.
30. Mary Slosson, "Anti-Kony Campaign in Turmoil after Filmmaker's Breakdown," Reuters, April 2, 2012, http://www.reuters.com/article/2012/04/02/us-usa-kony-future-idUSBRE83116Y20120402.
31. Dan Kane, "It's Public Money but Private Secrecy," *The Charlotte Observer*, July 6, 2011, 1A–4A.
32. Edelman, 2012 Edelman Trust Barometer Global results, http://www.slideshare.net/EdelmanInsights/2012-edelman-trust-barometer-global-deck.
33. *Webster's Encyclopedic Unabridged Dictionary of the English Language* (New York: Gramercy Books, 1994), 1917.
34. Charles Kibert, et al., 1.
35. Simon Bell and Stephen Morse, *Sustainability Indicators: Measuring the Immeasurable* (London: Earthscan Publications Limited, 2000), 9–13.
36. Nasrin R. Khalili, *Practical Sustainability: From Grounded Theory to Emerging Strategies* (New York: Palgrave Macmillian, 2011), 6–16.
37. *Webster's*, 377.

Chapter 4

1. Keith Michael Hearit and Kasie Mitchell Roberson, "Denial, Differentiation, and Apology: On the Use of Apologia in Crisis Management," *Handbook of Risk and Crisis Communication* (New York: Routledge, 2010), 544.
2. Robert R. Ulmer, Timothy L. Sellnow, and Matthew W. Seeger, *Effective Crisis Communication: Moving from Crisis to Opportunity* (2nd ed.) (Thousand Oaks, CA: Sage Publications, 2011), 9–13.
3. W. Timothy Coombs, *Ongoing Crisis Communication: Planning, Managing, and Responding* (2nd ed.) (Thousand Oaks, CA: Sage Publications, 2007), 17–20.
4. Robert L. Heath and H. Dan O'Hair, "The Significance of Crisis and Risk Communication," *Handbook of Risk and Crisis Communication* (New York: Routledge, 2010), 16.

5. Pamela Ferrante Walaski, *Risk and Crisis Communication* (Hoboken, NJ: John Wiley & Sons, 2011), 125.
6. Michel Ogrizek and Jean-Michel Guillery, *Communicating in a Crisis* (New York, Walter de Gruyter, 1999), 2–4.
7. Ted Hart, James M. Greenfield, Steve MacLaughlin, and Philip H. Geier, Jr., *Internet for Nonprofits Management* (Hoboken, NJ: John Wiley & Sons, 2010), 15.
8. Smith, Bucklin, & Associates, Robert H. Wilbur (ed.) *The Complete Guide to Nonprofit Management* (2nd ed.) (New York: John Wiley & Sons, 2000), 198.
9. Coombs, 141.
10. Barbara Kellerman, "When Should a Leader Apologize and When Not?", *Harvard Business Review*, April 2006, 81.
11. Gilpin, Dawn R., and Priscilla J. Murphy, *Crisis Management in a Complex World* (New York: Oxford University Press, 2008), 152.
12. Marion Pinsdorf, *All Crises Are Global: Managing to Escape the Chaos* (New York: Fordham University Press, 2004), 20.

Chapter 5

1. Edelman, "GoodPurpose 2012 Executive Summary," April 2012, 3.
2. Cone Communications, "Cone Releases First Cause Consumer Behavior Study," October 1, 2008, Cone Communications and Duke University's Fuqua School of Business, The 2008 Behavior Cause Study, October 1, 2008, http://www.coneinc.com/content1188.
3. Cone Communications, "More than Three-Quarters of Americans Say a Non-profit-Corporate Partnership Makes a Cause Stand Out," March 10, 2010, http://www.coneinc.com/stuff/contentmgr/files/0/a15fa8db491fa7480e129c545fea7b11/files/2010_cone_nonporfit_marketing_trend_tracker_release_and_fact_sheet.pdf.
4. Barkley, Boston Consulting Group, and Service Management Group, "Executive Summary," American Millennials: Deciphering the Enigma Generation, September 12, 2011, 7.
5. Sana-ur-Rehman Sheikh and Rian Beise-Zee, "Corporate Social Responsibility or Cause-Related Marketing? The Role of Cause Specificity of CSR," *Journal of Consumer Marketing*, Vol. 28, Issue 1 (2011): 29.
6. Jocelyne Daw, *Cause Marketing for Nonprofits* (Hoboken, NJ: John Wiley & Sons, 2006, xxviii.
7. Daw, xxx.
8. A. R. Andreasen, "Profits for Nonprofits: Find a Corporate Partner," *Harvard Business Review*, November–December 1996, 47–59.
9. Daw, 61.
10. Daw, 4.
11. Sue Adkins, *Cause Related Marketing: Who Cares Wins* (Boston: Elsevier Butterworth-Heinemann, 2004), 120.
12. Daw, 108.
13. Adkins, 231.
14. Cone Communications, *Past. Present. Future. The 25th Anniversary of Cause Marketing* (Boston, MA: Cone Communications, 2008), 42.
15. Adkins, 102.
16. Joe Waters and Joanna MacDonald, *Cause Marketing for Dummies* (Hoboken, NJ: Wiley Publishing, 2011), 4.
17. Nicky Amos, "The New World of Company Giving," *Corporate Responsibility Management*, August/September 2005, Vol. 2, Issue 1, 35.
18. Cone Communications, *Past. Present. Future*, 43.

19. Nicole Wallace, "Attitudes Toward Charities in Marketing Partnerships: A New Survey," The Chronicle of Philanthropy, March 10, 2010, http://philanthropy.com/blogs/prospecting/attitudes-toward-charities-in-marketing-partnerships-a-new-survey/21719.
20. Grahame Dowling, *Creating Corporation Reputations* (New York: Oxford University Press, 2002), 145.
21. Waters and MacDonald, 23.
22. Harnish Pringle and Marjorie Thompson, *Brand Spirit: How Cause-related Marketing Builds Brands* (New York: John Wiley & Sons, 1999), 49–64.

Chapter 6

1. Glen M. Broom and Bey-Ling Sha, *Cutlip & Center's Effective Public Relations* (11th ed.) (New York: Pearson Education, 2013), 172.
2. Heather Mansfield, *Social Media for Social Good* (New York: The McGraw-Hill Companies, 2012), xiii.
3. Olivier Blanchard, *Social Media ROI* (Boston: Pearson Education, Inc., 2011), 180.
4. Blanchard, 84.
5. Ruth Kinzey, "When a Policy for Social Media is a Good Thing," *The Triad Business Journal*, October 7, 2011, 17.
6. Beth Kanter and Allison H. Fine, *The Networked Nonprofit* (San Francisco: John Wiley & Sons, 2010), 151-161.
7. David Meerman Scott, *The New Rules of Marketing & PR* (Hoboken, NJ: John Wiley & Sons, 2011), 209.
8. Mansfield, 13.
9. Scott, 242.
10. Nancy Flynn, *Blog Rules* (New York: American Management Association, 2006), 86.
11. Flynn, 89.
12. Jennifer Aaker and Andy Smith, *The Dragonfly Effect* (San Francisco: Jossey-Bass, 2010), 6.
13. "About," LinkedIn, http://press.linkedin.com/about.
14. Sally J. Patterson and Janel M. Radtke, *Strategic Communications for Nonprofit Organizations* (2nd ed.) (Hoboken, NJ: John Wiley & Sons, 2009), 141.
15. Nitish Singh and Arun Pereira, *The Culturally Customized Web Site: Customizing Web Sites for the Global Marketplace* (Burlington, MA: Elseiver Butterworth-Heinemann, 2005), 1.
16. Allan Pressel, "Effective Web Design," Ted Hart, James M. Greenfield, Steve MacLaughlin, and Philip H. Geier, Jr., *Internet for Nonprofits Management* (Hoboken, NJ: John Wiley & Sons, 2010), 291.
17. Mansfield, 11.
18. Scott, 204.
19. "Frequently Asked Questions," YouTube, http://www.youtube.com/t/faq.
20. "Home page," Flickr, http://www.flickr.com.
21. "Home page," Shutterfly, http://www.shutterfly.com.
22. "About," Pinterest, http://pinterest.com/about/.
23. K.D. Paine, *Measure What Matters* (Hoboken, NJ: John Wiley & Sons, 2011), 191.
24. Michael Moume, "RSS Feeds: Are They Worth It?", Ezine, http://ezinearticles.com/?RSS-Feeds:-Are-They-Worth-It?&id=6289886.

Chapter 7

1. *Webster's Encyclopedic Unabridged Dictionary* (New York: Value House Random Publishing, 1996), 644.
2. William H. Macey, Benjamin Schneider, Karen M. Barbera, and Scott A. Young, *Employee Engagement: Tools for Analysis, Practice, and Competitive Advantage* (Malden, MA: Wiley-Blackwell, 2009), 4.
3. Blessing White, *Employee Engagement Report 2011* (Princeton, NJ: Blessing White, 2011), 3.
4. Macey, et al, 143-146.
5. Corporation for National and Community Service, "New Report: Americans Devote 8.1 Billion Hours to Volunteering in 2010," August 8, 2011, http://www.nationalservice.gov/about/newsroom/releases_detail.asp?tbl_pr_id=2026.
6. U.S. Bureau of Labor Statistics, "Volunteering in the United States 2011," February 22, 2012, http://www.bls.gov/news.release/volun.nr0.htm.
7. "Value of Volunteering Grows," *Philanthropy Journal*, April 6, 2012, http://www.philanthropyjournal.org/news/top-stories/value-volunteering-grows.
8. Emily Holder, "The Need for Inspiration: How Millennials Connect, Involve and Give to Nonprofits," *Philanthropy Journal*, June 14, 2012, http://www.philanthropyjournal.org/resources/marketingcommunications/need-inspiration-how-millennials-connect-involve-and-give-nonprofi.
9. *Millennial Impact Report 2012* (Greenwood, IN: Achieve and JGA, 2012), 4.
10. Gary M. Grobman, *The Nonprofit Handbook* (6th ed.) (Harrisburg, PA: White Hat Communication, 2011), 128.
11. Jill Friedman Fixler, Sandie Eichbert, and Gail Lorenz, *Boomer Volunteer Engagement: Collaborate Today, Thrive Tomorrow* (Bloomington, IN: Author House, 2008), 59.
12. Fixler et al., 111.
13. "Bank of America High Net Worth Philanthropy Study," http://mediaroom.bankofamerica.com/phoenix.zhtml?c=234503&p=mediaMention&id=294026.
15. "Wealthy Women Control Charitable Checkbooks," *Philanthropy Journal*, January 5, 2012, http://www.philanthropyjournal.org/news/top-stories-welathy-women-control-charitable-checkbooks.
14. The *2011 Study of High Net Worth Women's Philanthropy & The Impact of Women's Giving Networks* December 2011. Researched & written by The Center on Philanthropy at Indiana University Indiana & Purdue University Indianapolis, Indiana.
16. *The Millennial Impact Report*, 22–28.
17. Paul Marciano, *Carrots and Sticks Don't Work: Build a Culture of Employee Engagement with the Principles of RESPECT* (New York: McGraw-Hill, 2010), 80–81.
18. Macey, et al., 48.
19. Marciano, 175.
20. Bob Kelleher, *Louder than Words* (Portland, OR: BLKB Publishing, 2010), 180.
21. Peter Vogt, "Awareness to Action," *Communication World*, March-April, 2004, 22.
22. "Effective Communication Positively Impacts Employee Motivation Levels, Employee Advocacy Latest Ouch Point Survey from Opinion Research Corporation Suggests," March 9, 2009, http://www.reuters.com/article/2009/03/09/idUS101145+09-Mar-2009+BW20090309.
23. Society for Human Resource Management (SHRM), Employee Job Satisfaction and Engagement Survey, http://www.shrm.org/research/surveyfindings/articles/documents/11-0618%20job_satisfaction_fnl.pdf.
24. "Study: Workers' Morale Hurt Most by Communication Failures," Triangle Business Journal, Nov. 10, 2008, http://bizjournals.com/triangle/stories/2008/11/10/daily2.html.

25. *Watson Wyatt Worldwide, Driving Employee Engagement in a Global Workforce 2007/2008* (New York: Watson Wyatt Worldwide, 2008), 3.
26. *Dynamics of Cause Engagement* (Washington, DC: The Center for Social Impact Communication at Georgetown University and Ogilvy Public Relations Worldwide, 2011), 5.
26. *Dynamics of Cause Engagement*, 9.
28. Todd Cohen, "Nonprofits Have a Great Story to Tell," Inside Philanthropy, Jan. 9, 2012. http://philanthropyjournal.blogspot.com/search?q=nonprofits+have+a+great+story+to+tell.
29. Jim Haudan, The Art of Engagement (New York: McGraw-Hill, 2008), 91–92.
30. Edelman, Edelman's 2012 Trust Barometer, http://www.slideshare.net/edelman Insights/2012-edelman-trust-barometer-global-deck, 7.
31. *Dynamics of Cause Engagement*, 11.

Bibliography

Books, Journals, Newspapers, & Magazines

Aaker, Jennifer, Andy Smith, and Carlye Adler. *The Dragonfly Effect*. San Francisco: Jossey-Bass, 2010.

Adkins, Sue. *Cause Related Marketing: Who Cares Wins*. Boston: Elsevier Butterworth-Heinemann, 2004.

Adler, Stephen M. *Cause of Concern: Results-Oriented Cause Marketing*. Mason, OH: Thomson Learning Academic Resource, 2006.

Ahmed, Meena. *The Principles and Practice of Crisis Management*. New York: Palgrave Macmillan, 2006.

Amos, Nicky. "The New World of Company Giving." *Corporate Responsibility Management*, August/September 2005, Volume 2, Issue 1: 34–37.

Allison, Michael, and Jude Kaye. *Strategic Planning for Nonprofit Organizations* (2nd ed.). Hoboken, NJ: John Wiley & Sons, 2005.

Andersen, Erika. *Being Strategic*. New York: St. Martin's Press, 2009.

Anderson, Ray C. *Confessions of a Radical Industrialist: Profits, People, Purpose – Doing Business by Respecting the Earth*. New York: St. Martin Press, 2009.

Andreasen, A.R. "Profits for Nonprofits: Find a Corporate Partner." *Harvard Business Review,* November-December 1996: 47–59.

Arthur W. Page Society. *Restoring Trust in Business: Models in Action*. New York: Arthur W. Page Society, 2003.

Arthur W. Page Society. *Special Report: The Dynamic of Public Trust in Business – Emerging Opportunities for Leaders*. Darden, VA: Arthur W. Page Society and Business Roundtable Institute for Corporate Ethics, 2009.

Ash, David W., and Dvlad G. Dabija. *Planning for Real Time Event Response Management*. Upper Saddle River, NJ: Prentice Hall, 2000.

Austin, Erica Weintraub, and Bruce E. Pinkleton. *Strategic Public Relations Management*. Mahwah, NJ: Lawrence Erlbaum Associates, 2001.

Bangs, Jr., David H. *Business Plans Made Easy* (3rd ed.). Toronto, Ontario, Canada: Entrepreneur Media Inc., 2005.

Bangs, Jr., David H. *Nonprofits Made Easy*. Toronto, Ontario, Canada: Entrepreneur Press, 2006.

Banerjee, Preeta M., and Vanita Shastri. *Social Responsibility and Environmental Sustainability in Business*. Thousand Oaks, CA: Response Books, Sage Publications, 2010.

Barrett, Richard. *Building a Values-Driven Organization*. Burlington, MA: Butterworth-Heinemann, 2006.

Barton, Laurence. *Crisis in Organizations II.* Cincinnati: South-Western College Publishing, 2001.

Beesley, Michael, and Tom Evans. *Corporate Social Responsibility: A Reassessment.* London: Croom Helm Ltd., 1978.

Biegel, Len. *Never Say Never: The Complete Executive Guide to Crisis Management.* New York: Tower Press, 2007.

Bell, Jeanne, Jan Masaoka, and Steve Zimmerman. *Nonprofit Sustainability: Making Strategic Decisions for Financial Viability.* San Francisco: Jossey-Bass, 2010.

Bell, Simon, and Stephen Morse. *Sustainability Indicators: Measuring the Immeasurable.* Sterling, VA: Earthscan Publishing, 2000.

Below, Patrick J., George L. Morrisey, and Betty L. Acomb. *The Executive Guide to Strategic Planning.* San Francisco: Jossey-Bass, 1998.

Benn, Suzanne, and Dianne Bolton. *Key Concepts in Social Responsibility.* Thousand Oaks, CA: Sage Publications, 2011.

Berezin, Valerie. "Social Reporting: Getting a Clear Picture." *The Corporate Citizen,* Issue 4, 11–13.

Bertocci, David I. *Strategic Planning and Management: A Roadmap to Success.* New York: University Press of America, 2009.

Blanchard, Olivier. *Social Media ROI.* Boston, MA: Pearson Education, 2011.

Blessing White. *Employee Engagement Report 2011.* Princeton, NJ: Blessing White, 2011.

Block, Stephen. *Why Nonprofits Fail.* San Francisco: Jossey-Bass, 2004.

Blowfield, Michael, and Alan Murray. *Corporate Responsibility: A Critical Introduction.* New York: Oxford University Press, 2008.

Bonk, Kathy, Emily Tynes, Henry Griggs, and Phil Sparks, *Strategic Communications for Nonprofits: A Step-by-Step Guide to Working with the Media* (2nd ed.) (San Francisco: John Wiley & Sons, 2008).

Brennan, Bernie, and Lori Schafer. *Branded! How Retailers Engage Customers with Social Media and Mobility.* Hoboken: NJ: John Wiley & Sons, 2010.

Broom, Glen M., and Bey-Ling Sha. *Cutlip & Center's Effective Public Relations* (11th ed.). New York: Pearson Education, 2013.

Bryson, John M. *Strategic Planning for Public and Nonprofit Organizations* (3rd ed.). San Francisco: John Wiley & Sons, 2004.

Burke, Donald J., and Cary L. Cooper (eds.). *The Organization in Crisis.* Malden, MA: Blackwell Publishers, 2000.

Capon, Noel, John U. Farley, and James M. Hulbert. *Corporate Strategic Planning.* New York: Columbia University Press, 1987.

Carman, Joanne G., and Kimberly A. Fredericks (eds.). "Nonprofits and Evaluation." *New Directions for Evaluation,* Issue 119, Autumn, 1–119, 2008.

Cone Communications. "More Than Three-Quarters of Americans Say a Nonprofit Corporate Partnership Makes a Cause Stand Out." *Cone Trend Tracker,* March 10, 2010.

Cone Communications. *Past. Present. Future. The 25th Anniversary of Cause Marketing.* Boston: Cone Communications, 2008.

Connors, Tracy Daniel. *The Nonprofit Handbook: Management 2002 Supplement* (3rd ed.). New York: John Wiley & Sons, 2002.

Coombs, W. Timothy. *Ongoing Crisis Communication: Planning, Managing, and Responding* (2nd ed.). Thousand Oaks, CA: Sage Publications, 2007.

CQ Researcher. Issues for Depabe in Corporate Social Responsibility. Thousand Oaks, CA: Sage Publications, 2010.

Crandall, William, John A. Parnell, and John E. Spillan. *Crisis Management in the New Strategy Landscape.* Thousand Oaks, CA: Sage Publications, 2010.

Crowther, David, and Nicholas Capaldi (eds.). *The Ashgate Research Companion to Corporate Social Responsibility.* Burlington, VT: Ashgate Publishing Company, 2008.

Cutlip, Scott M., Allen H. Center, and Glen M. Broom. *Effective Public Relations* (8th ed.). Upper Saddle River, NJ: Prentice Hall, 2000.

Daw, Jocelyne S., and Carol Cone. *Breakthrough Nonprofit Branding: Seven Principles to Power Extraordinary Results.* Hoboken, NJ: John Wiley & Sons, 2011.

Dees, J. Gregory, Jed Emerson, and Peter Economy. *Enterprising Nonprofits.* New York: John Wiley & Sons, 2001.

Dooris, Michael J., John M. Kelley, and James F. Trainer (eds.). *Successful Strategic Planning.* San Francisco: Jossey-Bass, 2004.

Dowling, Grahame. *Creating Corporate Reputations: Identity, Image, and Performance.* New York: Oxford University Press, 2002.

Durham, Sarah. *Brandraising.* San Francisco: Jossey-Bass, 2010.

Dynamics of Cause Engagement. Washington, DC: The Center for Social Impact Communication at Georgetown University and Ogilvy Public Relations Worldwide, 2011.

Edelman. "Executive Summary." Goodpurpose 2012. New York: Edelman, April 2012.

Eisenberg, Pablo. *Challenges for Nonprofits and Philanthropy: The Courage to Change.* Medford, MA: Tufts University Press, 2005.

Esty, Daniel C., and Andrew S. Winston. *Green to Gold.* New Haven: Yale University Press, 2006.

Fink, Steven. *Crisis Management: Planning for the Inevitable.* New York: AMACOM, 1986.

Fixler, Jill Friedman, Sandie Eichberg, and Gail Lorenz. *Boomer Volunteer Engagement: Collaborate Today, Thrive Tomorrow.* Bloomington, IN: Author House, Inc., 2008.

Flynn, Nancy. *Blog Rules.* New York: AMACOM, 2006.

Fraher, Amy L. *Thinking Through the Crisis: Improving Teamwork and Leadership in High-Risk Fields.* New York: Cambridge University Press, 2011.

Fry, Fred L., Charles R. Stoner, and Laurence G. Weinzimmer. *Strategic Planning for Small Business Made Easy.* Toronto, Ontario, Canada: Entrepreneur Media, Inc., 2005.

Gardner, James R., Robert Rachlin, H. W. Allen Sweeny. *Handbook of Strategic Planning.* New York: John Wiley & Sons, 1986.

Gilpin, Dawn R., and Priscilla J. Murphy. *Crisis Management in a Complex World.* New York: Oxford University Press, 2008.

Giving USA. "Executive Summary." The Annual Report on Philanthropy for the Year 2011. Indianapolis, IN: The Indiana University Center on Philanthropy, 2012.

Goodstein, Leonard, Timothy M. Nolan, and William J. Pfeiffer. *Applied Strategic Planning: A Comprehensive Guide.* New York: McGraw Hill, 1993.

Gould, Daniella. "The Problem with Supplier Audits." *Corporate Responsibility Management*, Volume 1, Issue 1, August/September 2005.

Grobman, Gary M. *The Nonprofit Handbook* (6th ed.). Harrisburg, PA: White Hat Communication, 2011.

Grunig, Rudolf, and Richard Kuhn. *Process-based Strategic Planning.* Heidelberg, Germany: Springer-Verlag, 2011.

Guth, David W., and Charles Marsh. *Public Relations: A Values-Driven Approach.* Boston: Allyn & Bacon, 2000.

Handley, Ann, and C. C. Chapman. *Content Rules: How to Create Killer Blogs, Podcasts, Videos, Ebooks, Webinars (and More) that Engage Customers and Ignite Your Business.* Hoboken, NJ: John Wiley & Sons, 2011.

Hart, Ted, James M. Greenfield, Steve MacLaughlin, and Philip H. Greier, Jr. *Internet for Nonprofits Management: Strategies, Tools, and Trade Secrets.* Hoboken, NJ: John Wiley & Sons, 2010.

Harvard Business Essentials. Crisis Management: Master the Skills to Prevent Disasters. Boston: Harvard Business School Publishing Corporation, 2004.

Haudan, Jim. *The Art of Engagement: Bridging the Gap Between People and Possibilities.* New York: McGraw-Hill, 2008.

Heath, Robert L., and H. Dan O'Hair (eds.). *Handbook of Risk and Crisis Communication.* New York: Routledge, 2010.

Hellebust, Karsten G., and Joseph C. Krallinger. *Strategic Planning Workbook.* New York: John Wiley & Sons, 1989.

Henry, Rene A. *The Complete Guide to Crisis and Risk Communications … You'd Better Have a Hose if You Want to Put Out the Fire: Professional Tips, Tactics, Dos, Don'ts and Case Histories.* Windsor, CA: Gollywobbler Productions, 2000.

Hiebert, Ray Eldon (ed.). *Precision Public Relations.* New York: Longman, 1988.

Hitchcock, Darcy, and Marsha Willard. *The Step-by-Step Guide to Sustainability Planning.* Sterling, VA: Earthscan Publishing, 2008.

Hitchcock, Darcy, and Marsha Willard. *The Business Guide to Sustainability.* Sterling, VA: Earthscan Publishing, 2009.

Holloway, Clark. *Strategic Planning.* Chicago: Nelson-Hall, 1986.

Hoskins, Tony. "Tailoring CR Communication to Your Stakeholders." *Corporate Responsibility Management*, Volume 2, Issue 2, October/November 2005: 16–19.

Howard, Carole M., and Wilma K. Mathews. *On Deadline: Managing Media Relations* (3rd ed.). Prospect Heights, IL: Waveland Press, 2000.

Hund, Gretchen, Jill Engel-Cox, and Kim Fowler. *Communications Guide for Sustainable Development: How Interested parties Become Partners.* Columbus, OH: Battelle Press, 2004.

Hunt, Todd, and James E. Grunig. *Public Relations Techniques.* New York: Harcourt Brace College Publishers, 1994.

Husted, Bryan W., and David Bruce Allen. *Corporate Social Strategy: Stakeholder Engagement and Competitive Advantage.* New York: Cambridge University Press, 2011.

Jackson, Peggy M. *Nonprofit Strategic Planning: Leveraging Sarbanes-Oxley Best Practices.* Hoboken, NJ: John Wiley & Sons, 2007.

James, Erika Hayes, and Lynn Perry Wooten. *Leading Under Pressure: From Surviving to Thriving Before, During and After a Crisis.* New York: Routledge, Taylor & Francis Group, 2010.

Jordan, Stephen, and B. J. Parker. *Two Steps Forward, One Step Back: A Brief History of Corporate Citizenship and Corporate Social Responsibility.* Washington, DC: Business Civic Leadership Center, 2010.

Kane, Dan. "It's Public Money but Private Secrecy." *The Charlotte Observer*, July 6, 2011.

Kanter, Beth, and Allison H. Fine. *The Networked Nonprofit.* San Francisco: John Wiley & Sons, 2010.

Kaufman, Eileen Kohl. "Choosing a Reporting Standard." *Corporate Responsibility Management*, Volume 2, Issue 3, December/January 2006: 5.

Kaufman, Roger, Hugh Oakley-Browne, Ryan Watkins, and Doug Leigh. *Strategic Planning for Success: Aligning People, Performance, and Payoffs.* San Francisco: John Wiley & Sons, 2003.

Keegan, P. Burke. *Fundraising for Non-Profits.* New York: HarperCollins Publishers, 1990.

Kelleher, Bob. *Louder than Words.* Portland, WA: BLKB Publishing, 2010.

Kellerman, Barbara. "When Should a Leader Apologize and When Not?" *Harvard Business Review,* Volume 84, No. 4, April 200: 73–81.

Kendall, Robert. *Public Relations Campaign Strategies: Planning for Implementation* (2nd ed.). New York: HarperCollins College Publishers, 1996.

Kenny, Graham. *Strategic Planning and Performance Management: Develop and Measure Winning Strategy.* New York: Elsevier Butterworth Heinemann, 2005.

Khalili, Nasprin R. *Practical Sustainability: From Grounded Theory to Emerging Strategies.* New York: Palgrave Macmillan, 2011.

Kibert, Charles J., Martha C. Monroe, Anna L. Peterson, Richard R. Plate, and Leslie Paul Thiele. *Working Toward Sustainability: Ethical Decision Making in a Technological World.* Hoboken, NJ: John Wiley & Sons, 2012.

King, Samantha. *Pink Ribbons, Inc.* Minneapolis: University of Minnesota Press, 2006.

Kinzey, Ruth Ellen. "When a Policy for Social Media is a Good Thing." *The Triad Business Journal,* October 7, 2011: 14–15.

Kinzey, Ruth Ellen. *Using Public Relations Strategies to Promote Your Nonprofit Organization.* New York: Haworth Press, 1999.

Klewes, Joachim, and Robert Wreschniok (eds.). *Reputation Capital: Building and Maintaining Trust in the 21st Century.* New York: Springer, 2009.

Kotler, Philip, and Nancy Lee. *Corporate Social Responsibility: Doing the Most Good for Your Company and Your Cause.* Hoboken, NJ: John Wiley Sons, 2005.

Landor. *Perspectives 2012.* New York: Landor, 2012.

Landor, Burson Marsteller, Penn Schoen Berland, and BAV. *2012 Global Corporate Reputation Index.* New York: Landor, Burson Marsteller, Penn Schoen Berland and BAV, 2012.

Laszlo, Chris, and Nadya Zhexembayeva. *Embedded Sustainability: The Next Big Competitive Advantage.* Stanford, CA: Greenleaf Publishing, 2011.

Lautman, Kay Partney. *Direct Marketing for Nonprofits.* Gaithersburg, MD: Aspen Publishers, 2001.

Leibner, Josh, Mader Gershon, and Allen Weiss. *The Power of Strategic Commitment.* New York: AMACOM, 2009.

Lerbinger, Otto. *The Crisis Manager: Facing Risk and Responsibility.* Mahwah, NJ: Lawrence Erlbaum Associations, 1997.

Letts, Christine W., William P. Ryan, and Allen Grossman. *High Performance Nonprofit Organizations: Managing Upstream for Greater Impact.* New York: John Wiley & Sons, 1999.

Levine, Michael. *Selling Goodness.* Los Angeles: Renaissance Books, 1998.

Lippman, Walter. *Public Opinion.* New York: Free Press Paperbacks, 1997.

Little, Ken. The Complete Idiot's Guide to Socially Responsible Investing. New York: Alpha Books, 2008.

Littlejohn, Stephen. *Theories of Human Communication* (5th ed.). Boston: Wadsworth Publishing, 1996.

Lorange, Peter. *Implementation of Strategic Planning.* Englewood Cliffs, NJ: Prentice Hall, 1982.

Luecke, Richard. *Crisis Management: Master the Skills to Prevent Disaster.* Boston: Harvard Business School Press, 2004.

Macey, William H., Benjamin Schneider, Karen M. Barbera, and Scott A. Young. *Employee Engagement: Tools for Analysis, Practice, and Competitive Advantage.* Malden, MA: Wiley-Blackwell, 2009.

Mansfield, Heather. *A How-To guide for Nonprofits Social Media for Social Good.* New York: McGraw-Hill Companies, 2012.

Marchica, John. *The Accountable Organization: Reclaiming integrity, Restoring Trust.* Palo Alto, CA: Davies-Black Publishing, 2004.

Marciano, Paul L. *Carrots and Sticks Don't Work: Build a Culture of Employee Engagement with the Principles of RESPECT.* New York: McGraw-Hill, 2010.

McCarty, Thomas, Michael Jordan, and Daniel Probst. *Six Sigma for Sustainability.* New York: McGraw Hill, 2011.

Meyers, Kenneth N. *Total Contingency Planning for Disasters: Managing Risk ... Minimizing Loss ... Ensuring Business Continuity.* New York: John Wiley & Sons, 1993.

Millar, Dan P., and Robert L. Heath. *Responding to Crisis: A Rhetorical Approach to Crisis Communication.* Mahwah, NJ: Lawrence Erlbaum Associates, 2004.

Millennial Impact Report 2012. Greenwood, IN: Achieve and JGA, 2012.

Mirvis, Philip H., and Bradley K. Googins. *Moving to Next Generation Corporate Citizenship.* Berlin: Centrum for Corporate Citizenship Deutschland, 2009.

Moran, Gwen, and Sue Johnson. *The Complete Idiot's Guide to Business Plans.* New York: Penguin Group, 2005.

Ogrizek, Michel, and Jean-Michel Guillery. *Communicating in a Crisis.* New York: Walter de Gruyter, 1999.

Olsen, Erica. *Strategic Planning for Dummies.* Hoboken, NJ: Wiley Publishing, 2007.

Paine, Katie Delahaye. "It's 9 a.m., Do You Know Where Your Membership Is?" Speech presented at the American Society of Association Executives, Minneapolis, MN, August 18, 2004.

Paine, Katie Delahaye. *Measure What Matters.* Hoboken, NJ: John Wiley & Sons, 2011.

Patterson, Sally J. and Janel M. Radtke. *Strategic Communications for Nonprofit Organizations* (2nd ed.). Hoboken, NJ: John Wiley & Sons, 2009.

Pinsdorf, Marion. *All Crisis Are Global: Managing to Escape Chaos.* New York: Fordham University Press, 2004.

Pinson, Linda. *Anatomy of a Business Plan* (7th ed.). Tustin, CA: Out of Your Mind ... and into the Marketplace, 2008.

Ploof, Ron. *Read This First.* Bloomington, IN: iUniverse, 2009.

Price, Tom. *Issues for Debate in Corporate Social Responsibility.* Thousand Oaks, CA: Sage Publications, 2010.

Pringle, Hamish, and Marjorie Thompson. *Brand Spirit: How Cause-related Marketing Builds Brands.* New York: John Wiley & Sons, 1999.

Ralser, Tom. *ROI for Nonprofits: The New Key to Sustainability.* Hoboken, NJ: John Wiley & Sons, 2007.

Reiss, Alvin. *CPR for Nonprofits: Creative Strategies for Successful Fundraising, Marketing, Communications, and Management.* San Francisco: Jossey-Bass, 2000.

Ross, Robert D. *The Management of Public Relations: Analysis and Planning External Relations.* New York: John Wiley & Sons. 1977.

Sagini, Meshack M. *Strategic Planning and Management in Public Organizations.* Lanham, MD: University Press of America, 2007.

Scott, David Meerman. *The New Rules of Marketing and PR: How to Use News Releases, Blogs, Podcasting, Viral Marketing, & Online Media to Reach Buyers Directly.* Hoboken, NJ: John Wiley & Sons, 2007.

Scott, David Meerman. *Real-Time Marketing & PR: How to Instantly Engage Your Market, Connect with Customers, and Create Products that Grow Your Business Now.* Hoboken, NJ: John Wiley & Sons, 2011.

Seeger, Matthew W., Timothy Sellnow, and Robert R. Ulmer. *Communication and Organizational Crisis.* Westport, CT: Praeger, 2003.

Sheikh, Sana-ur-Rehman, and Rian Beise-Zee. "Corporate Social Responsibility or Cause-Related Marketing? The Role of Cause Specificity of CSR." *Journal of Consumer Marketing,* Volume 28, Issue 1 (2011): 27–39.

Shih, Clara. *The Facebook Era: Tapping online Social Networks to Build Better Products, Reach New Audiences, and Sell More Stuff.* Boston: Prentice Hall, 2009.

Shipley, David, and Will Schwalbe. *SEND.* New York: Alfred A. Knopf, 2008.

Sikich, Geary W. *Protecting Your Business in a Pandemic: Plans, Tools and Advice for Maintaining Business Continuity.* Westport, CT: Praeger, 2008.

Singh, Nitish, and Arun Pereira. *The Culturally Customized Web Site: Customizing Web Sites for the Global Marketplace.* Burlington, MA: Elsevier Butterworth-Heinemann, 2005.

Smith, Bucklin & Associates, Inc., Robert H. Wilbur (ed). *The Complete Guide to Nonprofit Management* (2nd ed.). New York: John Wiley & Sons, 2000.

Smith, Jeanette. *The New Publicity Kit.* New York: John Wiley & Sons, 1995.

Smith, Nick, Robert Woolan, and Catherine Zhour. *The Social Media Management Handbook.* Hoboken, NJ: John Wiley & Sons, 2011.

Sommerrock, Katharina. *Social Entrepreneurship Business Models: Incentive Strategies to Catalyze Public Goods Provision.* Hampshire, U.K.: Palgrave Macmillian, 2010.

Steiner, George, A. *Strategic Planning What Every Manager Must Know.* New York: The Free Press, 1979.

Stengel, Jim. *GROW.* New York: Crown Business, 2011.

Succeeding at Social Enterprise: Hard-Won Lessons for Nonprofits and Social Entrepreneurs. San Francisco: Jossey-Bass, 2010.

Swaim, Robert. *The Strategic Drucker.* San Francisco: John Wiley & Sons, 2010.

The Center on Philanthropy at Indiana University Indiana & Purdue University. *2011 Study of High Net Worth Women's Philanthropy & The Impact of Women's Giving Networks.* Indianapolis, IN: The Center on Philanthropy at Indiana University Indiana & Purdue University, 2011.

The Nonprofit Board Answer Book: A Practical Guide for Board Members and Chief Executives (2nd ed.). San Francisco: John Wiley & Sons, 2007.

Ulmer, Robert R., Timothy L. Sellnow, and Matthew W. Seeger. *Effective Crisis Communication: Moving from Crisis to Opportunity* (2nd ed.). Thousand Oaks, CA: Sage Publications, 2007.

Visser, Wayne. *The Age of Responsibility: CSR 2.0 and the New DNA of Business.* West Sussex, U.K.: John Wiley & Sons, 2011.

Vogt, Peter. "Awareness to Action." *Communication World,* March-April 2004: 22–26.

Waddock, Sandra. *Leading Corporation Citizens: Vision, Values, Value Added.* New York: McGraw Hill, 2002.

Walaski, Pamela (Ferrante). *Risk and Crisis Communications.* Hoboken, NJ: John Wiley & Sons, 2011.

Waters, Joe, and Joanna MacDonald. *Cause Marketing for Dummies.* Hoboken, NJ: Wiley Publishing, 2011.

Watson, Tom, and Paul Noble. *Evaluating Public Relations: A Best Practice Guide to Public Relations Planning, Research & Evaluation* (2nd ed.). Philadelphia, PA: Kogan Page, 2007.

Watson Wyatt Worldwide. *Driving Employee Engagement in a Global Workforce: 2007/2008*. New York: Watson Wyatt Worldwide, 2007.

Weber, Larry. *Marketing to the Social Web*. Hoboken, NJ: John Wiley & Sons, 2007.

Webster's Encyclopedic Unabridged Dictionary of the English Language. New York: Gramercy Books, 1996.

Weick, Karl E., and Kathleen M. Sutcliffe. *Managing the Unexpected: Assuring High Performance in an Age of Complexity*. San Francisco: Jossey-Bass, 2001.

Werbach, Adam. *Strategy for Sustainability*. Boston: Harvard Business Press, 2009.

Werther, William B., and David Chandler. *Strategic Corporate Social Responsibility: Stakeholders in a Global Environment*. Thousand Oaks, CA: Sage Publications, 2006.

Wilcox, Dennis L., Phillip H. Ault, and Warren K. Agee. *Public Relations: Strategies and Tactics* (5th ed.). New York: Addison Wesley Longman, 1998.

Wilson, Ian. *The New Rules of Corporate Conduct: Rewriting the Social Chapter*. Westport, CT: Quorum Books, 2000.

Wilson, Richard M. S., and Colin Golligan. *Strategic Marketing Management*. Boston: Butterworth Heinemann, 1997.

Wolk, Thomas. *Managing a Nonprofit Organization*. New York: Prentice Hall Press, 1990.

Wymer, Jr., Walter, Patricia Knowles, and Roger Gomes. *Nonprofit Marketing*. Thousand Oaks, CA: Sage Publications, 2006.

Wymer, Jr., Walter, and Sridhar Samu (eds.). *Nonprofit and Business Sector Collaboration: Social Enterprises, Cause-Related Marketing, Sponsorships, and Other Corporate-Nonprofit Dealings*. New York: The Haworth Press, 2003.

Zappala, Joseph M., and Ann R. Carden. *Public Relations Worktext: A Writing and Planning Resource* (2nd ed.). Mahwah, NJ: Lawrence Erlbaum Associates, 2004.

Ziegenfuss, Jr., James T. *Strategic Planning: Cases, Concepts, and Lessons* (2nd ed.). New York: University Press of America, 2006.

Online Resources

"Bank of America High Net Worth Philanthropy Study." http://mediaroom.bankofamerica.com/phoenix.zhtml?c=234503&p=mediaMention&id=394026.

Barkley. "Executive Summary." American Millennials: Deciphering the Enigma Generation. September 12, 2011. http://blog-barkleyus-com.s3.amazonaws.com/wp-content/uploads/2011/09/BarkleyMillennial-ResearchExecSummary.pdf.

Bhattacharya, C.B., Daniel Korschum, and Sankar Sen. "What Really Drives Value in Corporate Responsibility." McKinsey Quarterly, December 2011.http://www.mckinseyquaraterly.com/araticle_print.aspx.

Blessing White, "Employee Engagement Report 2011," December 2010, http://www.blessingwhite.com/EEE__report.asp.

Boston College Center for Corporate Citizenship and Reputation Institute. "Corporate Reputation and Social Responsibility Rankings: 2011 CRS Index". http://www.bcccc.net/pdf/CSRIReport2011.pdf.

Cause Marketing Forum. "Statistics Every Cause Marketer Should Know." http://www.causemarketingforum.com/site/c.bkLUKcOTLkK4E/b.6448131/k.262B/Statistics_Every_Cause_Marketer_Should_Know.htm.

Coffman, Julia. "Strategic Communications Audit." October 2004. http://www.mediae-valuationporject.org/WorkingPaper1.pdf.

Cohen, Todd. "Nonprofits Have a Great Story to Tell." *Inside Philanthropy*, January 9, 2012. http://philanthropyjournal.blogspot.com/search?g=nonprofits+have+a+great+story+to+tell.

Cone Communications. "Cone Releases First Cause Consumer Behavior Study." October 1, 2008. http://www.coneinc.com/content1188.

Corporation for National Community Service. "Volunteering in America." http://www.nationalservice.gov/about/volunteering/index.asp and http://www.volunteeringinamerica.gov/.

Corporation for National Community Service. "New Report: Americans Devote 8.1 Billion Hours to Volunteering in 2010." August 8, 2011. http://www.nationalservice.gov/about/newsroom/releases_detail.asp?tbl_pr_id=2026.

Edelman. "2012 Edelman Trust Barometer Global Results." http://www.slideshare.net/EdelmanInsights/2012-edelman-trust-barometer-global-deck.

Edelman. "U.S. Consumers Feel Most Responsible to Help, Yet Involvement in Societal Issues Declines for the First Time; Look to Marketers to Bridge the Gap." April 26, 2012. Cause Marketing News Headlines. http://www.causemarketingforum.com/site/apps/nlnet/content2.aspx?c=bkLUKcOTLkK4e&b=6420367&ct=11734301.

"Effective Communication Positively Impacts Employee Motivation Levels," Employee Advocacy Latest Ouch Point Survey from Opinion Research Corporation Suggests." Reuters. March 9, 2009. http://www.reuters.com/article/2009/03/09/idUS101145+09-Mar-2009+BW20090309.

Fitzgerald, David, and Drew Griffin. "Little of Charity's Money Going to Animals." CNN Investigative Unit, June 15, 2012. http://cnn.com/2012/06/14/us/animal-charity-investigation/index/html?iref=allsearch.

Fitzgerald, David, and Drew Griffin. "Tax Records Show Charities Spent Millions on Direct Mail." CNN Investigative Unit, May 18, 2012. http://cnn.com/2012/05/18/us/veterans-charity- marketing/index.html?iref=allsearch.

Flickr. "Home Page." Accessed July 29, 2012. http://www.flickr.com. Global Reporting Initiative. "About Sustainability Reporting." Global Reporting Initiative. http://www.globalreporting.org/information/sustainability-reporting/Pages/default.aspx.

Heath, Robert L., and Lan Ni. "Corporate Social Responsibility: Three R's." http://old.instituteforpr.org/essential_knowledge/detail/corporate-social-responsibility-three-rs/.

Holder, Emily. "The Need for Inspiration: How Millennials Connect, Involve and Give to Nonprofits." *Philanthropy Journal*, June 14, 2012. http://www.philanthropyjournal.org/resources/marketingcommunications/need-inspiration-how-millennials-connect-involve-and-give-nonprofi.

Institute for Public Relations. Proposed Interim Standards for Metrics in Traditional Media Analysis. June 7, 2012. www.instituteforpr.org/topics/proposed-interim-standards-for-metrics-in-traditional-media-analysis.

Internal Revenue Service. October 2011. http://www.irs.gov/pub/irs-pdf/p557.pdf.

Kliff, Sarah. "Susan G. Komen Foundation Revises Policy That Barred Planned Parenthood Funding." *The Washington Post*, February 3, 2012. http://www.washingtonpost.com/business/economy/komen-revises-funding-policy/2012/02/03/glQA-VRa3mQ_story.html.

Moume, Michael. "RSS Feeds: Are They Worth It?" Ezine. Accessed July 29, 2012. http://ezinearticles.com/?RSS-Feeds:-Are-They-Worth-It?&id=6289886.

"New Report: Americans Devote 8.1 Billion Hours to Volunteering in 2010." The Corporation for National and Community Service. August 8, 2011. http://www.nationalservice.gov/about/newsroom/releases_details.asp?tbl_pr_id=2026.

Pinterest. "About." http://pinterest.com/about/.

Reputation Institute. The 2012 U.S. ReTrack Pulse. http://www.reputationinstitute.com/thought-leadership/category/complimentary-reports-2012.

Salamon, Lester M., Stephanie L. Geller, and S. Wojciech Sokolowski. "Taxing the Tax-Exempt Sector – A Growing Danger for Nonprofit Organizations." John Hopkins University. Communique No. 21. http://ccss.jhu.edu/wp-content/uploads/downloads/2011/09/LP_Communique21_2011.pdf.

Shutterfly. http://www.shutterfly.com.

Slaper, Timothy F., and Tanya J. Hall. "The Triple Bottom Line: What Is It and How Does It Work?" *Indiana Business Review*, Spring 2011. http://www.ibrc.indiana.edu/ibr/2011/spring/article2.html.

Slosson, Mary. "Anti-Kony Campaign in Turmoil after Filmmaker's Breakdown." Reuters. April 2, 2012. http://www.reuters.com/article/2012/0002/us-usa-kony-futureidUSBRE83116Y20120402.

Society for Human Resource Management. 2011 Employee Job Satisfaction and Engagement. http://www.shrm.org/research/surveyfindings/articles/documents/11-0618%20job_satisfaction_fnl.pdf.

"Study: Workers' Morale Hurt Most by Communication Failures." *Triad Business Journal*, November 10, 2008. http://triangle.bizjournals.com/triangle/stories/2008/11/10/daily2.html.

The Nonprofit Times. "15 Ways to Power Cause Marketing Partnerships. October 5, 2011. http://www.thenonprofittimes.com/article/detail/15-ways-to-power-cause-marketing-partnerships-4117#.

United Nations. "Report of the World Commission on Environment and Development: Our Common Future." http://www.un-documents.net/wced-ocf.htm.

U.S. Bureau of Labor Statistics. "Volunteering in the United States, 2011." http://www.bls.gov/news.release/volun.nr0.htm/

"Value of Volunteering Grows." Philanthropy Journal, April 6, 2012. http://www.philanthropyjournal.org/new/top-stories/value-volunteering-grows."Volunteering in America," Corporation for National Community Service, http://www.nationalservice.gov/about/volunteering/index.asp and http://www.volunteeringinamerica.gov/.

"Volunteering in the United States – 2011." U.S. Bureau of Labor Statistics. February 22, 2012. http://www.bls.gov/news.release/volun.nr0.htm.

Wallace, Nicole. "Attitudes Toward Charities in Marketing Partnerships: A New Survey." The Chronicle of Philanthropy, March 10, 2010. http://philanthropy.com/blogs/prospecting/attitudes-toward-charities-in-marketing-partnerships-a-new-survey/21719.

Watson, Stuart, "United Way Settles Lawsuit with Former CEO." WCNC. http://www.wcnc.com/video/featuredvideos/United-Way-settles-discrimination-lawsuit-with-former-CEO-Gloria-Pace-King-111150384.html.

"Wealthy Women Control Charitable Checkbooks." Philanthropy Journal. January 5, 2012. http://www.philanthropyjournal.org/news/top-stories-wealthy-women-control-charitable-checkbooks.

Women Give 2012. Indianapolis, IN: Women's Philanthropy Institute, 2012. http://philanthropy.iupui.edu/files/research/womengive2012forrelease.pdf.

YouTube. "Frequently Asked Questions." Accessed July 31, 2012. http://www.youtube.com/t/faq.

Index